SIXTH EDITION

PROGRAMMING LOGIC AND DESIGN

INTRODUCTORY

JOYCE FARRELL

COURSE TECHNOLOGY
CENGAGE Learning™

Australia • Brazil • Japan • Korea • Mexico • Singapore • Spain • United Kingdom • United States

COURSE TECHNOLOGY
CENGAGE Learning™

Programming Logic and Design, Introductory, Sixth Edition
Joyce Farrell

Executive Editor: Marie Lee

Acquisitions Editor: Amy Jollymore

Managing Editor: Tricia Coia

Developmental Editor: Dan Seiter

Content Project Manager: Jennifer Feltri

Editorial Assistant: Zina Kresin

Marketing Manager: Bryant Chrzan

Art Director: Marissa Falco

Text Designer: Shawn Girsberger

Cover Designer: Cabbage Design Company

Cover Image: iStockphoto

Print Buyer: Julio Esperas

Copy Editor: Michael Beckett

Proofreader: Vicki Zimmer

Indexer: Alexandra Nickerson

Compositor: Integra

For product information and technology assistance, contact us at
Cengage Learning Customer & Sales Support, 1-800-354-9706
For permission to use material from this text or product, submit all requests online at **cengage.com/permissions**
Further permissions questions can be emailed to
permissionrequest@cengage.com

Library of Congress Control Number: 2009934819

ISBN-13: 978-0-5387-4477-5

ISBN-10: 0-538-74477-4

Course Technology
20 Channel Center Street
Boston, MA 02210
USA

Some of the product names and company names used in this book have been used for identification purposes only and may be trademarks or registered trademarks of their respective manufacturers and sellers.

Course Technology, a part of Cengage Learning, reserves the right to revise this publication and make changes from time to time in its content without notice.

Cengage Learning is a leading provider of customized learning solutions with office locations around the globe, including Singapore, the United Kingdom, Australia, Mexico, Brazil, and Japan. Locate your local office at:
www.cengage.com/global

Cengage Learning products are represented in Canada by Nelson Education, Ltd.

To learn more about Course Technology, visit
www.cengage.com/coursetechnology

Purchase any of our products at your local college store or at our preferred online store **www.ichapters.com**

Printed in Canada
1 2 3 4 5 6 7 14 13 12 11 10

Brief Contents

Preface ix

CHAPTER 1   An Overview of Computers and Programming . . 1

CHAPTER 2   Working with Data, Creating Modules,
and Designing High-Quality Programs 41

CHAPTER 3   Understanding Structure 92

CHAPTER 4   Making Decisions 133

CHAPTER 5   Looping 184

CHAPTER 6   Arrays 228

CHAPTER 7   File Handling and Applications 276

APPENDIX A   Understanding Numbering Systems
and Computer Codes. 325

APPENDIX B   Flowchart Symbols 334

APPENDIX C   Structures 335

APPENDIX D   Solving Difficult Structuring Problems . . . 337

APPENDIX E   Creating Print Charts 346

APPENDIX F   Two Variations on the Basic Structures—
case and do-while 348

Glossary 354

Index 362

Contents

Preface ix

CHAPTER 1 An Overview of Computers
and Programming 1

Understanding Computer Systems. 2
Understanding Simple Program Logic 5
Understanding the Program Development Cycle 8
   Understanding the Problem 8
   Planning the Logic 10
   Coding the Program 10
   Using Software to Translate the Program
     into Machine Language 11
   Testing the Program 12
   Putting the Program into Production 14
   Maintaining the Program 14
Using Pseudocode Statements and Flowchart Symbols 15
   Writing Pseudocode 15
   Drawing Flowcharts 17
   Repeating Instructions 18
Using a Sentinel Value to End a Program 20
Understanding Programming and User Environments 23
   Understanding Programming Environments 23
   Understanding User Environments 25
Understanding the Evolution of Programming Models 27
Chapter Summary 28
Key Terms 29
Review Questions 32
Exercises 37

CHAPTER 2 Working with Data, Creating Modules,
and Designing High-Quality Programs 41

Declaring and Using Variables and Constants. 42

Working with Variables 42

Naming Variables 44

Understanding Unnamed, Literal Constants
and their Data Types 45

Understanding the Data Types of Variables 46

Declaring Named Constants. 47

Assigning Values to Variables 48

Performing Arithmetic Operations 49

Understanding the Advantages of Modularization 52

Modularization Provides Abstraction 53

Modularization Allows Multiple Programmers
to Work on a Problem. 54

Modularization Allows You to Reuse Your Work 54

Modularizing a Program 55

Declaring Variables and Constants
within Modules 59

Understanding the Most Common Configuration
for Mainline Logic 61

Creating Hierarchy Charts 66

Features of Good Program Design. 68

Using Program Comments 69

Choosing Identifiers 71

Designing Clear Statements. 72

Writing Clear Prompts and Echoing Input 74

Maintaining Good Programming Habits 76

Chapter Summary .77

Key Terms 78

Review Questions .82

Exercises 86

CHAPTER 3   Understanding Structure **92**

Understanding Unstructured Spaghetti Code 93

Understanding the Three Basic Structures 95

Using a Priming Input to Structure a Program 103

Understanding the Reasons for Structure 110

Recognizing Structure 111

Structuring and Modularizing Unstructured Logic 115

Chapter Summary 121

Key Terms 122

Review Questions 123

Exercises 127

v

CHAPTER 4   Making Decisions **133**

Evaluating Boolean Expressions to Make Comparisons . . . 134
Using Relational Comparison Operators 137
    Avoiding a Common Error with Relational Operators. . . . 141
Understanding AND Logic 141
    Nesting AND Decisions for Efficiency 144
    Using the AND Operator 146
    Avoiding Common Errors in an AND Selection. 148
Understanding OR Logic 150
    Writing OR Decisions for Efficiency 152
    Using the OR Operator 153
    Avoiding Common Errors in an OR Selection 155
Making Selections within Ranges 159
    Avoiding Common Errors When Using Range Checks . . . 162
Understanding Precedence When Combining
AND and OR Operators 166
Chapter Summary 169
Key Terms 170
Review Questions 171
Exercises 177

CHAPTER 5   Looping **184**

Understanding the Advantages of Looping 185
Using a Loop Control Variable. 186
    Using a Definite Loop with a Counter 187
    Using an Indefinite Loop with a Sentinel Value 188
    Understanding the Loop in a Program's Mainline Logic. . . 190
Nested Loops 192
Avoiding Common Loop Mistakes 196
    Mistake: Neglecting to Initialize the
    Loop Control Variable. 197
    Mistake: Neglecting to Alter the
    Loop Control Variable. 198
    Mistake: Using the Wrong Comparison with the
    Loop Control Variable. 200
    Mistake: Including Statements Inside the Loop
    that Belong Outside the Loop 201
Using a for Loop 206
Common Loop Applications. 208
    Using a Loop to Accumulate Totals 208
    Using a Loop to Validate Data 211
    Limiting a Reprompting Loop 213

    Validating a Data Type 215
    Validating Reasonableness and Consistency of Data 216
  Chapter Summary 217
  Key Terms 218
  Review Questions 219
  Exercises 223

CHAPTER 6   Arrays **228**

  Understanding Arrays and How They Occupy
    Computer Memory 229
    How Arrays Occupy Computer Memory 229
  Manipulating an Array to Replace Nested Decisions 232
  Using Constants with Arrays 240
    Using a Constant as the Size of an Array 240
    Using Constants as Array Element Values 241
    Using a Constant as an Array Subscript 241
  Searching an Array 242
  Using Parallel Arrays 246
    Improving Search Efficiency 251
  Searching an Array for a Range Match 254
  Remaining within Array Bounds 258
  Using a for Loop to Process Arrays 261
  Chapter Summary 262
  Key Terms 263
  Review Questions 264
  Exercises 268

CHAPTER 7   File Handling and Applications **276**

  Understanding Computer Files 277
    Organizing Files 278
  Understanding the Data Hierarchy 279
  Performing File Operations 280
    Declaring a File 280
    Opening a File 281
    Reading Data From a File 281
    Writing Data to a File 283
    Closing a File 283
    A Program that Performs File Operations 283
  Understanding Sequential Files and Control Break Logic . . . 286
    Understanding Control Break Logic 287
  Merging Sequential Files 293
  Master and Transaction File Processing 303

Random Access Files 311
Chapter Summary 313
Key Terms 314
Review Questions 316
Exercises 320

viii

APPENDIX A   Understanding Numbering Systems
and Computer Codes **325**

APPENDIX B   Flowchart Symbols **334**

APPENDIX C   Structures **335**

APPENDIX D   Solving Difficult Structuring Problems . . . **337**

APPENDIX E   Creating Print Charts **346**

APPENDIX F   Two Variations on the Basic Structures—
case and do-while **348**

Glossary **354**

Index **362**

Preface

Programming Logic and Design, Introductory, Sixth Edition provides the beginning programmer with a guide to developing structured program logic. This textbook assumes no programming language experience. The writing is nontechnical and emphasizes good programming practices. The examples are business examples; they do not assume mathematical background beyond high school business math. Additionally, the examples illustrate one or two major points; they do not contain so many features that students become lost following irrelevant and extraneous details.

The examples in *Programming Logic and Design* have been created to provide students with a sound background in logic, no matter what programming languages they eventually use to write programs. This book can be used in a stand-alone logic course that students take as a prerequisite to a programming course, or as a companion book to an introductory programming text using any programming language.

Organization and Coverage

Programming Logic and Design, Introductory, Sixth Edition introduces students to programming concepts and enforces good style and logical thinking. General programming concepts are introduced in Chapter 1. Chapter 2 discusses using data and introduces two important concepts: modularization and creating high-quality programs. It is important to emphasize these topics early so that students start thinking in a modular way and concentrate on making their programs efficient, robust, easy to read, and easy to maintain.

Chapter 3 covers the key concepts of structure, including what structure is, how to recognize it, and most importantly, the advantages to writing structured programs. This early overview gives students a solid foundation for thinking in a structured way before they have to manage the details of the structures.

Chapters 4, 5, and 6 explore the intricacies of decision making, looping, and array manipulation. Chapter 7 provides details of file handling so students can create programs that handle a significant amount of data.

x

The first three appendices give students summaries of numbering systems, flowchart symbols, and structures. Additional appendices allow students to gain extra experience with structuring large unstructured programs, creating print charts, and understanding posttest loops and case structures.

Programming Logic and Design combines text explanation with flowcharts and pseudocode examples to provide students with alternative means of expressing structured logic. Numerous detailed, full-program exercises at the end of each chapter illustrate the concepts explained within the chapter, and reinforce understanding and retention of the material presented.

Programming Logic and Design distinguishes itself from other programming logic books in the following ways:

- It is written and designed to be non-language specific. The logic used in this book can be applied to any programming language.

- The examples are everyday business examples; no special knowledge of mathematics, accounting, or other disciplines is assumed.

- The concept of structure is covered earlier than in many other texts. Students are exposed to structure naturally, so they will automatically create properly designed programs.

- Text explanation is interspersed with flowcharts and pseudocode so students can become comfortable with both logic development tools and understand their interrelationship. Screen shots of running programs also are included, providing students with a clear and concrete image of the programs' execution.

- Complex programs are built through the use of complete business examples. Students see how an application is constructed from start to finish instead of studying only segments of programs.

Features

This edition of the text includes many features to help students become better programmers and understand the big picture in program development. Many new features have been added, and the popular features from the first five editions are still included.

Features maintained from previous editions include:

OBJECTIVES Each chapter begins with a list of objectives so the student knows the topics that will be presented in the chapter. In addition to providing a quick reference to topics covered, this feature provides a useful study aid.

FLOWCHARTS This book has plenty of figures and illustrations, including flowcharts, which provide the reader with a visual learning experience, rather than one that involves simply studying text. You can see examples of flowcharts beginning in Chapter 1.

PSEUDOCODE This book also includes numerous examples of pseudocode, which illustrate correct usage of the programming logic and design concepts being taught.

 NOTES These tips provide additional information—for example, another location in the book that expands on a topic, or a common error to watch out for.

 THE DON'T DO IT ICON It is sometimes illustrative to show an example of how NOT to do something—for example, having a dead code path in a program. However, students do not always read carefully and sometimes use logic similar to that shown in what is intended to be a "bad" example. When the instructor is critical, the frustrated student says, "But that's how they did it in the book!" Therefore, although the text will continue to describe bad examples, and the captions for the related figures will mention that they are bad examples, the book also includes a "Don't Do It" icon near the offending section of logic. This icon provides a visual jolt to the student, emphasizing that particular figures are NOT to be emulated.

THE TWO TRUTHS AND A LIE QUIZ This quiz appears after each chapter section, with answers provided. The quiz contains three statements based on the preceding section of text—two true and one false. Over the years, students have requested answers to problems, but we have hesitated to distribute them in case instructors want to use problems as assignments or test questions. These true-false mini-quizzes provide students with immediate feedback as they read, without "giving away" answers to the multiple-choice questions and programming problems later in the chapter.

 GAME ZONE EXERCISES These exercises are included at the end of each chapter. Students can create games as an additional entertaining way to understand key concepts presented in the chapter.

CHAPTER SUMMARIES Following each chapter is a summary that recaps the programming concepts and techniques covered in the chapter. This feature provides a concise means for students to review and check their understanding of the main points in each chapter.

KEY TERMS Each chapter lists key terms and their definitions; the list appears in the order the terms are encountered in the chapter. Along with the chapter summary, the list of key terms provides a snapshot overview of a chapter's main ideas. A glossary at the end of the book lists all the key terms in alphabetical order, along with working definitions.

DEBUGGING EXERCISES Because examining programs critically and closely is a crucial programming skill, each chapter includes a "Find the Bugs" section in which programming examples are presented that contain syntax errors and logical errors for the student to find and correct.

REVIEW QUESTIONS Twenty multiple-choice review questions appear at the end of every chapter to allow students to test their comprehension of the major ideas and techniques presented.

EXERCISES Multiple end-of-chapter flowcharting and pseudocoding exercises are included so students have more opportunities to practice concepts as they learn them. These exercises increase in difficulty and are designed to allow students to explore logical programming concepts. Each exercise can be completed using flowcharts, pseudocode, or both. In addition, instructors can assign the exercises as programming problems to be coded and executed in a particular programming language.

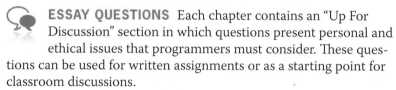 **ESSAY QUESTIONS** Each chapter contains an "Up For Discussion" section in which questions present personal and ethical issues that programmers must consider. These questions can be used for written assignments or as a starting point for classroom discussions.

New to this Edition!

VIDEO LESSONS Each chapter is accompanied by two or more video lessons that help explain an important chapter concept. A listing of the videos provided can be found on the inside back cover of this text. These videos are designed and narrated by the author and are available for free with a new book. (They can also be purchased separately at iChapters.com.)

If you have a new book, it will contain a URL and PIN code. Once you go to this URL and enter your PIN code, follow the prompts to locate the videos for this text. If you are a user of an online course cartridge, such as BlackBoard, WebCT, or Angel, you will also have access to these videos through that platform.

INCREASED EMPHASIS ON MODULARITY From the second chapter, students are encouraged to write code in concise, easily manageable, and reusable modules. Instructors have found that modularization is a technique that should be encouraged early to instill good habits and a clearer understanding of structure. This edition explains modularization early, using global variables instead of local passed and returned values, and saves parameter passing for later when the student has become more adept.

CLEARER EXPLANATIONS This edition has been rewritten to provide clearer, simpler explanations that are appropriate for the beginning programming student. As a result of the new, cleaner approach, the length of the book has been reduced.

NEW APPENDICES FOR EASY REFERENCE New appendices have been added that cover numbering systems, flowchart symbols, and structures.

DECREASED EMPHASIS ON CONTROL BREAKS Professional programmers should understand control break logic, but creating such logic is not as common a task as it was years ago. Therefore, the topic is still covered briefly as part of the file-handling chapter, but with reduced emphasis from previous editions of the book.

Instructor Resources

The following supplemental materials are available when this book is used in a classroom setting. All of the instructor resources available with this book are provided to the instructor on a single CD-ROM.

ELECTRONIC INSTRUCTOR'S MANUAL The Instructor's Manual that accompanies this textbook provides additional instructional material to assist in class preparation, including items such as Sample Syllabi, Chapter Outlines, Technical Notes, Lecture Notes, Quick Quizzes, Teaching Tips, Discussion Topics, and Key Terms.

EXAMVIEW® This textbook is accompanied by ExamView, a powerful testing software package that allows instructors to create and administer printed, computer (LAN-based), and Internet exams. ExamView includes hundreds of questions that correspond to the topics covered in this text, enabling students to generate detailed study guides that include page references for further review. The computer-based and Internet testing components allow students to take exams at their computers, and save the instructor time by grading each exam automatically.

POWERPOINT PRESENTATIONS This book comes with Microsoft PowerPoint slides for each chapter. These are included as a teaching aid for classroom presentation, to make available to students on your network for chapter review, or to be printed for classroom distribution. Instructors can add their own slides for additional topics they introduce to the class.

SOLUTIONS Suggested solutions to Review Questions and Exercises are provided on the Instructor Resources CD and may also be found on the Course Technology Web site at *www.cengage.com/coursetechnology*. The solutions are password protected.

DISTANCE LEARNING Course Technology offers WebCT and Blackboard courses for this text to provide the most complete and dynamic learning experience possible. When you add online content to one of your courses, you're adding a lot: automated tests, topic reviews, quick quizzes, and additional case projects with solutions. For more information on how to bring distance learning to your course, contact your Course Technology sales representative.

Software Options

You have the option to bundle software with your text! Please contact your Course Technology sales representative for more information.

MICROSOFT® OFFICE VISIO® PROFESSIONAL Visio is a diagramming program that helps users create flowcharts and diagrams easily while working through the text, enabling them to visualize concepts and learn more effectively.

VISUAL LOGIC™ This simple but powerful tool teaches programming logic and design without traditional high-level programming language syntax. Visual Logic uses flowcharts to explain essential programming concepts, including variables, input, assignment, output, conditions, loops, procedures, graphics, arrays, and files. It also has the ability to interpret and execute flowcharts, providing students with immediate and accurate feedback about their solutions. By executing student solutions, Visual Logic combines the power of a high-level language with the ease and simplicity of flowcharts.

Acknowledgments

I would like to thank all of the people who helped to make this book a reality, especially Dan Seiter, Development Editor, whose hard work and attention to detail have made this a high-quality textbook. I have worked with Dan for many years now, and he is indispensable in producing accurate and approachable technical instruction. Thanks also to Tricia Coia, Managing Editor; Amy Jollymore, Acquisitions Editor; Jennifer Feltri, Content Project Manager; and Green Pen QA, Technical Editors. I am grateful to be able to work with so many fine people who are dedicated to producing high-quality instructional materials.

I am grateful to the many reviewers who provided helpful and insightful comments during the development of this book, including John Buerck, Saint Louis University; Karen Cummings, McLennan Community College; and Clara Groeper, Illinois Central College.

Thanks, too, to my husband, Geoff, and our daughters, Andrea and Audrey, for their support. This book, as were all its previous editions, is dedicated to them.

–Joyce Farrell

About the Inside Front Cover

Check out our interviews with recent graduates who are now
working in the IT field. One is featured on the inside front cover
of this book. If you know people who recently landed a job in IT,
we'd like to interview them too! Send your suggestions via e-mail to
Amy Jollymore, Acquisitions Editor, at Amy.Jollymore@Cengage.com.

CHAPTER 1

An Overview of Computers and Programming

In this chapter, you will learn about:

- ◎ Computer systems
- ◎ Simple program logic
- ◎ The steps involved in the program development cycle
- ◎ Pseudocode statements and flowchart symbols
- ◎ Using a sentinel value to end a program
- ◎ Programming and user environments
- ◎ The evolution of programming models

Understanding Computer Systems

A **computer system** is a combination of all the components required to process and store data using a computer. Every computer system is composed of multiple pieces of hardware and software.

- **Hardware** is the equipment, or the physical devices, associated with a computer. For example, keyboards, mice, speakers, and printers are all hardware. The devices are manufactured differently for large mainframe computers, laptops, and even smaller computers that are embedded into products such as cars and thermostats, but the types of operations performed by different-sized computers are very similar. When you think of a computer, you often think of its physical components first, but for a computer to be useful it needs more than devices; a computer needs to be given instructions. Just as your stereo equipment does not do much until you provide music, computer hardware needs instructions that control how and when data items are input, how they are processed, and the form in which they are output or stored.

- **Software** is computer instructions that tell the hardware what to do. Software is **programs**: instructions written by programmers. You can buy prewritten programs that are stored on a disk or that you download from the Web. For example, businesses use word-processing and accounting programs, and casual computer users enjoy programs that play music and games. Alternatively, you can write your own programs. When you write software instructions, you are **programming**. This book focuses on the programming process.

 Software can be classified as application software or system software. **Application software** comprises all the programs you apply to a task—word-processing programs, spreadsheets, payroll and inventory programs, and even games. **System software** comprises the programs that you use to manage your computer, including operating systems such as Windows, Linux, or UNIX. This book focuses on the logic used to write application software programs, although many of the concepts apply to both types of software.

Together, computer hardware and software accomplish three major operations in most programs:

- **Input**—Data items enter the computer system and are put into memory, where they can be processed. Hardware devices that perform input operations include keyboards and mice. **Data items** include all the text, numbers, and other information that are processed by a computer.

 In business, much of the data used is facts and figures about such entities as products, customers, and personnel. However, data can also be items such as the choices a player makes in a game or the notes required by a music-playing program.

Many computer professionals distinguish between the terms *data*, which describes items that are input, and *information*, which describes data items that have been processed and sent to a device where people can read and interpret them. For example, your name, Social Security number, and hourly pay rate are data items when they are input to a program, but the same items are information after they have been processed and output on your paycheck.

- **Processing**—Processing data items may involve organizing or sorting them, checking them for accuracy, or performing calculations with them. The hardware component that performs these types of tasks is the **central processing unit**, or **CPU**.

- **Output**—After data items have been processed, the resulting information usually is sent to a printer, monitor, or some other output device so people can view, interpret, and use the results.

Some people consider storage as a fourth major computer operation. Instead of sending output to a device such as a printer, monitor, or speaker where a person can interpret it, you sometimes store output on **storage devices**, such as a disk or flash media. People cannot read data directly from these storage devices, but the devices hold information for later retrieval. When you send output to a storage device, sometimes it is used later as input for another program.

You write computer instructions in a computer **programming language**, such as Visual Basic, C#, C++, or Java. Just as some people speak English and others speak Japanese, programmers also write programs in different languages. Some programmers work exclusively in one language, whereas others know several programming languages and use the one that is best suited to the task at hand.

The instructions you write using a programming language are called **program code**; when you write instructions, you are **coding the program**.

Every programming language has rules governing its word usage and punctuation. These rules are called the language's **syntax**. If you ask, "How the geet too store do I?" in English, most people can figure out what you probably mean, even though you have not used proper English syntax—you have mixed up the word order, misspelled a word, and used an incorrect word. However, computers are not nearly as smart as most people; in this case, you might as well have asked the computer, "Xpu mxv ort dod nmcad bf B?" Unless the syntax is perfect, the computer cannot interpret the programming language instruction at all.

When you write a program, you usually type its instructions using a keyboard. When you type program instructions, they are stored in **computer memory**, which is a computer's temporary, internal

4

Random access memory, or **RAM**, is a form of internal, volatile memory. It is hardware on which the programs that are currently running and the data items that are currently being used are stored for quick access.

The program statements you write in a programming language are known as **source code**. The translated machine language statements are known as **object code**.

storage. Internal storage is **volatile**—its contents are lost when the computer is turned off or loses power. Usually, you want to be able to retrieve and perhaps modify the stored instructions later, so you also store them on a permanent storage device, such as a disk. Permanent storage devices are **nonvolatile**—that is, their contents are persistent and are retained even when power is lost.

After a computer program is stored in memory, it must be translated from your programming language statements to **machine language** that represents the millions of on/off circuits within the computer. Each programming language uses a piece of software, called a **compiler** or an **interpreter**, to translate your program code into machine language. Machine language is also called **binary language**, and is represented as a series of 0s and 1s. The compiler or interpreter that translates your code tells you if any programming language component has been used incorrectly. Syntax errors are relatively easy to locate and correct because the compiler or interpreter you use highlights every syntax error. If you write a computer program using a language such as C++ but spell one of its words incorrectly or reverse the proper order of two words, the software lets you know that it found a mistake by displaying an error message as soon as you try to translate the program.

Although there are differences in how compilers and interpreters work, their basic function is the same—to translate your programming statements into code the computer can use. When you use a compiler, an entire program is translated before it can execute; when you use an interpreter, each instruction is translated just prior to execution. Usually, you do not choose which type of translation to use—it depends on the programming language. However, there are some languages for which both compilers and interpreters are available.

Only after program instructions are successfully translated to machine code can the computer carry out the program instructions. When instructions are carried out, a program **runs**, or **executes**. In a typical program, some input will be accepted, some processing will occur, and results will be output.

Besides the popular full-blown programming languages such as Java and C++, many programmers use **scripting languages** (also called **scripting programming languages** or **script languages**) such as Python, Lua, Perl, and PHP. Scripts written in these languages usually can be typed directly from a keyboard and are stored as text rather than as binary executable files. Scripting language programs are interpreted line by line each time the program executes, instead of being stored in a compiled (binary) form.

Understanding Simple Program Logic

A program with syntax errors cannot execute. A program with no syntax errors can execute, but might contain **logical errors**, and produce incorrect output as a result. For a program to work properly, you must give the instructions to the computer in a specific sequence, you must not leave any instructions out, and you must not add extraneous instructions. By doing this, you are developing the **logic** of the computer program.

Suppose you instruct someone to make a cake as follows:

Don't Do It
Don't bake a cake like this!

```
Get a bowl
Stir
Add two eggs
Add a gallon of gasoline
Bake at 350 degrees for 45 minutes
Add three cups of flour
```

Even though you have used the English language syntax correctly, the cake-baking instructions are out of sequence, some instructions are missing, and some instructions belong to procedures other than baking a cake. If you follow these instructions, you are not going to make an edible cake, and you most likely will end up with a disaster. Logical errors are much more difficult to locate than syntax errors—it is easier for you to determine whether "eggs" is spelled incorrectly in a recipe than it is for you to tell if there are too many eggs or if they are added too soon.

 The dangerous cake-baking instructions are shown with a Don't Do It icon. You will see this icon when the book contains an unrecommended programming practice that is used as an example of what *not* to do.

 If you misspell a programming language word, you commit a syntax error, but if you use an otherwise correct word that does not make sense in the current context, programmers say you have committed a **semantic error**. Either way, the program will not execute.

After you learn French, you automatically know, or can easily figure out, many Spanish words. Similarly, after you learn one programming language, it is much easier to understand several other languages.

You will learn about the odd elimination of the space between words like my and Number in Chapter 2.

Programmers use an asterisk to indicate multiplication. You will learn more about arithmetic statements in Chapter 2.

Just as baking directions can be given correctly in Mandarin, Urdu, or Spanish, the same program logic can be expressed in any number of programming languages. Because this book is not concerned with any specific language, the programming examples could have been written in Visual Basic, C++, or Java. For convenience, this book uses instructions written in English!

Most simple computer programs include steps that perform input, processing, and output. Suppose you want to write a computer program to double any number you provide. You can write such a program in a programming language such as Visual Basic or Java, but if you were to write it using English-like statements, it would look like this:

```
input myNumber
set myAnswer = myNumber * 2
output myAnswer
```

The number-doubling process includes three instructions:

- The instruction to input myNumber is an example of an input operation. When the computer interprets this instruction, it knows to look to an input device to obtain a number. When you work in a specific programming language, you write instructions that tell the computer which device to access for input. For example, when a user enters a number as data for a program, the user might click on the number with a mouse, type it from a keyboard, or speak it into a microphone. Logically, however, it doesn't really matter which hardware device is used, as long as the computer knows to look for a number. When the number is retrieved from an input device, it is placed in the computer's memory at the location named myNumber. The location myNumber is a variable. A **variable** is a named memory location whose value can vary—for example, the value of myNumber might be 3 when the program is used for the first time and 45 when it is used the next time.

From a logical perspective, when you input a value, the hardware device is irrelevant. The same is true in your daily life. If you follow the instruction "Get eggs for the cake," it does not really matter if you purchase them from a store or harvest them from your own chickens—you get the eggs either way. There might be different practical considerations to getting the eggs, just as there are for getting data from a large database as opposed to an inexperienced user. For now, this book is only concerned with the logic of the operation, not the minor details.

- The instruction set myAnswer = myNumber * 2 is an example of a processing operation. Mathematical operations are not the only kind of processing operations, but they are very typical. As with input operations, the type of hardware used for processing is irrelevant—after you write a program, it can be used on computers of different brand names, sizes, and speeds. The instruction takes the value stored in memory at the myNumber location, multiplies it by 2, and stores the result in another memory location named myAnswer.

- In the number-doubling program, the output myAnswer instruction is an example of an output operation. Within a particular program, this statement could cause the output to appear on the monitor (which might be a flat-panel plasma screen or a cathode-ray tube), or the output could go to a printer (which could be laser or ink-jet), or the output could be written to a disk or DVD. The logic of the output process is the same no matter what hardware device you use. When this instruction executes, the value stored in memory at the location named myAnswer is sent to an output device.

Watch the video *A Simple Program*.

Computer memory consists of millions of numbered locations where data can be stored. The memory location of **myNumber** has a specific numeric address—for example, 48604. Your program associates **myNumber** with that address. Every time you refer to **myNumber** within a program, the computer retrieves the value at the associated memory location. When you write programs, you seldom need to be concerned with the value of the memory address; instead, you simply use the easy-to-remember name you created.

Computer programmers often refer to memory addresses using hexadecimal notation, or base 16. Using this system, they might use a value like 42FF01A to refer to a memory address. Despite the use of letters, such an address is still a hexadecimal number. Appendix A contains information on this numbering system.

TWO TRUTHS & A LIE

Understanding Simple Program Logic

1. A program with syntax errors can execute but might produce incorrect results.

2. Although the syntax of programming languages differs, the same program logic can be expressed in different languages.

3. Most simple computer programs include steps that perform input, processing, and output.

The false statement is #1. A program with syntax errors cannot execute; a program with no syntax errors can execute, but might produce incorrect results.

Understanding the Program Development Cycle

A programmer's job involves writing instructions (such as those in the doubling program in the preceding section), but a professional programmer usually does not just sit down at a computer keyboard and start typing. Figure 1-1 illustrates the **program development cycle**, which can be broken down into at least seven steps:

1. Understand the problem.

2. Plan the logic.

3. Code the program.

4. Use software (a compiler or interpreter) to translate the program into machine language.

5. Test the program.

6. Put the program into production.

7. Maintain the program.

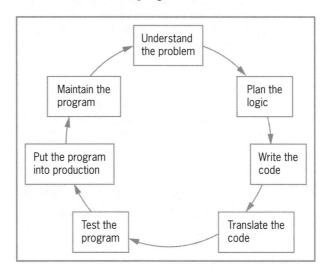

Figure 1-1 The program development cycle

Understanding the Problem

Professional computer programmers write programs to satisfy the needs of others, called **users** or **end users**. Examples could include a Human Resources department that needs a printed list of all employees, a Billing department that wants a list of clients who are 30 or more days overdue on their payments, and an Order department that needs a Web site to provide buyers with an online shopping cart in which to gather their orders. Because programmers are providing a service to these users, programmers must first understand what the users want. Although when a program runs, you usually think of the logic as a cycle of input-processing-output operations; when you plan a program, you think of the output first. After you understand what the desired result is, you can plan what to input and process to achieve it.

Suppose the director of Human Resources says to a programmer, "Our department needs a list of all employees who have been here over five years, because we want to invite them to a special thank-you dinner." On the surface, this seems like a simple request. An experienced programmer, however, will know that the request is incomplete. For example, you might not know the answers to the following questions about which employees to include:

- Does the director want a list of full-time employees only, or a list of full- and part-time employees together?

- Does she want people who have worked for the company on a month-to-month contractual basis over the past five years, or only regular, permanent employees?

- Do the listed employees need to have worked for the organization for five years as of today, as of the date of the dinner, or as of some other cutoff date?

- What about an employee who, for example, worked three years, took a two-year leave of absence, and has been back for three years?

The programmer cannot make any of these decisions; the user (in this case, the Human Resources director) must address these questions.

More decisions still might be required. For example:

- What data should be included for each listed employee? Should the list contain both first and last names? Social Security numbers? Phone numbers? Addresses?

- Should the list be in alphabetical order? Employee ID number order? Length-of-service order? Some other order?

- Should the employees be grouped by any criteria, such as department number or years of service?

Several pieces of documentation are often provided to help the programmer understand the problem. **Documentation** consists of all the supporting paperwork for a program; it might include items such as original requests for the program from users, sample output, and descriptions of the data items available for input.

The term *end user* distinguishes those who actually use and benefit from a software product from others in an organization who might purchase, install, or have other contact with the software.

Watch the video *The Program Development Cycle, Part 1.*

Really understanding the problem may be one of the most difficult aspects of programming. On any job, the description of what the user needs may be vague—worse yet, users may not really know what they want, and users who think they know frequently change their minds after seeing sample output. A good programmer is often part counselor, part detective!

Planning the Logic

You may hear programmers refer to planning a program as "developing an algorithm." An **algorithm** is the sequence of steps necessary to solve any problem.

The heart of the programming process lies in planning the program's logic. During this phase of the process, the programmer plans the steps of the program, deciding what steps to include and how to order them. You can plan the solution to a problem in many ways. The two most common planning tools are flowcharts and pseudocode. Both tools involve writing the steps of the program in English, much as you would plan a trip on paper before getting into the car or plan a party theme before shopping for food and favors.

You will learn more about flowcharts and pseudocode later in this chapter.

The programmer shouldn't worry about the syntax of any particular language at this point, but should focus on figuring out what sequence of events will lead from the available input to the desired output. Planning the logic includes thinking carefully about all the possible data values a program might encounter and how you want the program to handle each scenario. The process of walking through a program's logic on paper before you actually write the program is called **desk-checking**. You will learn more about planning the logic throughout this book; in fact, the book focuses on this crucial step almost exclusively.

In addition to flowcharts and pseudocode, programmers use a variety of other tools to help in program development. One such tool is an **IPO chart**, which delineates input, processing, and output tasks. Some object-oriented programmers also use **TOE charts**, which list tasks, objects, and events.

Coding the Program

After the logic is developed, only then can the programmer write the program. Hundreds of programming languages are available. Programmers choose particular languages because some have built-in capabilities that make them more efficient than others at handling certain types of operations. Despite their differences, programming languages are quite alike in their basic capabilities—each can handle input operations, arithmetic processing, output operations, and other standard functions. The logic developed to solve a programming problem can be executed using any number of languages. Only after choosing a language must the programmer be concerned with proper punctuation and the correct spelling of commands—in other words, using the correct *syntax*.

Some very experienced programmers can successfully combine logic planning and program coding in one step. This may work for planning and writing a very simple program, just as you can plan and write a postcard to a friend using one step. A good term paper or a Hollywood screenplay, however, needs planning before writing—and so do most programs.

Which step is harder: planning the logic or coding the program? Right now, it may seem to you that writing in a programming language is a very difficult task, considering all the spelling and syntax rules you must learn. However, the planning step is actually more difficult. Which is more difficult: thinking up the twists and turns to the plot of a best-selling mystery novel, or writing a translation of an existing novel from English to Spanish? And who do you think gets paid more, the writer who creates the plot or the translator? (Try asking friends to name any famous translator!)

Using Software to Translate the Program into Machine Language

Even though there are many programming languages, each computer knows only one language: its machine language, which consists of 1s and 0s. Computers understand machine language because they are made up of thousands of tiny electrical switches, each of which can be set in either the on or off state, which is represented by a 1 or 0, respectively.

When you learn the syntax of a programming language, the commands you learn will work on any machine on which the language software has been installed. However, your commands are translated to machine language, which differs depending on your computer make and model.

Languages like Java or Visual Basic are available for programmers because someone has written a translator program (a compiler or interpreter) that changes the programmer's English-like **high-level programming language** into the **low-level machine language** that the computer understands. If you write a programming language statement incorrectly (for example, by misspelling a word, using a word that doesn't exist in the language, or using "illegal" grammar), the translator program doesn't know how to proceed and issues an error message identifying a **syntax error**, which is a misuse of a language's grammar rules. Although making errors is never desirable, syntax errors are not a major concern to programmers, because the compiler or interpreter catches every syntax error and displays a message that notifies you of the problem. The computer will not execute a program that contains even one syntax error.

Typically, a programmer develops a program's logic, writes the code, and compiles the program, receiving a list of syntax errors. The programmer then corrects the syntax errors and compiles the program again. Correcting the first set of errors frequently reveals new errors that originally were not apparent to the compiler. For example, if you could use an English compiler and submit the sentence "The dg chase

Watch the video *The Program Development Cycle, Part 2.*

After a program has been translated into machine language, the machine language program is saved and can be run any number of times without repeating the translation step. You only need to retranslate your code if you make changes to your source code statements.

the cat," the compiler at first might point out only one syntax error. The second word, "dg," is illegal because it is not part of the English language. Only after you corrected the word to "dog" would the compiler find another syntax error on the third word, "chase," because it is the wrong verb form for the subject "dog." This doesn't mean "chase" is necessarily the wrong word. Maybe "dog" is wrong; perhaps the subject should be "dogs," in which case "chase" is right. Compilers don't always know exactly what you mean, nor do they know what the proper correction should be, but they do know when something is wrong with your syntax.

When writing a program, a programmer might need to recompile the code several times. An executable program is created only when the code is free of syntax errors. When you run an executable program, it typically also might require input data. Figure 1-2 shows a diagram of this entire process.

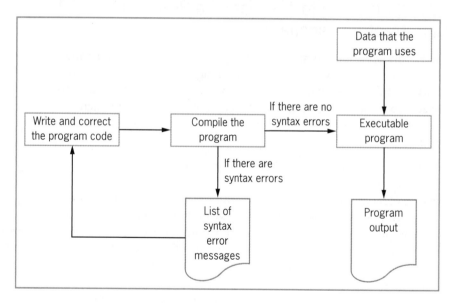

Figure 1-2 Creating an executable program

Testing the Program

A program that is free of syntax errors is not necessarily free of logical errors. A logical error results when you use a syntactically correct statement but use the wrong one for the current context. For example, the English sentence "The dog chases the cat," although syntactically perfect, is not logically correct if the dog chases a ball or the cat is the aggressor.

Once a program is free of syntax errors, the programmer can test it—that is, execute it with some sample data to see whether the results are logically correct. Recall the number-doubling program:

```
input myNumber
set myAnswer = myNumber * 2
output myAnswer
```

If you execute the program, provide the value 2 as input to the program, and the answer 4 is displayed, you have executed one successful test run of the program.

However, if the answer 40 is displayed, maybe the program contains a logical error. Maybe the second line of code was mistyped with an extra zero, so that the program reads:

```
input myNumber
set myAnswer = myNumber * 20
output myAnswer
```

Don't Do It
The programmer typed "20" instead of "2".

Placing 20 instead of 2 in the multiplication statement caused a logical error. Notice that nothing is syntactically wrong with this second program—it is just as reasonable to multiply a number by 20 as by 2—but if the programmer intends only to double myNumber, then a logical error has occurred.

 The process of finding and correcting program errors is called **debugging**.

Programs should be tested with many sets of data. For example, if you write the program to double a number, then enter 2 and get an output value of 4, that doesn't necessarily mean you have a correct program. Perhaps you have typed this program by mistake:

Don't Do It
The programmer typed "+" instead of "*".

```
input myNumber
set myAnswer = myNumber + 2
output myAnswer
```

An input of 2 results in an answer of 4, but that doesn't mean your program doubles numbers—it actually only adds 2 to them. If you test your program with additional data and get the wrong answer—for example, if you enter 7 and get an answer of 9—you know there is a problem with your code.

Selecting test data is somewhat of an art in itself, and it should be done carefully. If the Human Resources department wants a list of the names of five-year employees, it would be a mistake to test the program with a small sample file of only long-term employees. If no newer employees are part of the data being used for testing, you do not really know if the program would have eliminated them

Chapter 4 contains more information on testing programs.

from the five-year list. Many companies do not know that their software has a problem until an unusual circumstance occurs—for example, the first time an employee has more than nine dependents, the first time a customer orders more than 999 items at a time, or when (as well-documented in the popular press) a new century begins.

Putting the Program into Production

Once the program is tested adequately, it is ready for the organization to use. Putting the program into production might mean simply running the program once, if it was written to satisfy a user's request for a special list. However, the process might take months if the program will be run on a regular basis, or if it is one of a large system of programs being developed. Perhaps data-entry people must be trained to prepare the input for the new program; users must be trained to understand the output; or existing data in the company must be changed to an entirely new format to accommodate this program. **Conversion**, the entire set of actions an organization must take to switch over to using a new program or set of programs, can sometimes take months or years to accomplish.

Maintaining the Program

After programs are put into production, making necessary changes is called **maintenance**. Maintenance can be required for many reasons: new tax rates are legislated, the format of an input file is altered, or the end user requires additional information not included in the original output specifications, to name a few. Frequently, your first programming job will require maintaining previously written programs. When you maintain the programs others have written, you will appreciate the effort the original programmer put into writing clear code, using reasonable variable names, and documenting his or her work. When you make changes to existing programs, you repeat the development cycle. That is, you must understand the changes, then plan, code, translate, and test them before putting them into production. If a substantial number of program changes are required, the original program might be retired, and the program development cycle might be started for a new program.

Watch the video *The Program Development Cycle, Part 3.*

TWO TRUTHS & A LIE

Understanding the Program Development Cycle

1. Understanding the problem that must be solved can be one of the most difficult aspects of programming.

2. The two most commonly used logic-planning tools are flowcharts and pseudocode.

3. Flowcharting a program is a very different process if you use an older programming language instead of a newer one.

The false statement is #3. Despite their differences, programming languages are quite alike in their basic capabilities—each can handle input operations, arithmetic processing, output operations, and other standard functions. The logic developed to solve a programming problem can be executed using any number of languages.

Using Pseudocode Statements and Flowchart Symbols

When programmers plan the logic for a solution to a programming problem, they often use one of two tools: pseudocode (pronounced "sue-doe-code") or flowcharts. **Pseudocode** is an English-like representation of the logical steps it takes to solve a problem. A **flowchart** is a pictorial representation of the same thing. *Pseudo* is a prefix that means "false," and to *code* a program means to put it in a programming language; therefore, *pseudocode* simply means "false code," or sentences that appear to have been written in a computer programming language but do not necessarily follow all the syntax rules of any specific language.

Writing Pseudocode

You have already seen examples of statements that represent pseudocode earlier in this chapter, and there is nothing mysterious about them. The following five statements constitute a pseudocode representation of a number-doubling problem:

```
start
  input myNumber
  set myAnswer = myNumber * 2
  output myAnswer
stop
```

Using pseudocode involves writing down all the steps you will use in a program. Usually, programmers preface their pseudocode with a beginning statement like start and end it with a terminating statement like stop. The statements between start and stop look like English and are indented slightly so that start and stop stand out. Most programmers do not bother with punctuation such as periods at the end of pseudocode statements, although it would not be wrong to use them if you prefer that style. Similarly, there is no need to capitalize the first word in a sentence, although you might choose to do so. This book follows the conventions of using lowercase letters for verbs that begin pseudocode statements and omitting periods at the end of statements.

Pseudocode is fairly flexible because it is a planning tool, and not the final product. Therefore, for example, you might prefer any of the following:

- Instead of start and stop, some pseudocode developers would use the terms begin and end.

- Instead of writing input myNumber, some developers would write get myNumber or read myNumber.

- Instead of writing set myAnswer = myNumber * 2, some developers would write calculate myAnswer = myNumber times 2 or compute myAnswer as myNumber doubled.

- Instead of writing output myAnswer, many pseudocode developers would write display myAnswer, print myAnswer, or write myAnswer.

The point is, the pseudocode statements are instructions to retrieve an original number from an input device and store it in memory where it can be used in a calculation, and then to get the calculated answer from memory and send it to an output device so a person can see it. When you eventually convert your pseudocode to a specific programming language, you do not have such flexibility because specific syntax will be required. For example, if you use the C# programming language and write the statement to output the answer, you will code the following:

```
Console.Write (myAnswer);
```

The exact use of words, capitalization, and punctuation are important in the C# statement, but not in the pseudocode statement.

Drawing Flowcharts

Some professional programmers prefer writing pseudocode to drawing flowcharts, because using pseudocode is more similar to writing the final statements in the programming language. Others prefer drawing flowcharts to represent the logical flow, because flowcharts allow programmers to visualize more easily how the program statements will connect. Especially for beginning programmers, flowcharts are an excellent tool to help them visualize how the statements in a program are interrelated.

17

 You can draw a flowchart by hand or use software, such as Microsoft Word and Microsoft PowerPoint, that contains flowcharting tools. You can use several other software programs, such as Visio and Visual Logic, specifically to create flowcharts.

When you create a flowchart, you draw geometric shapes that contain the individual statements and that are connected with arrows. You use a parallelogram to represent an **input symbol**, which indicates an input operation. You write an input statement in English inside the parallelogram, as shown in Figure 1-3.

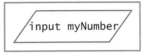

Figure 1-3   Input symbol

Arithmetic operation statements are examples of processing. In a flowchart, you use a rectangle as the **processing symbol** that contains a processing statement, as shown in Figure 1-4.

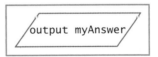

Figure 1-4   Processing symbol

 Because the parallelogram is used for both input and output, it is often called the **input/output symbol** or **I/O symbol**.

To represent an output statement, you use the same symbol as for input statements—the **output symbol** is a parallelogram, as shown in Figure 1-5.

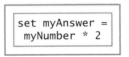

Figure 1-5   Output symbol

 Some software programs that use flowcharts (such as Visual Logic) use a left-slanting parallelogram to represent output. As long as the flowchart creator and the flowchart reader are communicating, the actual shape used is irrelevant. This book will follow the most standard convention of always using the right-slanting parallelogram for both input and output.

To show the correct sequence of these statements, you use arrows, or **flowlines**, to connect the steps. Whenever possible, most of a flowchart should read from top to bottom or from left to right on a page. That's the way we read English, so when flowcharts follow this convention, they are easier for us to understand.

Appendix B contains a summary of all the flowchart symbols you will see in this book.

Programmers seldom create both pseudocode and a flowchart for the same problem. You usually use one or the other. In a large program, you might even prefer to use pseudocode for some parts and draw a flowchart for others.

18

To be complete, a flowchart should include two more elements: **terminal symbols**, or start/stop symbols, at each end. Often, you place a word like start or begin in the first terminal symbol and a word like end or stop in the other. The standard terminal symbol is shaped like a racetrack; many programmers refer to this shape as a lozenge, because it resembles the shape of the medication you might use to soothe a sore throat. Figure 1-6 shows a complete flowchart for the program that doubles a number, and the pseudocode for the same problem. You can see from the figure that the flowchart and pseudocode statements are the same—only the presentation format differs.

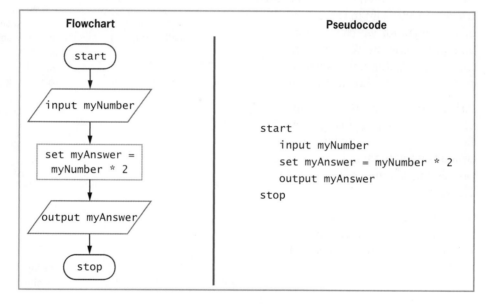

Figure 1-6   Flowchart and pseudocode of program that doubles a number

Repeating Instructions

After the flowchart or pseudocode has been developed, the programmer only needs to: (1) buy a computer, (2) buy a language compiler, (3) learn a programming language, (4) code the program, (5) attempt to compile it, (6) fix the syntax errors, (7) compile it again, (8) test it with several sets of data, and (9) put it into production.

"Whoa!" you are probably saying to yourself. "This is simply not worth it! All that work to create a flowchart or pseudocode, and *then* all those other steps? For five dollars, I can buy a pocket calculator that will double any number for me instantly!" You are absolutely right. If this were a real computer program, and all it did was double the value of a number, it would not be worth the effort. Writing a computer program would be worthwhile only if you had many—let's say 10,000—numbers to double in a limited amount of time—let's say the next two minutes.

Unfortunately, the number-doubling program represented in Figure 1-6 does not double 10,000 numbers; it doubles only one. You could execute the program 10,000 times, of course, but that would require you to sit at the computer and tell it to run the program over and over again. You would be better off with a program that could process 10,000 numbers, one after the other.

One solution is to write the program shown in Figure 1-7 and execute the same steps 10,000 times. Of course, writing this program would be very time consuming; you might as well buy the calculator.

When you tell a friend how to get to your house, you might write a series of instructions or you might draw a map. Pseudocode is similar to written, step-by-step instructions; a flowchart, like a map, is a visual representation of the same thing.

19

```
start
   input myNumber
   set myAnswer = myNumber * 2
   output myAnswer
   input myNumber
   set myAnswer = myNumber * 2
   output myAnswer
   input myNumber
   set myAnswer = myNumber * 2
   output myAnswer
   ...and so on for 9,997 more times
```

Don't Do It
You would never want to write such a repetitious list of instructions.

Figure 1-7   Inefficient pseudocode for program that doubles 10,000 numbers

A better solution is to have the computer execute the same set of three instructions over and over again, as shown in Figure 1-8. The repetition of a series of steps is called a **loop**. With this approach, the computer gets a number, doubles it, displays the answer, and then starts over again with the first instruction. The same spot in memory, called myNumber, is reused for the second number and for any subsequent numbers. The spot in memory named myAnswer is reused each time to store the result of the multiplication operation. The logic illustrated in the flowchart in Figure 1-8 contains a major problem—the sequence of instructions never ends. This programming situation is known as an **infinite loop**—a repeating flow of logic with no end. You will learn one way to handle this problem later in this chapter; you will learn a superior way in Chapter 3.

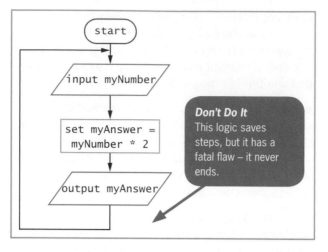

Figure 1-8 Flowchart of infinite number-doubling program

Using a Sentinel Value to End a Program

The logic in the flowchart for doubling numbers, shown in Figure 1-8, has a major flaw—the program contains an infinite loop. If, for example, the input numbers are being entered at the keyboard, the program will keep accepting numbers and outputting doubles forever. Of course, the user could refuse to type any more numbers. But the computer is very patient, and if you refuse to give it any more numbers, it will sit and wait forever. When you finally type a number, the program will double it, output the result, and wait for another. The program cannot progress any further while it is waiting for input; meanwhile, the program is occupying computer memory and tying up operating system resources. Refusing to enter any more numbers is not a practical solution. Another way to end the program is simply to turn off the computer. But again, that's neither the best way nor an elegant solution.

A superior way to end the program is to set a predetermined value for myNumber that means "Stop the program!" For example, the programmer and the user could agree that the user will never need to know the double of 0, so the user could enter a 0 to stop. The program could then test any incoming value contained in myNumber and, if it is a 0, stop the program. Testing a value is also called **making a decision**.

You represent a decision in a flowchart by drawing a **decision symbol**, which is shaped like a diamond. The diamond usually contains a question, the answer to which is one of two mutually exclusive options—often yes or no. All good computer questions have only two mutually exclusive answers, such as yes and no or true and false. For example, "What day of the year is your birthday?" is not a good computer question because there are 366 possible answers. However, "Is your birthday June 24?" is a good computer question because, for everyone in the world, the answer is either yes or no.

 A yes-or-no decision is called a **binary decision**, because there are two possible outcomes.

The question to stop the doubling program should be "Is the value of myNumber just entered equal to 0?" or "myNumber = 0?" for short. The complete flowchart will now look like the one shown in Figure 1-9.

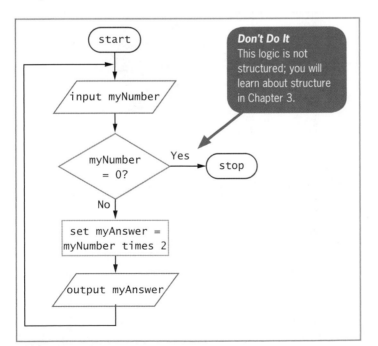

Figure 1-9   Flowchart of number-doubling program with sentinel value of 0

One drawback to using 0 to stop a program, of course, is that it won't work if the user does need to find the double of 0. In that case, some other data-entry value that the user will never need, such as 999 or −1, could be selected to signal that the program should end. A preselected value that stops the execution of a program is often called a **dummy value** because it does not represent real data, but just a signal to stop. Sometimes, such a value is called a **sentinel value** because it represents an entry or exit point, like a sentinel who guards a fortress.

Not all programs rely on user data entry from a keyboard; many read data from an input device, such as a disk. When organizations store data on a disk or other storage device, they do not commonly use a dummy value to signal the end of the file. For one thing, an input record might have hundreds of fields, and if you store a dummy record in every file, you are wasting a large quantity of storage on "nondata." Additionally, it is often difficult to choose sentinel values for fields in a company's data files. Any balanceDue, even a zero or a negative number, can be a legitimate value, and any customerName, even "ZZ", could be someone's name. Fortunately, programming languages can recognize the end of data in a file automatically, through a code that is stored at the end of the data. Many programming languages use the term **eof** (for "end of file") to refer to this marker that automatically acts as a sentinel. This book, therefore, uses eof to indicate the end of data whenever using a dummy value is impractical or inconvenient. In the flowchart shown in Figure 1-10, the eof question is shaded.

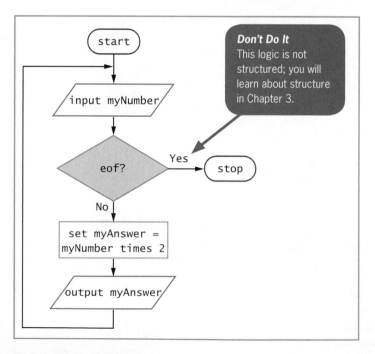

Figure 1-10   Flowchart using eof

TWO TRUTHS & A LIE

Using a Sentinel Value to End a Program

1. A program that contains an infinite loop is one that never ends.

2. A preselected value that stops the execution of a program is often called a dummy value or a sentinel value.

3. Many programming languages use the term fe (for "file end") to refer to a marker that automatically acts as a sentinel.

The false statement is #3. The term eof (for "end of file") is the common term for a file sentinel.

Understanding Programming and User Environments

Many approaches can be used to write and execute a computer program. When you plan a program's logic, you can use a flowchart or pseudocode, or a combination of the two. When you code the program, you can type statements into a variety of text editors. When your program executes, it might accept input from a keyboard, mouse, microphone, or any other input device, and when you provide a program's output, you might use text, images, or sound. This section describes the most common environments you will encounter as a new programmer.

Understanding Programming Environments

When you plan the logic for a computer program, you can use paper and pencil to create a flowchart, or you might use software that allows you to manipulate flowchart shapes. If you choose to write pseudocode, you can do so by hand or by using a word-processing program. To enter the program into a computer so you can translate and execute it, you usually use a keyboard to type program statements into an editor. You can type a program into one of the following:

- A plain text editor

- A text editor that is part of an integrated development environment

A **text editor** is a program that you use to create simple text files. It is similar to a word processor, but without as many features. You can use a text editor such as Notepad that is included with Microsoft Windows. Figure 1-11 shows a C# program in Notepad that accepts a number and doubles it. An advantage to using a simple text editor to type and save a program is that the completed program does not require much disk space for storage. For example, the file shown in Figure 1-11 occupies only 314 bytes of storage.

> This line contains a prompt that tells the user what to enter. You will learn more about prompts in Chapter 2.

```
NumberDoublingProgram.cs - Notepad

File  Edit  Format  View  Help

using System;
public class NumberDoublingProgram
{
    public static void Main()
    {
        int myNumber;
        int myAnswer;
        Console.Write("Please enter a number >> ");
        myNumber = Convert.ToInt32(Console.ReadLine());
        myAnswer = myNumber * 2;
        Console.WriteLine(myAnswer);
    }
}
```

Figure 1-11   A C# number-doubling program in Notepad

You can use the editor of an **integrated development environment (IDE)** to enter your program. An IDE is a software package that provides an editor, compiler, and other programming tools. For example, Figure 1-12 shows a C# program in the **Microsoft Visual Studio IDE**, an environment that contains tools useful for creating programs in Visual Basic, C++, and C#.

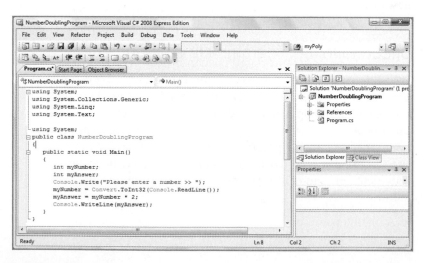

Figure 1-12   A C# number-doubling program in Visual Studio

Using an IDE is helpful to programmers because IDEs usually provide features similar to those you find in many word processors. In particular, an IDE's editor commonly includes such features as the following:

- It uses different colors to display various language components, making elements like data types easier to identify.

- It highlights syntax errors visually for you.

- It employs automatic statement completion; when you start to type a statement, the IDE suggests a likely completion, which you can accept with a keystroke.

- It provides tools that allow you to step through a program's execution one statement at a time so you can more easily follow the program's logic and determine the source of any errors.

When you use the IDE to create and save a program, you occupy much more disk space than when using a plain text editor. For example, the program in Figure 1-12 occupies more than 49,000 bytes of disk space.

Although various programming environments might look different and offer different features, the process of using them is very similar. When you plan the logic for a program using pseudocode or a flowchart, it does not matter which programming environment you will use to write your code, and when you write the code in a programming language, it does not matter which environment you use to write it.

Understanding User Environments

A user might execute a program you have written in any number of environments. For example, a user might execute the number-doubling program from a command line like the one shown in Figure 1-13. A **command line** is a location on your computer screen at which you type text entries to communicate with the computer's operating system. In the program in Figure 1-13, the user is asked for a number, and the results are displayed.

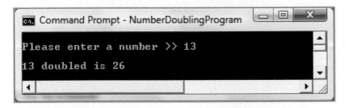

Figure 1-13 Executing a number-doubling program in a command-line environment

Many programs are not run at the command line in a text environment, but are run using a **graphical user interface**, or **GUI** (pronounced "gooey"), which allows users to interact with a program in a graphical environment. When running a GUI program, the user might type input into a text box or use a mouse or other pointing device to select options on the screen. Figure 1-14 shows a number-doubling program that performs exactly the same task as the one in Figure 1-13, but this program uses a GUI.

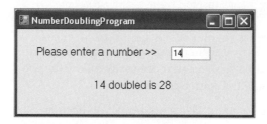

Figure 1-14 Executing a number-doubling program in a GUI environment

A command-line program and a GUI program might be written in the same programming language. (For example, the programs shown in Figures 1-13 and 1-14 were both written using C#.) However, no matter which environment is used to write or execute a program, the logical process is the same. The two programs in Figures 1-13 and 1-14 both accept input, perform multiplication, and perform output. In this book, you will not concentrate on which environment is used to type a program's statements, nor will you care about the type of environment the user will see. Instead, you will be concerned with the logic that applies to all programming situations.

TWO TRUTHS & A LIE

Understanding Programming and User Environments

1. You can type a program into an editor that is part of an integrated development environment, but using a plain text editor provides you with more programming help.

2. When a program runs from the command line, a user types text to provide input.

3. Although GUI and command-line environments look different, the logic processes of input, processing, and output apply to both program types.

The false statement is #1. An integrated development environment provides more programming help than a plain text editor.

Understanding the Evolution of Programming Models

People have been writing modern computer programs since the 1940s. The oldest programming languages required programmers to work with memory addresses and to memorize awkward codes associated with machine languages. Newer programming languages look much more like natural language and are easier to use, partly because they allow programmers to name variables instead of using awkward memory addresses. Also, newer programming languages allow programmers to create self-contained modules or program segments that can be pieced together in a variety of ways. The oldest computer programs were written in one piece, from start to finish, but modern programs are rarely written that way—they are created by teams of programmers, each developing reusable and connectable program procedures. Writing several small modules is easier than writing one large program, and most large tasks are easier when you break the work into units and get other workers to help with some of the units.

Currently, two major models or paradigms are used by programmers to develop programs and their procedures. One technique, **procedural programming**, focuses on the procedures that programmers create. That is, procedural programmers focus on the actions that are carried out—for example, getting input data for an employee and writing the calculations needed to produce a paycheck from the data. Procedural programmers would approach the job of producing a paycheck by breaking down the process into manageable subtasks.

The other popular programming model, **object-oriented programming**, focuses on objects, or "things," and describes their features (or attributes) and their behaviors. For example, object-oriented programmers might design a payroll application by thinking about employees and paychecks, and describing their attributes (e.g. employees have names and Social Security numbers, and paychecks have names and check amounts). Then the programmers would think about the behaviors of employees and paychecks, such as employees getting raises and adding dependents and paychecks being calculated and output. Object-oriented programmers would then build applications from these entities.

With either approach, procedural or object oriented, you can produce a correct paycheck, and both models employ reusable program modules. The major difference lies in the focus the programmer takes during the earliest planning stages of a project. For now, this book focuses on procedural programming techniques. The skills you gain in programming procedurally—declaring variables, accepting input, making decisions, producing output, and so on—will serve you well whether you eventually write programs in a procedural or object-oriented fashion, or in both.

Ada Byron Lovelace predicted the development of software in 1843; she is often regarded as the first programmer. The basis for most modern software was proposed by Alan Turing in 1935.

You will learn to create program modules in Chapter 2.

You can write a procedural program in any language that supports object orientation. The opposite is not always true.

Object-oriented programming employs a large vocabulary; you can learn this terminology in Chapter 10 of the comprehensive version of this book.

28

TWO TRUTHS & A LIE

Understanding the Evolution of Programming Models

1. The oldest computer programs were written in many separate modules.

2. Procedural programmers focus on actions that are carried out by a program.

3. Object-oriented programmers focus on a program's objects and their attributes and behaviors.

The false statement is #1. The oldest programs were written in a single piece; newer programs are divided into modules.

Chapter Summary

- Together, computer hardware (physical devices) and software (instructions) accomplish three major operations: input, processing, and output. You write computer instructions in a computer programming language that requires specific syntax; the instructions are translated into machine language by a compiler or interpreter. When both the syntax and logic of a program are correct, you can run, or execute, the program to produce the desired results.

- For a program to work properly, you must develop correct logic. Logical errors are much more difficult to locate than syntax errors.

- A programmer's job involves understanding the problem, planning the logic, coding the program, translating the program into machine language, testing the program, putting the program into production, and maintaining it.

- When programmers plan the logic for a solution to a programming problem, they often use flowcharts or pseudocode. When you draw a flowchart, you use parallelograms to represent input and output operations, and rectangles to represent processing. Programmers also use decisions to control repetition of instruction sets.

- To avoid creating an infinite loop when you repeat instructions, you can test for a sentinel value. You represent a decision in a flowchart by drawing a diamond-shaped symbol that contains a question, the answer to which is either yes or no.

- You can type a program into a plain text editor or one that is part of an integrated development environment. When a program's data values are entered from a keyboard, they can be entered at the command line in a text environment or in a GUI. Either way, the logic is similar.

- Procedural and object-oriented programmers approach problems differently. Procedural programmers concentrate on the actions performed with data. Object-oriented programmers focus on objects and their behaviors and attributes.

Key Terms

A **computer system** is a combination of all the components required to process and store data using a computer.

Hardware is the collection of physical devices that comprise a computer system.

Software consists of the programs that tell the computer what to do.

Programs are sets of instructions for a computer.

Programming is the act of developing and writing programs.

Application software comprises all the programs you apply to a task.

System software comprises the programs that you use to manage your computer.

Input describes the entry of data items into computer memory using hardware devices such as keyboards and mice.

Data items include all the text, numbers, and other information processed by a computer.

Processing data items may involve organizing them, checking them for accuracy, or performing mathematical operations on them.

The **central processing unit**, or **CPU**, is the hardware component that processes data.

Output describes the operation of retrieving information from memory and sending it to a device, such as a monitor or printer, so people can view, interpret, and work with the results.

Storage devices are types of hardware equipment, such as disks, that hold information for later retrieval.

Programming languages, such as Visual Basic, C#, C++, Java, or COBOL, are used to write programs.

Program code is the set of instructions a programmer writes in a programming language.

Coding the program is the act of writing programming language instructions.

The **syntax** of a language is its grammar rules.

Computer memory is the temporary, internal storage within a computer.

Volatile describes storage whose contents are lost when power is lost.

Nonvolatile describes storage whose contents are retained when power is lost.

Random access memory (RAM) is temporary, internal computer storage.

Machine language is a computer's on/off circuitry language.

A **compiler** or **interpreter** translates a high-level language into machine language and tells you if you have used a programming language incorrectly.

Binary language is represented using a series of 0s and 1s.

Source code is the statements a programmer writes in a programming language.

Object code is translated machine language.

To **run** or **execute** a program is to carry out its instructions.

Scripting languages (also called **scripting programming languages** or **script languages**) such as Python, Lua, Perl, and PHP are used to write programs that are typed directly from a keyboard. Scripting languages are stored as text rather than as binary executable files.

A **logical error** occurs when incorrect instructions are performed, or when instructions are performed in the wrong order.

You develop the **logic** of the computer program when you give instructions to the computer in a specific sequence, without omitting any instructions or adding extraneous instructions.

A **semantic error** occurs when a correct word is used in an incorrect context.

A **variable** is a named memory location whose value can vary.

The **program development cycle** consists of the steps that occur during a program's lifetime.

Users (or **end users**) are people who employ and benefit from computer programs.

Documentation consists of all the supporting paperwork for a program.

An **algorithm** is the sequence of steps necessary to solve any problem.

An **IPO chart** is a program development tool that delineates input, processing, and output tasks.

A **TOE chart** is a program development tool that lists tasks, objects, and events.

Desk-checking is the process of walking through a program solution on paper.

A **high-level programming language** supports English-like syntax.

Machine language is the **low-level language** made up of 1s and 0s that the computer understands.

A **syntax error** is an error in language or grammar.

Debugging is the process of finding and correcting program errors.

Conversion is the entire set of actions an organization must take to switch over to using a new program or set of programs.

Maintenance consists of all the improvements and corrections made to a program after it is in production.

Pseudocode is an English-like representation of the logical steps it takes to solve a problem.

A **flowchart** is a pictorial representation of the logical steps it takes to solve a problem.

An **input symbol** indicates an input operation and is represented by a parallelogram in flowcharts.

A **processing symbol** indicates a processing operation and is represented by a rectangle in flowcharts.

An **output symbol** indicates an output operation and is represented by a parallelogram in flowcharts.

An **input/output symbol** or **I/O symbol** is represented by a parallelogram in flowcharts.

Flowlines, or arrows, connect the steps in a flowchart.

A **terminal symbol**, or start/stop symbol, is used at each end of a flowchart. Its shape is a lozenge.

A **loop** is a repetition of a series of steps.

An **infinite loop** occurs when repeating logic cannot end.

Making a decision is the act of testing a value.

A **decision symbol** is shaped like a diamond and used to represent decisions in flowcharts.

A **binary decision** is a yes-or-no decision with two possible outcomes.

A **dummy value** is a preselected value that stops the execution of a program.

A **sentinel value** is a preselected value that stops the execution of a program.

The term **eof** means "end of file."

A **text editor** is a program that you use to create simple text files; it is similar to a word processor, but without as many features.

An **integrated development environment (IDE)** is a software package that provides an editor, compiler, and other programming tools.

Microsoft Visual Studio IDE is a software package that contains useful tools for creating programs in Visual Basic, C++, and C#.

A **command line** is a location on your computer screen at which you type text entries to communicate with the computer's operating system.

A **graphical user interface**, or **GUI** (pronounced "gooey"), allows users to interact with a program in a graphical environment.

Procedural programming is a programming model that focuses on the procedures that programmers create.

Object-oriented programming is a programming model that focuses on objects, or "things," and describes their features (or attributes) and their behaviors.

Review Questions

1. Computer programs are also known as _____.

   a. hardware

   b. software

   c. data

   d. information

2. The major computer operations include _____.

   a. hardware and software

   b. input, processing, and output

   c. sequence and looping

   d. spreadsheets, word processing, and data communications

3. Visual Basic, C++, and Java are all examples of computer _____.

   a. operating systems

   b. hardware

   c. machine languages

   d. programming languages

4. A programming language's rules are its _____.

   a. syntax

   b. logic

   c. format

   d. options

5. The most important task of a compiler or interpreter is to _____.

   a. create the rules for a programming language

   b. translate English statements into a language the computer can understand, such as Java

   c. translate programming language statements into machine language

   d. execute machine language programs to perform useful tasks

6. Which of the following is temporary, internal storage?

   a. CPU

   b. hard disk

   c. keyboard

   d. memory

7. Which of the following pairs of steps in the programming process is in the correct order?

    a. code the program, plan the logic

    b. test the program, translate it into machine language

    c. put the program into production, understand the problem

    d. code the program, translate it into machine language

8. The programmer's most important task before planning the logic of a program is to _____.

    a. decide which programming language to use

    b. code the problem

    c. train the users of the program

    d. understand the problem

9. The two most commonly used tools for planning a program's logic are _____.

    a. flowcharts and pseudocode

    b. ASCII and EBCDIC

    c. Java and Visual Basic

    d. word processors and spreadsheets

10. Writing a program in a language such as C++ or Java is known as _____ the program.

    a. translating

    b. coding

    c. interpreting

    d. compiling

11. An English-like programming language such as Java or Visual Basic is a _____ programming language.

    a. machine-level

    b. low-level

    c. high-level

    d. binary-level

12. Which of the following is an example of a syntax error?

    a. producing output before accepting input

    b. subtracting when you meant to add

    c. misspelling a programming language word

    d. all of the above

13. Which of the following is an example of a logical error?

    a. performing arithmetic with a value before inputting it

    b. accepting two input values when a program requires only one

    c. dividing by 3 when you meant to divide by 30

    d. all of the above

14. The parallelogram is the flowchart symbol representing _____.

    a. input

    b. output

    c. both a and b

    d. none of the above

15. In a flowchart, a rectangle represents _____.

    a. input

    b. a sentinel

    c. a question

    d. processing

16. In flowcharts, the decision symbol is a _____.

    a. parallelogram

    b. rectangle

    c. lozenge

    d. diamond

36

17. The term "eof" represents _____.

    a. a standard input device

    b. a generic sentinel value

    c. a condition in which no more memory is available for storage

    d. the logical flow in a program

18. When you use an IDE instead of a simple text editor to develop a program, _____.

    a. the logic is more complicated

    b. the logic is simpler

    c. the syntax is different

    d. some help is provided

19. When you write a program that will run in a GUI environment as opposed to a command-line environment, _____.

    a. the logic is very different

    b. some syntax is different

    c. you do not need to plan the logic

    d. users are more confused

20. As compared to procedural programming, with object-oriented programming _____.

    a. the programmer's focus differs

    b. you cannot use some languages, such as Java

    c. you do not accept input

    d. you do not code calculations; they are created automatically

Exercises

1. Match the definition with the appropriate term.

    1. Computer system devices   a. compiler

    2. Another word for programs   b. syntax

    3. Language rules   c. logic

    4. Order of instructions   d. hardware

    5. Language translator   e. software

2. In your own words, describe the steps to writing a computer program.

3. Match the term with the appropriate shape.

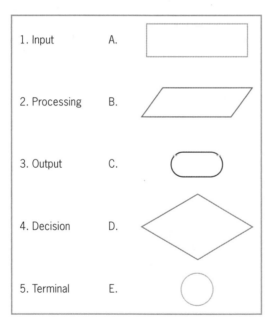

4. Draw a flowchart or write pseudocode to represent the logic of a program that allows the user to enter a value. The program multiplies the value by 10 and outputs the result.

5. Draw a flowchart or write pseudocode to represent the logic of a program that allows the user to enter a value for the radius of a circle. The program calculates the diameter by multiplying the radius by 2, and then calculates the circumference by multiplying the diameter by 3.14. The program outputs both the diameter and the circumference.

6. Draw a flowchart or write pseudocode to represent the logic of a program that allows the user to enter two values. The program outputs the sum of the two values.

7. Draw a flowchart or write pseudocode to represent the logic of a program that allows the user to enter three values. The values represent hourly pay rate, the number of hours worked this pay period, and percentage of gross salary that is withheld. The program multiplies the hourly pay rate by the number of hours worked, giving the gross pay. Then, it multiplies the gross pay by the withholding percentage, giving the withholding amount. Finally, it subtracts the withholding amount from the gross pay, giving the net pay after taxes. The program outputs the net pay.

 ## Find the Bugs

8. Since the early days of computer programming, program errors have been called "bugs." The term is often said to have originated from an actual moth that was discovered trapped in the circuitry of a computer at Harvard University in 1945. Actually, the term "bug" was in use prior to 1945 to mean trouble with any electrical apparatus; even during Thomas Edison's life, it meant an "industrial defect." However, the term "debugging" is more closely associated with correcting program syntax and logic errors than with any other type of trouble.

    Your student disk contains files named DEBUG01-01.txt, DEBUG01-02.txt, and DEBUG01-03.txt. Each file starts with some comments that describe the problem. Comments are lines that begin with two slashes (//). Following the comments, each file contains pseudocode that has one or more bugs you must find and correct.

Game Zone

9. In 1952, A. S. Douglas wrote his University of Cambridge Ph.D. dissertation on human-computer interaction, and created the first graphical computer game—a version of Tic-Tac-Toe. The game was programmed on an EDSAC vacuum-tube mainframe computer. The first computer game is generally assumed to be "Spacewar!", developed in 1962 at MIT; the first commercially available video game was "Pong," introduced by Atari in 1972. In 1980, Atari's "Asteroids" and "Lunar Lander" became the first video games to be registered with the U. S. Copyright Office. Throughout the 1980s, players spent hours with games that now seem very simple and unglamorous; do you recall playing "Adventure," "Oregon Trail," "Where in the World Is Carmen Sandiego?," or "Myst"?

Today, commercial computer games are much more complex; they require many programmers, graphic artists, and testers to develop them, and large management and marketing staffs are needed to promote them. A game might cost many millions of dollars to develop and market, but a successful game might earn hundreds of millions of dollars. Obviously, with the brief introduction to programming you have had in this chapter, you cannot create a very sophisticated game. However, you can get started.

Mad Libs© is a children's game in which players provide a few words that are then incorporated into a silly story. The game helps children understand different parts of speech because they are asked to provide specific types of words. For example, you might ask a child for a noun, another noun, an adjective, and a past-tense verb. The child might reply with such answers as "table," "book," "silly," and "studied." The newly created Mad Lib might be:

> Mary had a little *table*
>
> Its *book* was *silly* as snow
>
> And everywhere that Mary *studied*
>
> The *table* was sure to go.

Create the logic for a Mad Lib program that accepts five words from input, then creates and displays a short story or nursery rhyme that uses those words.

Up for Discussion

10. Which is the better tool for learning programming—flowcharts or pseudocode? Cite any educational research you can find.

11. What is the image of the computer programmer in popular culture? Is the image different in books than in TV shows and movies? Would you like that image for yourself?

CHAPTER 2

Working with Data, Creating Modules, and Designing High-Quality Programs

In this chapter, you will learn about:

- ◎ Declaring and using variables and constants
- ◎ Assigning values to variables
- ◎ The advantages of modularization
- ◎ Modularizing a program
- ◎ The most common configuration for mainline logic
- ◎ Hierarchy charts
- ◎ Some features of good program design

Declaring and Using Variables and Constants

As you learned in Chapter 1, data items include all the text, numbers, and other information that are processed by a computer. When you input data items into a computer, they are stored in variables in memory where they can be processed and converted to information that is output.

When you write programs, you work with data in three different forms: variables; literals, or unnamed constants; and named constants.

Watch the video
*Declaring
Variables and
Constants.*

Working with Variables

Variables are named memory locations whose contents can vary or differ over time. For example, in the number-doubling program in Figure 2-1, myNumber and myAnswer are variables. At any moment in time, a variable holds just one value. Sometimes, myNumber holds 2 and myAnswer holds 4; at other times, myNumber holds 6 and myAnswer holds 12. The ability of variables to change in value is what makes computers and programming worthwhile. Because one memory location can be used repeatedly with different values, you can write program instructions once and then use them for thousands of separate calculations. *One* set of payroll instructions at your company produces each individual's paycheck, and *one* set of instructions at your electric company produces each household's bill.

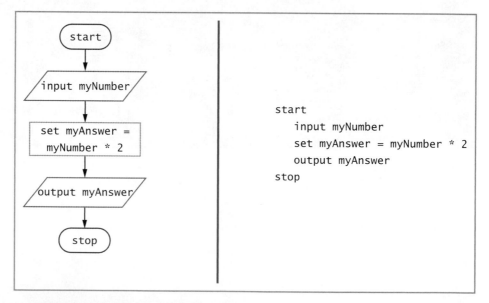

```
start
    input myNumber
    set myAnswer = myNumber * 2
    output myAnswer
stop
```

Figure 2-1   Flowchart and pseudocode for the number-doubling program

In most programming languages, before you can use any variable, you must include a declaration for it. A **declaration** is a statement that provides a data type and an identifier for a variable. An **identifier** is a variable's name. A data item's **data type** is a classification that describes the following:

The process of naming program variables and assigning a type to them is called **making declarations**, or **declaring variables**.

- What values can be held by the item

- How the item is stored in computer memory

- What operations can be performed on the data item

In this book, two data types will be used: num and string. When you declare a variable, you provide both a data type and an identifier. Optionally, you can declare a starting value for any variable. Declaring a starting value is known as **initializing the variable**. For example, each of the following statements is a valid declaration. Two of the statements include initializations, and two do not:

Later in this chapter, you will learn that you select identifiers for program modules as well as for variables.

```
num mySalary
num yourSalary = 14.55
string myName
string yourName = "Juanita"
```

Figure 2-2 shows the number-doubling program from Figure 2-1 with the added declarations shaded. Variables must be declared before they are used in a program for the first time.

```
start
  Declarations
    num myNumber
    num myAnswer
  input myNumber
  set myAnswer = myNumber * 2
  output myAnswer
stop
```

Figure 2-2 Flowchart and pseudocode of number-doubling program with variable declarations

43

Some languages require all variables to be declared at the beginning of the program; others allow variables to be declared anywhere as long as they are declared before their first use. This book will follow the convention of declaring all variables together.

44

In many programming languages, if you declare a variable and do not initialize it, the variable contains an unknown value until it is assigned a value. A variable's unknown value is commonly called **garbage**. In many languages it is illegal to use a garbage-holding variable in an arithmetic statement or to display it as output. Even if you work with a language that allows you to display garbage, it serves no purpose to do so and constitutes a logical error. When you create a variable without assigning it an initial value (as with myNumber and myAnswer in Figure 2-2), your intention is to assign a value later—for example, by receiving one as input or placing the result of a calculation there.

Naming Variables

Although some languages use a default value for some variables (such as assigning 0 to any unassigned numeric variable), this book will assume that an unassigned variable holds garbage.

The number-doubling example in Figure 2-2 requires two variables: myNumber and myAnswer. Alternatively, these variables could be named userEntry and programSolution, or inputValue and twiceTheValue. As a programmer, you choose reasonable and descriptive names for your variables. The language interpreter then associates the names you choose with specific memory addresses.

Every computer programming language has its own set of rules for creating identifiers. Most languages allow letters and digits within variable names. Some languages allow hyphens in variable names, such as hourly-wage, and some allow underscores, as in hourly_wage. Other languages allow neither. Some languages allow dollar signs or other special characters in variable names (for example, hourly$); others allow foreign-alphabet characters, such as π or Ω.

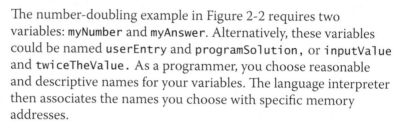
You can also refer to a variable name as a **mnemonic**. In everyday language, a mnemonic is a memory device, like the musical reference "Every good boy does fine," which makes it easier to remember the notes that occupy the lines on the staff in sheet music. In programming, a variable name is a device that makes it easier to reference a memory address.

Each programming language has a few (perhaps 80) reserved **keywords** that are not allowed as variable names because they are part of the language's syntax. When you learn a programming language, you will learn its list of keywords.

Different languages put different limits on the length of variable names, although in general, the length of identifiers in newer languages is virtually unlimited. In many languages, identifiers are case sensitive, so HoUrLyWaGe, hourlywage, and hourlyWage are three separate variable names. The format used in the last example, in which the variable starts with a lowercase letter and any subsequent word begins with an uppercase letter, is called **camel casing**—variable names such as hourlyWage have a "hump" in the middle. The variable names in this book are shown using camel casing.

When the first letter of a variable name is uppercase, as in `HourlyWage`, the format is known as **Pascal casing**. Adopting a naming convention for variables and using it consistently will help make your programs easier to read and understand.

Even though every language has its own rules for naming variables, you should not concern yourself with the specific syntax of any particular computer language when designing the logic of a program. The logic, after all, works with any language. The variable names used throughout this book follow only two rules:

1. *Variable names must be one word.* The name can contain letters, digits, hyphens, underscores, or any other characters you choose, with the exception of *spaces*. Therefore, r is a legal variable name, as are `rate` and `interestRate`. The variable name `interest rate` is not allowed because of the space.

2. *Variable names should have some appropriate meaning.* This is not a formal rule of any programming language. When computing an interest rate in a program, the computer does not care if you call the variable g, u84, or `fred`. As long as the correct numeric result is placed in the variable, its actual name doesn't really matter. However, it's much easier to follow the logic of a statement like `set finalBalance = initialInvestment * interestRate`, than a statement like `set f = i * r`, or `set someBanana = j89 * myFriendLinda`. When a program requires changes, which could be months or years after you write the original version, you and your fellow programmers will appreciate clear, descriptive variable names in place of cryptic identifiers.

Notice that the flowchart in Figure 2-2 follows the preceding two rules for variables: both variable names, `myNumber` and `myAnswer`, are one word without embedded spaces, and they have appropriate meanings. Some programmers name variables after friends or create puns with them, but computer professionals consider such behavior unprofessional and amateurish.

Understanding Unnamed, Literal Constants and their Data Types

Computers deal with two basic types of data—text and numeric. When you use a specific numeric value, such as 43, within a program, you write it using the digits and no quotation marks. A specific numeric value is often called a **numeric constant**

Almost all programming languages prohibit variable names that start with a digit. This book follows the most common convention of starting variable names with a letter.

When you write a program using an editor that is packaged with a compiler in an IDE, the compiler may display variable names in a different color from the rest of the program. This visual aid helps your variable names stand out from words that are part of the programming language.

Another general rule in all programming languages is that variable names may not begin with a digit, although usually they may contain digits. Thus, in most languages `budget2013` is a legal variable name, but `2013Budget` is not.

When you store a numeric value in computer memory, additional characters such as dollar signs and commas are not input or stored. Those characters can be added to output for readability, but then the output is a string and not a number.

(or **literal numeric constant**) because it does not change—a 43 always has the value 43. When you use a specific text value, or string of characters, such as "Amanda", you enclose the **string constant** (or **literal string constant**) within quotation marks. The constants 43 and "Amanda" are examples of **unnamed constants**—they do not have identifiers like variables do.

Understanding the Data Types of Variables

Like literals, variables can also be different data types.

- A **numeric variable** is one that can hold digits and have mathematical operations performed on it. Also, you usually have the option of having a numeric variable hold a decimal point and a sign indicating positive or negative. In the statement set myAnswer = myNumber * 2, both myAnswer and myNumber are numeric variables; that is, their intended contents are numeric values, such as 6 and 3, 14.8 and 7.4, or −18 and −9.

String values are also called **alphanumeric values** because they can contain alphabetic characters, numbers, and punctuation. Numeric values, however, cannot contain alphabetic characters.

- A **string variable** can hold text, such as letters of the alphabet, and other special characters, such as punctuation marks. If a working program contains the statement set lastName = "Lincoln", then lastName is a string variable. A string variable can also hold digits either with or without other characters. For example, "235 Main Street" and "86" are both strings. A string like "86" is stored differently than the numeric value 86, and you cannot perform arithmetic with the string.

Computers handle string data differently from the way they handle numeric data. You may have experienced these differences if you have used application software such as spreadsheets or database programs. For example, in a spreadsheet, you cannot sum a column of words. Similarly, every programming language requires that you distinguish variables as to their correct type, and that you use each type of variable appropriately.

Some languages allow for several types of numeric data. Languages such as C++, C#, Visual Basic, and Java distinguish between **integer** (whole number) numeric variables and **floating-point** (fractional) numeric variables that contain a decimal point. (Floating-point numbers are also called **real numbers**.) Thus, in some languages, the values 4 and 4.3 would be stored in different types of numeric variables.

Object-oriented programming languages allow you to create new data types called classes. Classes are covered in all object-oriented programming language textbooks, as well as in Chapter 10 of the comprehensive version of this book.

You can assign data to a variable only if it is the correct type. If you declare taxRate as a numeric variable and inventoryItem as a string, then the following statements are valid:

```
set taxRate = 2.5
set inventoryItem = "monitor"
```

The following are invalid because the type of data being assigned does ot match the variable type:

```
set taxRate = "2.5"
set inventoryItem = 2.5
```

Don't Do It
If `taxRate` is numeric and `inventoryItem` is a string, then these assignments are invalid.

Watch the video *Understanding Data Types.*

In addition to setting a variable to a constant value, you can set it to the value of another variable of the same data type. If `taxRate` and `oldRate` are both numeric, and `inventoryItem` and `orderedItem` are both strings, then the following are valid:

```
set taxRate = oldRate
set orderedItem = inventoryItem
```

Declaring Named Constants

Besides variables, most programming languages allow you to create named constants. A **named constant** is similar to a variable, except it can be assigned a value only once. You use a named constant when you want to assign a useful name to a value that will never be changed during a program's execution. Using named constants makes your programs easier to understand by eliminating magic numbers. A **magic number** is an unnamed constant, like 0.06, whose purpose is not immediately apparent.

For example, if a program uses a sales tax rate of 6%, you might want to declare a named constant as follows:

```
num SALES_TAX = 0.06
```

You then might use SALES_TAX in a program statement similar to the following:

```
set taxAmount = price * SALES_TAX
```

The way in which named constants are declared differs among programming languages. This book follows the convention of using all uppercase letters in constant identifiers, and using underscores to separate words for readability. Using these conventions makes named constants easier to recognize.

When you declare a named constant, program maintenance becomes easier. For example, if the value of the sales tax changes from 0.06 to 0.07 in the future, and you have declared a named constant SALES_TAX, then you only need to change the value assigned to the named constant at the beginning of the program, and all references to SALES_TAX are automatically updated. If you have used the unnamed literal 0.06 instead, you would have to search for every instance of the value and replace it with the new one.

In many languages a constant must be assigned its value when it is declared, but in some languages, a constant can be assigned its value later. In both cases, however, a constant's value can never be changed after the first assignment. This book follows the convention of initializing all constants when they are declared.

Sometimes, using unnamed literal constants is appropriate in a program, especially if their meaning is clear to most readers. For example, in a program that calculates half of a value by dividing by two, you might choose to use the literal 2 instead of incurring the extra time and memory costs of creating a named constant HALF and assigning 2 to it. Extra costs that result from adding variables or instructions to a program are known as **overhead**.

48

TWO TRUTHS & A LIE

Declaring and Using Variables and Constants

1. A variable's data type describes the kind of values the variable can hold and the types of operations that can be performed with it.

2. If name is a string variable, then the statement set name = "Ed" is valid.

3. If salary is a numeric variable, then the statement set salary = "12.50" is valid.

The false statement is #3. If salary is a numeric variable, then the statement set salary = 12.50 (with no quotation marks) is valid. If salary is a string variable, then the statement set salary = "12.50" is valid.

Assigning Values to Variables

The assignment operator is an example of a **binary operator**, meaning it requires two operands—one on each side.

When you create a flowchart or pseudocode for a program that doubles numbers, you can include a statement such as the following:

```
set myAnswer = myNumber * 2
```

Such a statement is an **assignment statement**. This statement incorporates two actions. First, the computer calculates the arithmetic value of myNumber * 2. Second, the computed value is stored in the myAnswer memory location.

An operator that works from right to left, like the assignment operator, has **right-associativity** or **right-to-left associativity**.

The equal sign is the **assignment operator**. The assignment operator always operates from right to left; the value of the expression to the right of the operator is evaluated before the assignment to the operand on the left occurs. The operand to the right of an assignment statement can be a value, a formula, a named constant, or a variable. The operand to the left of an assignment operator must be a name that represents a memory address—the name of the location where the result will be stored.

For example, if you have declared a numeric variable named someNumber, then each of the following is a valid assignment statement:

```
set someNumber = 2
set someNumber = 3 + 7
```

Additionally, if you have declared another numeric variable named someOtherNumber and assigned a value to it, then each of the following is a valid assignment statement:

```
set someNumber = someOtherNumber
set someNumber = someOtherNumber * 5
```

In each case, the expression to the right of the assignment operator is evaluated and stored at the location referenced on the left side.

The result to the left of an assignment operator is called an **lvalue**. The *l* is for left. Lvalues are always memory address identifiers.

Don't Do It
The operand to the left of an assignment operator must represent a memory address.

The following statements, however, are *not* valid:

```
set 2 + 4 = someNumber
set someOtherNumber * 10 = someNumber
```

In each of these cases, the value to the left of the assignment operator is not a memory address, so the statements are invalid.

When you write pseudocode or draw a flowchart, it might help you to use the word "set" in assignment statements, as shown here, to emphasize that the left-side value is being set. However, in most programming languages, the word "set" is not used, and assignment statements take the following form:

```
someNumber = 2
someNumber = someOtherNumber
```

Because the abbreviated form is how assignments appear in most languages, it is used for the rest of this book.

Performing Arithmetic Operations

Most programming languages use the following standard arithmetic operators:

Many languages also support operators that calculate the remainder after division (often the percent sign, %) and that raise a number to a higher power (often the carat, ^).

- + (plus sign)—addition

- – (minus sign)—subtraction

- * (asterisk)—multiplication

- / (slash)—division

For example, the following statement adds two test scores and assigns the sum to a variable named `totalScore`:

```
totalScore = test1 + test2
```

The following adds 10 to `totalScore` and stores the result in `totalScore`:

```
totalScore = totalScore + 10
```

In other words, this example increases the value of `totalScore`. This last example looks odd in algebra because it might appear to say that the value of `totalScore` and `totalScore` plus 10 are equivalent. You must remember that the equal sign is the assignment operator, and that the statement is actually taking the original value of `totalScore`,

49

The assignment operator has a very low precedence. Therefore, in a statement such as d = e * f + g, the operations on the right of the assignment operator are always performed before the final assignment to the variable on the left.

When you learn a specific programming language, you will learn about all the operators that are used in that language. Many programming language books contain a table that specifies the relative precedence of every operator used in the language.

adding 10 to it, and assigning the result to the memory address on the left of the operator, which is totalScore.

In programming languages, you can combine arithmetic statements. When you do, every operator follows **rules of precedence** (also called the **order of operations**) that dictate the order in which operations in the same statement are carried out. The rules of precedence for the basic arithmetic statements are as follows:

- Expressions within parentheses are evaluated first. If there are multiple sets of parentheses, the expression within the innermost parentheses is evaluated first.

- Multiplication and division are evaluated next, from left to right.

- Addition and subtraction are evaluated next, from left to right.

For example, consider the following two arithmetic statements:

```
firstAnswer = 2 + 3 * 4
secondAnswer = (2 + 3) * 4
```

After these statements execute, the value of firstAnswer is 14. According to the rules of precedence, multiplication is carried out before addition, so 3 is multiplied by 4, giving 12, and then 2 and 12 are added, and 14 is assigned to firstAnswer. The value of secondAnswer, however, is 20, because the parentheses force the contained addition operation to be performed first. The 2 and 3 are added, producing 5, and then 5 is multiplied by 4, producing 20.

Forgetting about the rules of arithmetic precedence, or forgetting to add parentheses when you need them, can cause logical errors that are difficult to find in programs. For example, the following statement might appear to average two test scores:

```
average = score1 + score2 / 2
```

However, it does not. Because division has a higher precedence than addition, the preceding statement takes half of score2, adds it to score1, and stores the result in average. The correct statement is:

```
average = (score1 + score2) / 2
```

You are free to add parentheses even when you don't need them to force a different order of operations; sometimes you use them just to make your intentions clearer. For example, the following statements operate identically:

```
totalPriceWithTax = price + price * TAX_RATE
totalPriceWithTax = price + (price * TAX_RATE)
```

In both cases, price is multiplied by TAX_RATE first, then it is added to price, and finally the result is stored in totalPriceWithTax. Because multiplication occurs before addition on the right side of the assignment operator, both statements are the same. However, if you feel the statement with the parentheses makes your intentions clearer to someone reading your program, then you should use them.

All the arithmetic operators have **left-to-right associativity**. This means that operations with the same precedence take place from left to right. Consider the following statement:

```
answer = a + b + c * d / e - f
```

Multiplication and division have higher precedence than addition or subtraction, so the multiplication and division are carried out from left to right as follows:

Watch the video *Arithmetic Operator Precedence.*

c is multiplied by d, and the result is divided by e, giving a new result.

Therefore, the statement becomes:

```
answer = a + b + (temporary result just calculated) - f
```

Then, addition and subtraction are carried out from left to right as follows:

a and b are added, the temporary result is added, and then f is subtracted. The final result is then assigned to answer.

Another way to say this is that the following two statements are equivalent:

```
answer = a + b + c * d / e - f
answer = a + b + ((c * d) / e) - f
```

Table 2-1 summarizes the precedence and associativity of the five most frequently used operators.

Operator symbol	Operator name	Precedence (compared to other operators in this table)	Associativity
=	Assignment	Lowest	Right-to-left
+	Addition	Medium	Left-to-right
−	Subtraction	Medium	Left-to-right
*	Multiplication	Highest	Left-to-right
/	Division	Highest	Left-to-right

Each operator in Table 2-1 is a binary operator.

Table 2-1 Precedence and associativity of five common operators

52

TWO TRUTHS & A LIE

Assigning Values to Variables

1. The assignment operator always operates from right to left; programmers say it has right-associativity or right-to-left associativity.

2. The operand to the right of an assignment operator must be a name that represents a memory address.

3. The following adds 5 to a variable named points:

   points = points + 5

The false statement is #2. The operand to the left of an assignment operator must be a name that represents a memory address—the name of the location where the result will be stored. Any operand on the right of an assignment operator can be a memory address (a variable) or a constant.

Understanding the Advantages of Modularization

 You can learn about modules that receive and return data in Chapter 9 of the comprehensive version of this book.

Programmers seldom write programs as one long series of steps. Instead, they break down the programming problem into reasonable units, and tackle one small task at a time. These reasonable units are called **modules**. Programmers also refer to them as **subroutines**, **procedures**, **functions**, or **methods**.

 The name that programmers use for their modules usually reflects the programming language they use. For example, Visual Basic programmers use "procedure" (or "subprocedure"). C and C++ programmers call their modules "functions," whereas C#, Java, and other object-oriented language programmers are more likely to use "method." Programmers in COBOL, RPG, and BASIC (all older languages) are most likely to use "subroutine."

The process of breaking down a large program into modules is called **modularization**. You are never required to modularize a large program in order to make it run on a computer, but there are at least three reasons for doing so:

 Reducing a large program into more manageable modules is sometimes called **functional decomposition**.

- Modularization provides abstraction.

- Modularization allows multiple programmers to work on a problem.

- Modularization allows you to reuse your work more easily.

Modularization Provides Abstraction

One reason modularized programs are easier to understand is that they enable a programmer to see the big picture. **Abstraction** is the process of paying attention to important properties while ignoring nonessential details. Abstraction is selective ignorance. Life would be tedious without abstraction. For example, you can create a list of things to accomplish today:

```
Do laundry
Call Aunt Nan
Start term paper
```

Without abstraction, the list of chores would begin:

```
Pick up laundry basket
Put laundry basket in car
Drive to Laundromat
Get out of car with basket
Walk into Laundromat
Set basket down
Find quarters for washing machine
. . . and so on.
```

You might list a dozen more steps before you finish the laundry and move on to the second chore on your original list. If you had to consider every small, low-level detail of every task in your day, you would probably never make it out of bed in the morning. Using a higher-level, more abstract list makes your day manageable. Abstraction makes complex tasks look simple.

Abstract artists create paintings in which they see only the "big picture"—color and form—and ignore the details. Abstraction has a similar meaning among programmers.

Likewise, some level of abstraction occurs in every computer program. Fifty years ago, a programmer had to understand the low-level circuitry instructions the computer used. But now, newer high-level programming languages allow you to use English-like vocabulary in which one broad statement corresponds to dozens of machine instructions. No matter which high-level programming language you use, if you display a message on the monitor, you are never required to understand how a monitor works to create each pixel on the screen. You write an instruction like `output message` and the details of the hardware operations are handled for you.

Modules provide another way to achieve abstraction. For example, a payroll program can call a module named `computeFederalWithholdingTax()`. When you call this module from your program, you use one statement; the module itself might contain dozens of statements. You can write the mathematical details of the module later, someone else can write them, or you can purchase them from an outside source. When you plan your main payroll program, your only concern is that a federal withholding tax will have to be calculated; you save the details for later.

Modularization Allows Multiple Programmers to Work on a Problem

When you dissect any large task into modules, you gain the ability to more easily divide the task among various people. Rarely does a single programmer write a commercial program that you buy. Consider any word-processing, spreadsheet, or database program you have used. Each program has so many options, and responds to user selections in so many possible ways, that it would take years for a single programmer to write all the instructions. Professional software developers can write new programs in weeks or months, instead of years, by dividing large programs into modules and assigning each module to an individual programmer or team.

Modularization Allows You to Reuse Your Work

If a module is useful and well written, you may want to use it more than once within a program or in other programs. For example, a routine that verifies the validity of dates is useful in many programs written for a business (e.g., a month value is valid if it is not lower than 1 or higher than 12, a day value is valid if it is not lower than 1 or higher than 31 if the month is 1, and so on). If a computerized personnel file contains each employee's birth date, hire date, last promotion date, and termination date, the date-validation module can be used four times with each employee record. Other programs in an organization can also use the module, including programs that ship customer orders, plan employees' birthday parties, and calculate when loan payments should be made. If you write the date-checking instructions so they are entangled with other statements in a program, they are difficult to extract and reuse. On the other hand, if you place the instructions in their own module, the unit is easy to use and portable to other applications. The feature of modular programs that allows individual modules to be used in a variety of applications is known as **reusability**.

You can find many real-world examples of reusability. When you build a house, you don't invent plumbing and heating systems; you incorporate systems with proven designs. This certainly reduces the time and effort it takes to build a house. The plumbing and electrical systems you choose are in service in other houses, so they also improve the reliability of your house's systems—they have been tested under a variety of circumstances and have been proven to function correctly. **Reliability** is the feature of programs that assures you a module has been tested and proven to function correctly. Reliable software saves time and money. If you create the functional components of your programs as stand-alone modules and test them in your current programs, much of the work will already be done when you use the modules in future applications.

TWO TRUTHS & A LIE

Understanding the Advantages of Modularization

1. Modularization eliminates abstraction, a feature that makes programs more confusing.

2. Modularization makes it easier for multiple programmers to work on a problem.

3. Modularization allows you to reuse your work more easily.

The false statement is #1. Modularization enables abstraction, which allows you to see the big picture.

Modularizing a Program

Most programs consist of a **main program**, which contains the basic steps, or the **mainline logic**, of the program. The main program then accesses modules that provide more refined details.

When you create a module, you include the following:

- A header—A **module's header** includes the module identifier and possibly other necessary identifying information.

- A body—A **module's body** contains all the statements in the module.

- A return statement—A **module's return statement** marks the end of the module and identifies the point at which control returns to the program or module that called the module.

 In most programming languages, if you do not include a return statement at the end of a module, the logic will still return. This book follows the convention of explicitly including a return statement with every module.

Naming a module is similar to naming a variable. The rules for naming modules are slightly different in every programming language, but in this text, module names follow the same two rules used for variable identifiers:

- Module names must be one word.

- Module names should have some meaning.

As you learn more about modules in specific programming languages, you will find that you sometimes place variable names within the parentheses of module names. Any variables enclosed in the parentheses contain information you want to send to the module. For now, the parentheses we use at the end of module names will be empty.

A module can call another module, and the called module can call another. The number of chained calls is limited only by the amount of memory available on your computer.

When you call a module, the action is similar to putting a DVD player on pause. You abandon your primary action (watching a video), take care of some other task (for example, making a sandwich), and then return to the main task exactly where you left off.

Although it is not a requirement of any programming language, it frequently makes sense to use a verb as all or part of a module's name, because modules perform some action. Typical module names begin with action words such as `get`, `calculate`, and `display`. When you program in visual languages that use screen components such as buttons and text boxes, the module names frequently contain verbs representing user actions, such as `click` or `drag`.

Additionally, in this text, module names are followed by a set of parentheses. This will help you distinguish module names from variable names. This style corresponds to the way modules are named in many programming languages, such as Java, C++, and C#.

When a main program wants to use a module, it "calls" the module's name. The flowchart symbol used to call a module is a rectangle with a bar across the top. You place the name of the module you are calling inside the rectangle.

Some programmers use a rectangle with stripes down each side to represent a module in a flowchart, and this book uses that convention if a module is external to a program. For example, prewritten, built-in modules that generate random numbers, compute standard trigonometric functions, and sort values are often external to your programs. However, if the module is one being created as part of the program, the book uses a rectangle with a single stripe across the top.

In a flowchart, you draw each module separately with its own sentinel symbols. The symbol that is the equivalent of the `start` symbol in a program contains the name of the module. This name must be identical to the name used in the calling program. The symbol that is the equivalent of the `stop` symbol in a program does not contain `stop`; after all, the program is not ending. Instead, the module ends with a "gentler," less final term, such as `exit` or `return`. These words correctly indicate that when the module ends, the logical progression of statements will exit the module and return to the calling program. Similarly, in pseudocode, you start each module with its name, and end with a `return` or `exit` statement; the module name and return statements are vertically aligned and all the module statements are indented between them.

For example, consider the program in Figure 2-3, which does not contain any modules. It accepts a customer's name and balance due as input and produces a bill. At the top of the bill, the company's name and address are displayed on three lines, which are followed by the customer's name and balance due. To display the company name and address, you can simply include three `output` statements in the mainline logic of a program, as shown in Figure 2-3, or you can modularize the program by creating both the mainline logic and a `displayAddressInfo()` module, as shown in Figure 2-4.

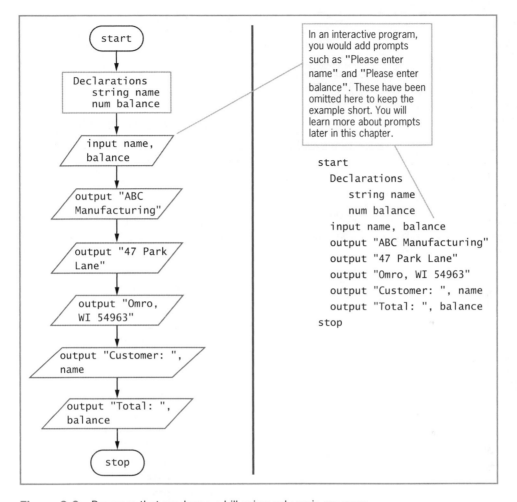

In an interactive program, you would add prompts such as "Please enter name" and "Please enter balance". These have been omitted here to keep the example short. You will learn more about prompts later in this chapter.

```
start
    Declarations
        string name
        num balance
    input name, balance
    output "ABC Manufacturing"
    output "47 Park Lane"
    output "Omro, WI 54963"
    output "Customer: ", name
    output "Total: ", balance
stop
```

Figure 2-3 Program that produces a bill using only main program

In Figure 2-4, when the `displayAddressInfo()` module is called, logic transfers from the main program to the `displayAddressInfo()` module, as shown by the large red arrow in both the flowchart and the pseudo-code. There, each module statement executes in turn before logical control is transferred back to the main program, where it continues with the statement that follows the module call, as shown by the large blue arrow.

Neither of the programs in Figures 2-3 and 2-4 is superior to the other in terms of functionality; both perform exactly the same tasks in the same order. However, you may prefer the modularized version of the program for at least two reasons:

- First, the main program remains short and easy to follow because it contains just one statement to call the module, rather than three separate **output** statements to perform the work of the module.

Programmers say the statements that are contained in a module have been **encapsulated**.

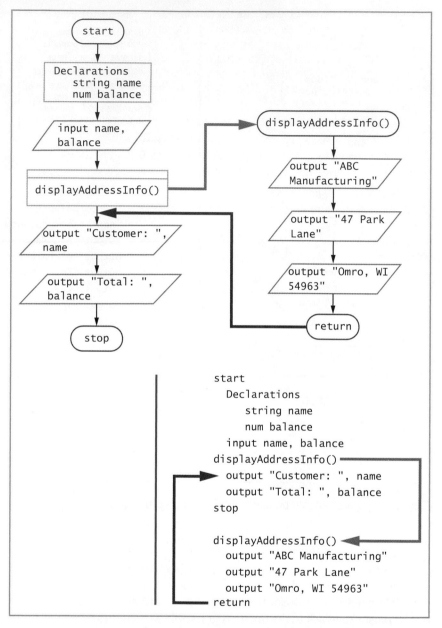

Figure 2-4   Program that produces a bill using main program that calls displayAddressInfo() module

- Second, a module is easily reusable. After you create the address information module, you can use it in any application that needs the company's name and address. In other words, you do the work once, and then you can use the module many times.

A potential drawback to creating modules and moving between them is the overhead incurred. The computer keeps track of the correct memory address to which it should return after executing a module by recording the memory address in a location known as the **stack**. This process requires a small amount of computer time and resources. In most cases, the advantage to creating modules far outweighs the small amount of overhead required.

Determining when to break down any particular program into modules does not depend on a fixed set of rules; it requires experience and insight. Programmers do follow some guidelines when deciding how far to break down modules, or how much to put in each of them. Some companies may have arbitrary rules, such as "a module's instructions should never take more than a page," or "a module should never have more than 30 statements," or "never have a module with only one statement." Rather than use such arbitrary rules, a better policy is to place together statements that contribute to one specific task. The more the statements contribute to the same job, the greater the **functional cohesion** of the module. A routine that checks the validity of a date variable's value, or one that asks a user for a value and accepts it as input, is considered cohesive. A routine that checks date validity, deducts insurance premiums, and computes federal withholding tax for an employee would be less cohesive.

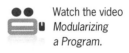 Watch the video *Modularizing a Program.*

Declaring Variables and Constants within Modules

You can place any statements within modules, including input, processing, and output statements. You can also include variable and constant declarations within modules. For example, you might decide to modify the billing program shown in Figure 2-4 so it looks like the one in Figure 2-5. In this version of the program, three named constants that hold the three lines of company data are declared within the displayAddressInfo() module. (See shading.)

The variables and constants declared in a module are usable only within the module. Programmers say the data items are **visible** only within the module in which they are declared. That means the program only recognizes them there. Programmers say that variables and constants declared within a module are **in scope** only within that module. Programmers also say that variables and constants are **local** to the module in which they are declared. In other words, when the strings LINE1, LINE2, and LINE3 are declared in the displayAddressInfo() module in Figure 2-5, they are not recognized and cannot be used by the main program.

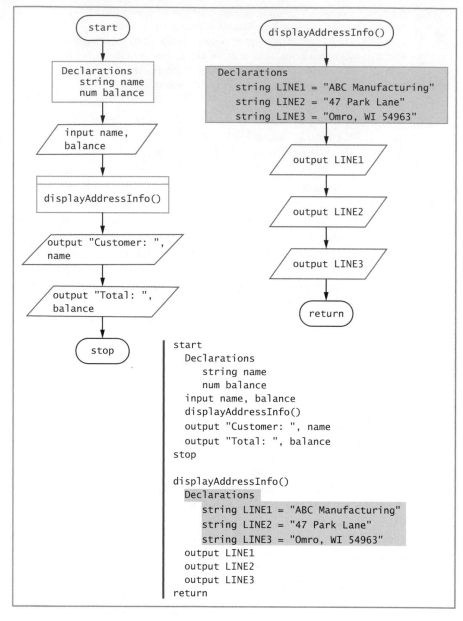

```
start
   Declarations
      string name
      num balance
   input name, balance
   displayAddressInfo()
   output "Customer: ", name
   output "Total: ", balance
stop

displayAddressInfo()
   Declarations
      string LINE1 = "ABC Manufacturing"
      string LINE2 = "47 Park Lane"
      string LINE3 = "Omro, WI 54963"
   output LINE1
   output LINE2
   output LINE3
return
```

Figure 2-5   The billing program with constants declared within the module

One of the motivations for creating modules is that separate modules are easily reusable in multiple programs. If the displayAddressInfo() module will be used by several programs within the organization, it makes sense that the definitions for its variables and constants must come with it. This makes the modules more **portable**; that is, they are self-contained units that are easily transported.

Besides local variables and constants, you can create global variables and constants. **Global** variables and constants are known to the entire program; they are said to be declared at the **program level**. That means they are visible to and usable in all the modules called by the program. The opposite is not true—variables and constants declared within a module are not usable elsewhere; they are visible only to that module. In this book, variables and constants declared in the main program will be global. (For example, in Figure 2-5, the main program variables `name` and `balance` are global variables, although in this case they are not used in any modules.) For the most part, this book will use only global variables and constants so that the examples are easier to follow and you can concentrate on the main logic.

Many programmers do not approve of using global variables and constants. They are used here so you can more easily understand modularization without yet learning the techniques of sending local variables from one module to another. Chapter 9 of the comprehensive version of this book will describe how you can make every variable local.

61

TWO TRUTHS & A LIE

Modularizing a Program

1. Most programs contain a main program, which contains the mainline logic; this program then accesses other modules or subroutines.

2. A calling program calls a module's name when it wants to use the module.

3. Whenever a main program calls a module, the logic transfers to the module; when the module ends, the program ends.

The false statement is #3. When a module ends, the logical flow transfers back to the main calling program and resumes where it left off.

Understanding the Most Common Configuration for Mainline Logic

In Chapter 1, you learned that a procedural program contains procedures that follow one another in sequence. The mainline logic of almost every procedural computer program can follow a general structure that consists of four distinct parts:

1. Declarations include data types, identifiers, and (sometimes) initial values for global variables and constants.

2. **Housekeeping tasks** include any steps you must perform at the beginning of a program to get ready for the rest of the program. They can include tasks such as displaying instructions

Inputting the first data item is always part of the housekeeping module. You will learn the theory behind this practice in Chapter 3.

Chapter 7 covers file handling, including what it means to open and close a file.

You learned that repetitions are called loops in Chapter 1.

In Chapter 1, you learned that when input data comes from a file, the end-of-file sentinel value is commonly called eof.

to users, displaying report headings, opening any files the program requires, and inputting the first piece of data.

3. **Detail loop tasks** do the core work of the program. When a program processes many records, detail loop tasks execute repeatedly for each set of input data until there are no more. For example, in a payroll program, the same set of calculations is executed repeatedly until a check has been produced for each employee.

4. **End-of-job tasks** are the steps you take at the end of the program to finish the application. You can call these finish-up or clean-up tasks. They might include displaying totals or other final messages and closing any open files.

Figure 2-6 shows the relationship of these three typical program parts. Notice how the housekeeping() and endOfJob() tasks are executed just once, but the detailLoop() tasks repeat as long as the eof condition has not been met. The flowchart uses an arrow to show how the detailLoop() module repeats; the pseudocode uses the words while and endwhile to contain statements that execute in a loop. You will learn more about the while and endwhile terms in subsequent chapters; for now, understand that they are a way of expressing repeated actions.

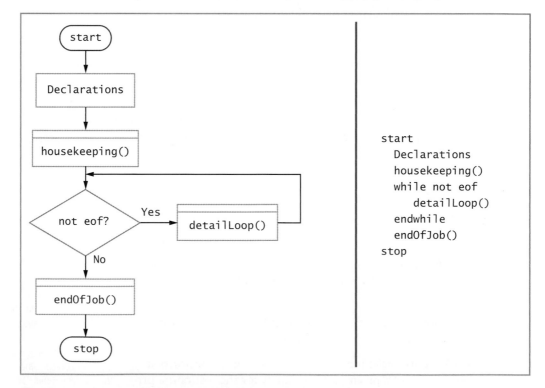

Figure 2-6   Flowchart and pseudocode of mainline logic for a typical procedural program

Many everyday tasks follow the three-module format just described. For example, a candy factory opens in the morning, and the machines are started and filled with ingredients. These housekeeping tasks occur just once at the start of the day. Then, repeatedly during the day, candy is manufactured. This process might take many steps, each of which occurs many times. These are the steps in the detail loop. Then, at the end of the day, the machines are cleaned and shut down. These are the end-of-job tasks.

The module names used in Figure 2-6 can be any legal identifiers you choose. The point is that almost all programs have start-up and finishing tasks that surround the major repetitive program work.

63

Not all programs take the format of the logic shown in Figure 2-6, but many do. Keep this general "shape" in mind as you think about how you might organize many programs. For example, Figure 2-7 shows a sample payroll report for a small company. A user enters employee names until there are no more to enter, at which point the user enters "XXX". As long as the entered name is not "XXX", the user enters the employee's weekly gross pay. Deductions are computed as a flat 25 percent of the gross pay, and the statistics for each employee are output. The user enters another name, and as long as it is not "XXX", the process continues. Examine the logic in Figure 2-8 to identify the components in the housekeeping, detail loop, and end-of-job tasks. You will learn more about the payroll report program in the next few chapters. For now, concentrate on the big picture of how a typical application works.

Payroll Report

Name	Gross	Deductions	Net
Andrews	1000.00	250.00	750.00
Brown	1400.00	350.00	1050.00
Carter	1275.00	318.75	956.25
Young	1100.00	275.00	825.00

***End of report

Figure 2-7   Sample payroll report

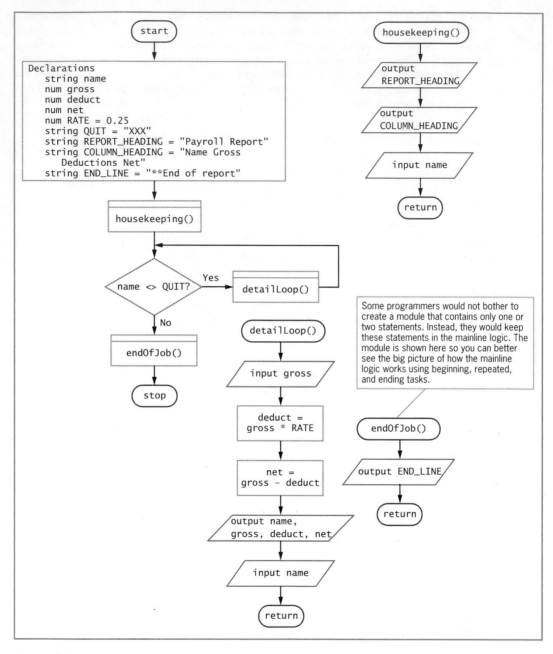

Figure 2-8 Logic for payroll report

```
start
   Declarations
       string name
       num gross
       num deduct
       num net
       num RATE = 0.25
       string QUIT = "XXX"
       string REPORT_HEADING = "Payroll Report"
       string COLUMN_HEADING = "Name  Gross  Deductions  Net"
       string END_LINE = "**End of report"
   housekeeping()
   while not name = QUIT
      detailLoop()
   endwhile
   endOfJob()
stop

housekeeping()
   output REPORT_HEADING
   output COLUMN_HEADING
   input name
return

detailLoop()
   input gross
   deduct = gross * RATE
   net = gross - deduct
   output name, gross, deduct, net
   input name
return

endOfJob()
   output END_LINE
return
```

Figure 2-8   Logic for payroll report (continued)

TWO TRUTHS & A LIE

Understanding the Most Common Configuration for Mainline Logic

1. Housekeeping tasks include any steps you must perform at the beginning of a program to get ready for the rest of the program.

2. The detail loop of a program contains the housekeeping and finishing tasks.

3. The end-of-job tasks are the steps you take at the end of the program to finish the application.

The false statement is #2. The detail loop executes repeatedly, once for every record. The loop executes after housekeeping tasks are completed and before end-of-job tasks are executed.

Creating Hierarchy Charts

You may have seen hierarchy charts for organizations, such as the one in Figure 2-9. The chart shows who reports to whom, not when or how often they report.

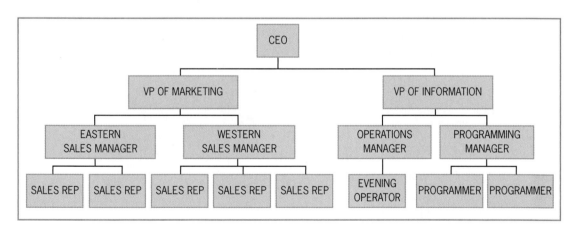

Figure 2-9 An organizational hierarchy chart

When a program has several modules calling other modules, programmers often use a program **hierarchy chart** that operates in a similar manner to show the overall picture of how modules are related to one another. A hierarchy chart does not tell you what tasks are to be performed *within* a module, *when* the modules are called, *how* a module executes, or *why* they are called—that information is in the flowchart or pseudocode. A hierarchy chart tells you only *which* modules exist within a program and *which* modules call others. The hierarchy chart for the program in Figure 2-8 looks like Figure 2-10. It shows that the main module calls three others—`housekeeping()`, `detailLoop()`, and `endOfJob()`.

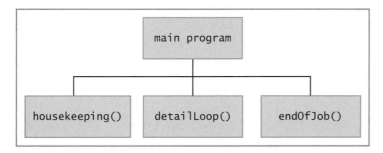

Figure 2-10   Hierarchy chart of payroll report program in Figure 2-8

Figure 2-11 shows an example of a hierarchy chart for the billing program of a mail-order company. The hierarchy chart is for a more complicated program, but like the payroll report chart in Figure 2-10, it supplies module names and a general overview of the tasks to be performed, without specifying any details.

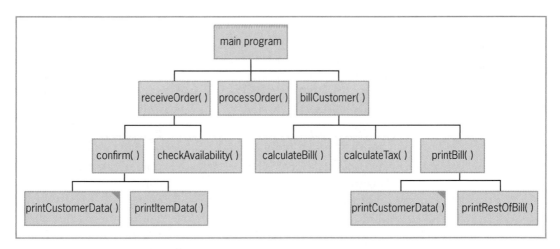

Figure 2-11   Billing program hierarchy chart

Because program modules are reusable, a specific module may be called from several locations within a program. For example, in the billing program hierarchy chart in Figure 2-11, you can see that the `printCustomerData()` module is used twice. By convention, you

Hierarchy charts are used in procedural programming, but other types of diagrams frequently are used in object-oriented environments. Chapter 13 of the comprehensive edition of this book describes the Unified Modeling Language, which is a set of diagrams you use to describe a system.

blacken a corner of each box that represents a module used more than once. This action alerts readers that any change to this module will affect more than one location.

A hierarchy chart can be both a planning tool for developing the overall relationship of program modules before you write them and a documentation tool to help others see how modules are related after a program is written. For example, if a tax law changes, a programmer might be asked to rewrite the `calculateTax()` module in the billing program diagrammed in Figure 2-11. As the programmer changes the `calculateTax()` module, the hierarchy chart shows other dependent routines that might be affected. If a change is made to `printCustomerData()`, the programmer is alerted that changes will occur in multiple locations. A hierarchy chart is useful for "getting the big picture" in a complex program.

TWO TRUTHS & A LIE

Creating Hierarchy Charts

1. You can use a hierarchy chart to illustrate modules' relationships.

2. A hierarchy chart tells you what tasks are to be performed within a module.

3. A hierarchy chart tells you only which modules call other modules.

The false statement is #2. A hierarchy chart tells you nothing about tasks performed within a module; it only depicts how modules are related to each other.

Features of Good Program Design

As your programs become larger and more complicated, the need for good planning and design increases. Think of an application you use, such as a word processor or a spreadsheet. The number and variety of user options are staggering. Not only would it be impossible for a single programmer to write such an application, but without thorough planning and design, the components would never work together properly. Ideally, each program module you design needs to work well as a stand-alone module and as an element of larger systems. Just as a house with poor plumbing or a car with bad brakes is fatally flawed, a computer-based application can be highly functional only if each component is designed well. Walking through your program's logic on paper (called desk-checking, as you learned in Chapter 1) is an important step to achieving superior programs. Additionally, you can implement several design features while creating programs that can make the programs easier to write and maintain:

- You should use program comments where appropriate.

- Your identifiers should be well-chosen.

- You should strive to design clear statements within your programs and modules.

- You should write clear prompts and echo input.

- You should continue to maintain good programming habits as you develop your programming skills.

Using Program Comments

When you write programs, you might often want to insert program comments. **Program comments** are written explanations that are not part of the program logic but that serve as documentation for readers of the program. In other words, they are nonexecuting statements that help readers understand programming statements. The syntax used to create program comments differs among programming languages. This book starts comments in pseudocode with two front slashes. For example, Figure 2-12 contains comments that explain the origins and purposes of some variables in a real estate program.

 Program comments are a type of **internal documentation.** This term distinguishes them from supporting documents outside the program, which are called **external documentation.** Appendix D discusses other types of documentation.

```
Declarations
    num sqFeet
        // sqFeet is an estimate provided by the seller of the property
    num pricePerFoot
        // pricePerFoot is determined by current market conditions
    num lotPremium
        // lotPremium depends on amenities such as whether lot is waterfront
```

Figure 2-12   Pseudocode that declares some variables and includes comments

In a flowchart, you can use an annotation symbol to hold information that expands on what is stored within another flowchart symbol. An **annotation symbol** is most often represented by a three-sided box that is connected to the step it references by a dashed line. Annotation symbols are used to hold comments, or sometimes statements that are too long to fit neatly into a flowchart symbol. For example, Figure 2-13 shows how a programmer might use some annotation symbols in a flowchart for a payroll program.

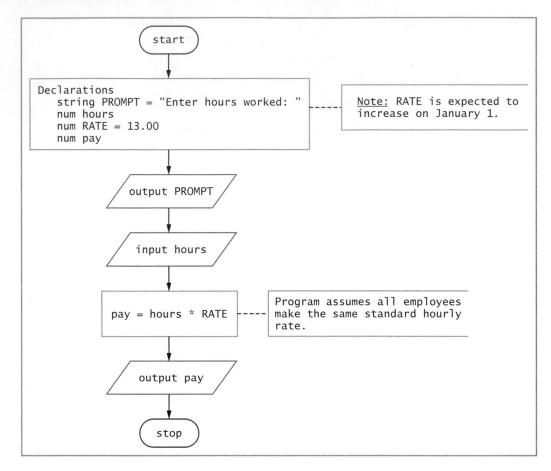

Figure 2-13 Flowchart that includes some annotation symbols

You probably will use program comments in your coded programs more frequently than you use them in pseudocode or flowcharts. For one thing, flowcharts and pseudocode are more English-like than the code in some languages, so your statements might be less cryptic. Also, your comments will remain in the program as part of the program documentation, but your planning tools are likely to be discarded once the program goes into production.

A drawback to comments is that they must be kept current as a program is modified. Outdated comments can provide misleading information about a program's status.

Including program comments is not necessary to create a working program, but comments can help you to remember the purpose of variables or to explain complicated calculations. Some students do not like to include comments in their programs because it takes time to type them and they aren't part of the "real" program, but the programs you write in the future probably will require some comments. When you acquire your first programming job and modify a program written by another programmer, you will appreciate well-placed comments that explain complicated sections of the code.

Choosing Identifiers

The selection of good identifiers is an often-overlooked element in program design. When you write programs, you choose identifiers for variables, constants, and modules. Choosing good names for these components makes your programming job easier and makes it easier for others to understand your work.

Some general guidelines include the following:

- Although it is not required in any programming language, it usually makes sense to give a variable or a constant a name that is a noun (or a combination of an adjective and a noun) because it represents a thing. Similarly, it makes sense to give a module an identifier that is a verb, or a combined verb and noun, because a module takes action.

- Use meaningful names. Creating a data item named `someData` or a module named `firstModule()` makes a program cryptic. Not only will others find it hard to read your programs, but you will forget the purpose of these identifiers even within your own programs. All programmers occasionally use short, nondescriptive names such as `x` or `temp` in a quick program; however, in most cases, data and module names should be meaningful. Programmers refer to programs that contain meaningful names as **self-documenting**. This means that even without further documentation, the program code explains itself to readers.

Don't forget that not all programmers share your culture. An abbreviation whose meaning seems obvious to you might be cryptic to someone in a different part of the world.

- Usually, you should use pronounceable names. A variable name like `pzf` is neither pronounceable nor meaningful. A name that looks meaningful when you write it might not be as meaningful when someone else reads it; for instance, `preparead()` might mean "Prepare ad" to you, but "Prep a read" to others. Look at your names critically to make sure they are pronounceable. Very standard abbreviations do not have to be pronounceable. For example, most businesspeople would interpret `ssn` as Social Security number.

To save typing time when you develop a program, you can use a short name like `efn`. After the program operates correctly, you can use a text editor's Search and Replace feature to replace your coded name with a more meaningful name such as `employeeFirstName`.

- Be judicious in your use of abbreviations. You can save a few keystrokes when creating a module called `getStat()`, but is its purpose to find the state in which a city is located, input some statistics, or determine the status of some variables? Similarly, is a variable named `fn` meant to hold a first name, file number, or something else?

Many IDEs support an automatic statement-completion feature that saves typing time. After the first time you use a name like `employeeFirstName`, you need to type only the first few letters before the compiler editor offers a list of available names from which to choose. The list is constructed from all the names you have used that begin with the same characters.

- Usually, avoid digits in a name. Zeroes get confused with the letter "O", and lowercase "l"s are misread as the numeral 1. Of course, use your judgment: budgetFor2012 probably will not be misinterpreted.

- Use the system your language allows to separate words in long, multiword variable names. For example, if the programming language you use allows dashes or underscores, then use a module name like initialize-data() or initialize_data(), which is easier to read than initializedata(). Another option is to use camel casing to create an identifier such as initializeData(). If you use a language that is case sensitive, it is legal but confusing to use variable names that differ only in case. For example, if a single program contains empName, EmpName, and Empname, confusion is sure to follow.

Many languages support a Boolean data type, which you assign to variables meant to hold only true or false. Using a form of "to be" in identifiers for Boolean variables is appropriate.

- Consider including a form of the verb *to be*, such as *is* or *are*, in names for variables that are intended to hold a status. For example, use isFinished as a variable that holds a "Y" or "N" to indicate whether a file is exhausted. The shorter name finished is more likely to be confused with a module that executes when a program is done.

- Many programmers follow the convention of naming constants using all uppercase letters, inserting underscores between words for readability. In this chapter you saw examples such as LINE1.

Programmers sometimes create a **data dictionary**, which is a list of every variable name used in a program, along with its type, size, and description. When a data dictionary is created, it becomes part of the program documentation.

- Organizations sometimes enforce different rules for programmers to follow when naming variables. It is your responsibility to find out the conventions used in your organization and to adhere to them. As an example, some organizations use a variable-naming convention called **Hungarian notation**, in which a variable's data type or other information is stored as part of the name. For example, a numeric field might always start with the prefix num, as in numAge or numSalary.

When you begin to write programs, the process of determining what data variables, constants, and modules you need and what to name them all might seem overwhelming. The design process is crucial, however. When you acquire your first professional programming assignment, the design process might very well be completed already. Most likely, your first assignment will be to write or modify one small member module of a much larger application. The more the original programmers stuck to these guidelines, the better the original design was, and the easier your job of modification will be.

Designing Clear Statements

In addition to adding program comments and selecting good identifiers, you can use the following tactics to contribute to the clarity of the statements within your programs:

- Avoid confusing line breaks.

- Use temporary variables to clarify long statements.

Avoiding Confusing Line Breaks

Some older programming languages require that program statements be placed in specific columns. Most modern programming languages are free-form; you can arrange your lines of code any way you see fit. As in real life, with freedom comes responsibility; when you have flexibility in arranging your lines of code, you must take care to make sure your meaning is clear. With free-form code, programmers are allowed to place two or three statements on a line, or, conversely, to spread a single statement across multiple lines. Both make programs harder to read. All the pseudocode examples in this book use appropriate, clear spacing and line breaks.

Using Temporary Variables to Clarify Long Statements

When you need several mathematical operations to determine a result, consider using a series of temporary variables to hold intermediate results. A **temporary variable** (or a **work variable**) is not used for input or output, but instead is just a working variable that you use during a program's execution. For example, Figure 2-14 shows two ways to calculate a value for a real estate salespersonCommission variable. Each module achieves the same result—the salesperson's commission is based on the square feet multiplied by the price per square foot, plus any premium for a lot with special features, such as a wooded or waterfront lot. However, the second example uses two temporary variables: basePropertyPrice and totalSalePrice. When the computation is broken down into less complicated, individual steps, it is easier to see how the total price is calculated. In calculations with even more computation steps, performing the arithmetic in stages would become increasingly helpful.

 Programmers might say using temporary variables, like the second example in Figure 2-14, is *cheap*. When executing a lengthy arithmetic statement, even if you don't explicitly name temporary variables, the programming language compiler creates them behind the scenes (although without descriptive names), so declaring them yourself does not cost much in terms of program execution time.

```
// Using a single statement to compute commission
salespersonCommission = (sqFeet * pricePerFoot + lotPremium) * commissionRate

// Using multiple statements to compute commission
basePropertyPrice = sqFeet * pricePerFoot
totalSalePrice = basePropertyPrice + lotPremium
salespersonCommission = totalSalePrice * commissionRate
```

Figure 2-14   Two ways of achieving the same salespersonCommission result

Writing Clear Prompts and Echoing Input

When program input should be retrieved from a user, you almost always want to provide a prompt for the user. A **prompt** is a message that is displayed on a monitor to ask the user for a response and perhaps explain how that response should be formatted. Prompts are used both in command-line and GUI interactive programs.

For example, suppose a program asks a user to enter a catalog number for an item the user is ordering. The following prompt is not very helpful:

```
Please enter a number.
```

The following prompt is more helpful:

```
Please enter a five-digit catalog order number.
```

The following prompt is even more helpful:

```
The five-digit catalog order number appears to the right of
the item's picture in the catalog. Please enter it now.
```

When program input comes from a stored file instead of a user, prompts are not needed. However, when a program expects a user response, prompts are valuable. For example, Figure 2-15 shows the flowchart and pseudocode for the beginning of the bill-producing program shown earlier in this chapter. If the input was coming from a data file, no prompt would be required, and the logic might look like the logic in Figure 2-15.

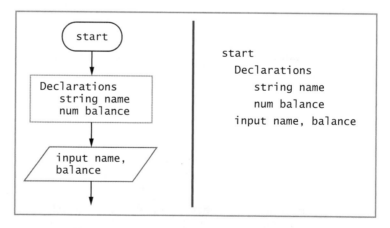

Figure 2-15 Beginning of a program that accepts a name and balance as input

However, if the input was coming from a user, including prompts would be helpful. You could supply a single prompt such as "Please enter a customer's name and balance due", but inserting more requests into a prompt generally makes it less likely that the user can remember to enter all the parts or enter them in the correct order. It is almost always best to include a separate prompt for each item to be entered. Figure 2-16 shows an example.

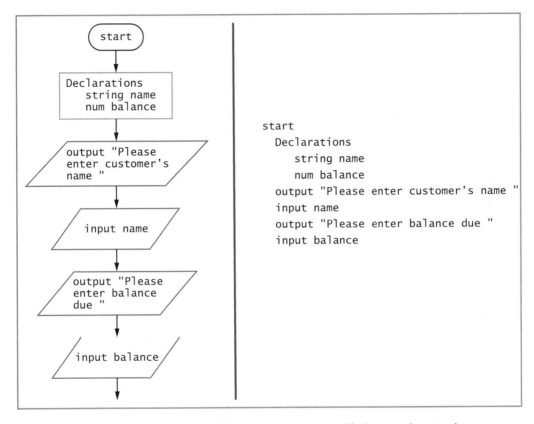

```
start
   Declarations
      string name
      num balance
   output "Please enter customer's name "
   input name
   output "Please enter balance due "
   input balance
```

Figure 2-16 Beginning of a program that accepts a name and balance as input and uses a separate prompt for each item

Users also find it helpful when you echo their input. **Echoing input** is the act of repeating input back to a user either in a subsequent prompt or in output. For example, Figure 2-17 shows how the second prompt in Figure 2-16 can be improved by echoing the user's first piece of input data in the second prompt. When a user runs the program that is started in Figure 2-17 and enters "Green" for the customer name, the second prompt will not be "Please enter balance due". Instead, it will be "Please enter balance due for Green". For example, if a clerk was about to enter the balance for the wrong customer, the mention of "Green" might be enough to alert the clerk to the potential error.

 Notice the space before the ending quote in the prompt "Please enter balance due for ". The space will appear between "for" and the last name.

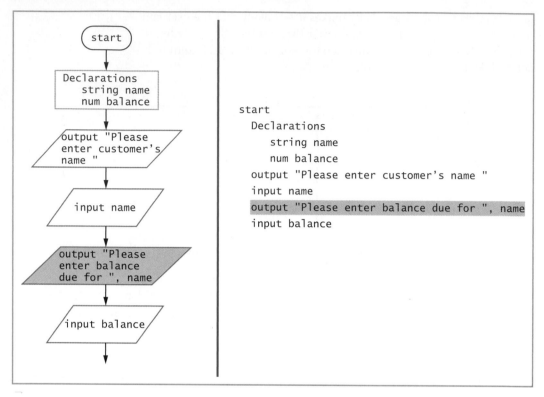

```
start
   Declarations
      string name
      num balance
   output "Please enter customer's name "
   input name
   output "Please enter balance due for ", name
   input balance
```

Figure 2-17   Beginning of a program that accepts a customer's name and uses it in the second prompt

Maintaining Good Programming Habits

When you learn a programming language and begin to write lines of program code, it is easy to forget the principles you have learned in this text. Having some programming knowledge and a keyboard at your fingertips can lure you into typing lines of code before you think things through. But every program you write will be better if you plan before you code. If you maintain the habit of first drawing flowcharts or writing pseudocode, as you have learned here, your future programming projects will go more smoothly. If you desk-check your program logic on paper before starting to type statements in a programming language, your programs will run correctly sooner. If you think carefully about the variable and module names you use, and design your program statements to be easy to read and use, your programs will be easier to develop and maintain.

77

TWO TRUTHS & A LIE

Features of Good Program Design

1. A program comment is a message that is displayed on a monitor to ask the user for a response and perhaps explain how that response should be formatted.

2. It usually makes sense to give each variable a name that contains a noun and to give each module a name that contains a verb.

3. Echoing input can help a user to confirm that a data item was entered correctly.

The false statement is #1. A program comment is a written explanation that is not part of the program logic but that serves as documentation for those reading the program. A prompt is a message that is displayed on a monitor to ask the user for a response and perhaps explain how that response should be formatted.

Chapter Summary

- Variables are named memory locations, the contents of which can vary. Before you can use a variable in any program, you must include a declaration for it. A declaration includes a data type and an identifier. Every computer programming language has its own set of rules for naming variables; however, all variable names must be written as one word without embedded spaces, and should have appropriate meaning. Data types include numeric and string. A named constant is similar to a variable, except it can be assigned a value only once.

- The equal sign is the assignment operator; it is used in an assignment statement. The assignment operator has right-associativity or right-to-left associativity. Most programming languages use +, −, *, and / as the four standard arithmetic operators. Every operator follows rules of precedence that dictate the order in which operations in the same statement are carried out; multiplication and division always take precedence over addition and subtraction. The rules of precedence can be overridden using parentheses.

- Programmers break down programming problems into reasonable units called modules, subroutines, procedures, functions, or methods. To execute a module, you call it from another program or module. Any program can contain an unlimited number of modules, and each module can be called an unlimited number of times. Modularization provides abstraction, allows multiple programmers to work on a problem, and makes it easier for you to reuse your work.

- When you create a module, you include a header, a body, and a return statement. When a main program wants to use a module, it "calls" the module's name. The flowchart symbol used to call a module is a rectangle with a bar across the top. In a flowchart, you draw each module separately with its own sentinel symbols. You can place any statements within modules, including input, processing, and output statements, and variable and constant declarations. The variables and constants declared in a module are usable only within the module; they are local to the module. Global variables and constants are those that are known to the entire program.

- The mainline logic of almost every procedural computer program can follow a general structure that consists of four distinct parts: declarations, housekeeping tasks, detail loop tasks, and end-of-job tasks.

- You can use a hierarchy chart to illustrate modules' relationships. A hierarchy chart tells you which modules exist within a program and which modules call others.

- As your programs become larger and more complicated, the need for good planning and design increases. You should use program comments where appropriate. Choose identifiers wisely, strive to design clear statements within your programs and modules, write clear prompts and echo input, and continue to maintain good programming habits as you develop your programming skills.

Key Terms

A **declaration** is a statement that provides a data type and an identifier for a variable.

An **identifier** is a variable's name.

A data item's **data type** is a classification that describes what values can be assigned, how the variable is stored, and what types of operations can be performed with the variable.

Making declarations or **declaring variables** describes the process of naming variables and assigning a data type to them.

Initializing a variable is the act of assigning its first value, often at the same time the variable is created.

Garbage describes the unknown value stored in an unassigned variable.

Keywords comprise the limited word set that is reserved in a language.

A **mnemonic** is a memory device; variable identifiers act as mnemonics for hard-to-remember memory addresses.

Camel casing is the format for naming variables in which the initial letter is lowercase, multiple-word variable names are run together, and each new word within the variable name begins with an uppercase letter.

Pascal casing is the format for naming variables in which the initial letter is uppercase, multiple-word variable names are run together, and each new word within the variable name begins with an uppercase letter.

A **numeric constant** (or **literal numeric constant**) is a specific numeric value.

A **string constant** (or **literal string constant**) is a specific group of characters enclosed within quotation marks.

An **unnamed constant** is a literal numeric or string value.

Alphanumeric values can contain alphabetic characters, numbers, and punctuation.

A **numeric variable** is one that can hold digits, have mathematical operations performed on it, and usually can hold a decimal point and a sign indicating positive or negative.

An **integer** is a whole number.

A **floating-point** number is a number with decimal places.

Real numbers are floating-point numbers.

A **string variable** can hold text that includes letters, digits, and special characters such as punctuation marks.

A **named constant** is similar to a variable, except that its value cannot change after the first assignment.

A **magic number** is an unnamed constant whose purpose is not immediately apparent.

Overhead describes the extra resources a task requires.

80

An **assignment statement** assigns a value from the right of an assignment operator to the variable or constant on the left of the assignment operator.

The **assignment operator** is the equal sign; it is used to assign a value to the variable or constant on its left.

A **binary operator** is an operator that requires two operands—one on each side.

Right-associativity and **right-to-left associativity** describe operators that evaluate the expression to the right first.

An **lvalue** is the memory address identifier to the left of an assignment operator.

Rules of precedence dictate the order in which operations in the same statement are carried out.

The **order of operations** describes the rules of precedence.

Left-to-right associativity describes operators that evaluate the expression to the left first.

Modules are small program units that you can use together to make a program. Programmers also refer to modules as **subroutines**, **procedures**, **functions**, or **methods**.

Modularization is the process of breaking down a program into modules.

Functional decomposition is the act of reducing a large program into more manageable modules.

Abstraction is the process of paying attention to important properties while ignoring nonessential details.

Reusability is the feature of modular programs that allows individual modules to be used in a variety of applications.

Reliability is the feature of modular programs that assures you a module has been tested and proven to function correctly.

A **main program** runs from start to stop and calls other modules.

The **mainline logic** is the logic that appears in a program's main module; it calls other modules.

A **module's header** includes the module identifier and possibly other necessary identifying information.

A **module's body** contains all the statements in the module.

A **module's return statement** marks the end of the module and identifies the point at which control returns to the program or module that called the module.

Encapsulation is the act of containing a task's instructions in a module.

A **stack** is a memory location in which the computer keeps track of the correct memory address to which it should return after executing a module.

The **functional cohesion** of a module is a measure of the degree to which all the module statements contribute to the same task.

Visible describes the state of data items when a module can recognize them.

In scope describes the state of data that is visible.

Local describes variables that are declared within the module that uses them.

A **portable** module is one that can more easily be reused in multiple programs.

Global describes variables that are known to an entire program.

Global variables are declared at the **program level**.

Housekeeping tasks include steps you must perform at the beginning of a program to get ready for the rest of the program.

Detail loop tasks of a program include the steps that are repeated for each set of input data.

End-of-job tasks hold the steps you take at the end of the program to finish the application.

A **hierarchy chart** is a diagram that illustrates modules' relationships to each other.

Program comments are written explanations that are not part of the program logic but that serve as documentation for those reading the program.

Internal documentation is documentation within a coded program.

External documentation is documentation that is outside a coded program.

An **annotation symbol** contains information that expands on what appears in another flowchart symbol; it is most often represented by a three-sided box that is connected to the step it references by a dashed line.

Self-documenting programs are those that contain meaningful data and module names that describe the programs' purpose.

Hungarian notation is a variable-naming convention in which a variable's data type or other information is stored as part of its name.

A **data dictionary** is a list of every variable name used in a program, along with its type, size, and description.

A **temporary variable** (or a **work variable**) is a working variable that you use to hold intermediate results during a program's execution.

A **prompt** is a message that is displayed on a monitor to ask the user for a response and perhaps explain how that response should be formatted.

Echoing input is the act of repeating input back to a user either in a subsequent prompt or in output.

Review Questions

1. What does a declaration provide for a variable?

    a. a name

    b. a data type

    c. both of the above

    d. none of the above

2. A variable's data type describes all of the following *except* _____.

    a. what values the variable can hold

    b. how the variable is stored in memory

    c. what operations can be performed with the variable

    d. the scope of the variable

3. The value stored in an uninitialized variable is
   _____.

   a. garbage

   b. null

   c. compost

   d. its identifier

4. The value 3 is a _____.

   a. numeric variable

   b. numeric constant

   c. string variable

   d. string constant

5. The assignment operator _____.

   a. is a binary operator

   b. has left-to-right associativity

   c. is most often represented by a colon

   d. two of the above

6. Which of the following is true about arithmetic precedence?

   a. Multiplication has a higher precedence than division.

   b. Operators with the lowest precedence always have left-to-right associativity.

   c. Division has higher precedence than subtraction.

   d. all of the above

7. Which of the following is a term used as a synonym for "module" in any programming language?

   a. method

   b. procedure

   c. both of these

   d. none of these

8. Which of the following is a reason to use modularization?

   a. Modularization avoids abstraction.

   b. Modularization reduces overhead.

   c. Modularization allows you to more easily reuse your work.

   d. Modularization eliminates the need for syntax.

9. What is the name for the process of paying attention to important properties while ignoring nonessential details?

   a. abstraction

   b. extraction

   c. extinction

   d. modularization

10. Every module has all of the following *except* _____.

    a. a header

    b. local variables

    c. a body

    d. a return statement

11. Programmers say that one module can _____ another, meaning that the first module causes the second module to execute.

    a. declare

    b. define

    c. enact

    d. call

12. The more that a module's statements contribute to the same job, the greater the _____ of the module.

    a. structure

    b. modularity

    c. functional cohesion

    d. size

13. In most modern programming languages, when a variable or constant is declared in a module, the variable or constant is _____ in that module.

    a. global

    b. invisible

    c. in scope

    d. undefined

14. Which of the following is *not* a typical housekeeping task?

    a. displaying instructions

    b. printing summaries

    c. opening files

    d. displaying report headings

15. Which module in a typical program will execute the most times?

    a. the housekeeping module

    b. the detail loop

    c. the end-of-job module

    d. It is different in every program.

16. A hierarchy chart tells you _____.

    a. what tasks are to be performed within each program module

    b. when a module executes

    c. which routines call which other routines

    d. all of the above

17. What are nonexecuting statements that programmers place within their code to explain program statements in English?

    a. comments

    b. pseudocode

    c. trivia

    d. user documentation

18. Program comments are _____.

    a. required to create a runnable program

    b. a form of external documentation

    c. both of the above

    d. none of the above

19. Which of the following is valid advice for naming variables?

    a. To save typing, make most variable names one or two letters.

    b. To avoid conflict with names that others are using, use unusual or unpronounceable names.

    c. To make names easier to read, separate long words by using underscores or capitalization for each new word.

    d. To maintain your independence, shun the conventions of your organization.

20. A message that asks a user for input is a _____.

    a. comment

    b. prompt

    c. echo

    d. declaration

Exercises

1. Explain why each of the following names does or does not seem like a good variable name to you.

    a. c

    b. cost

    c. costAmount

    d. cost amount

    e. cstofdngbsns

    f. costOfDoingBusinessThisFiscalYear

    g. costYear2012

    h. 2012YearCost

2. If myAge and yourRate are numeric variables, and departmentName is a string variable, which of the following statements are valid assignments? If a statement is not valid, explain why not.

    a. myAge = 23

    b. myAge = yourRate

    c. myAge = departmentName

    d. myAge = "departmentName"

    e. 42 = myAge

    f. yourRate = 3.5

    g. yourRate = myAge

    h. yourRate = departmentName

    i. 6.91 = yourRate

    j. departmentName = Personnel

    k. departmentName = "Personnel"

    l. departmentName = 413

    m. departmentName = "413"

    n. departmentName = myAge

    o. departmentName = yourRate

    p. 413 = departmentName

    q. "413" = departmentName

3. Assume that cost = 10 and price = 12. What is the value of each of the following expressions?

    a. price − cost * 2

    b. 15 + price − 3 * 2

    c. (price + cost) * 3

    d. 4 − 3 * 2 + cost

    e. cost * ((price − 8) + 5) + 100

4. Draw a typical hierarchy chart for a paycheck-producing program. Try to think of at least 10 separate modules that might be included. For example, one module might calculate an employee's dental insurance premium.

5. a. Draw the hierarchy chart and then plan the logic for a program for the sales manager of The Couch Potato Furniture Company. The manager needs a program to determine the profit on any item sold. Input includes the wholesale price and retail price for an item. The output is the item's profit, which is the retail price minus the wholesale price. Use three modules. The main program declares global variables and calls housekeeping, detail, and end-of-job modules. The housekeeping module prompts for and accepts a wholesale price. The detail module prompts for and accepts the retail price, computes the profit, and displays the result. The end-of-job module displays the message "Thanks for using this program".

   b. Revise the profit-determining program so that it runs continuously for any number of items. The detail loop executes continuously while the wholesale price is not 0; in addition to calculating the profit, it prompts the user for and gets the next wholesale price. The end-of-job module executes after 0 is entered for the wholesale price.

6. a. Draw the hierarchy chart and then plan the logic for a program that calculates the gown size a student needs for a graduation ceremony. The program uses three modules. The first prompts a user for and accepts the student's height in inches. The second module accepts the student's weight in pounds and converts the student's height to centimeters and weight to grams. Then, it calculates the graduation gown size needed by adding 1/3 of the weight in grams to the value of the height in centimeters. The program's output is the gown size the student should order. There are 2.54 centimeters in an inch and 453.59 grams in a pound. Use named constants wherever you think they are appropriate. The last module displays the message "End of job".

   b. Revise the size-determining program to execute continuously until the user enters 0 for the height in inches.

7. Draw the hierarchy chart and design the logic for a program that contains housekeeping, detail loop, and end-of-job modules, and that calculates the service charge customers owe for writing a bad check. The main program declares any needed global variables and constants and calls the other modules. The housekeeping module displays a prompt for and accepts a customer's last name. While the user does not enter "ZZZZ" for the name, the detail loop accepts the amount of the check in dollars and cents. The service charge is computed as $20 plus 2 percent of the check amount. The detail loop also displays the service charge and then prompts the user for the next customer's name. The end-of-job module, which executes after the user enters the sentinel value for the name, displays a message that indicates the program is complete.

8. Draw the hierarchy chart and design the logic for a program for the owner of Bits and Pieces Manufacturing Company, who needs to calculate an employee's projected salary following a raise. The input is the name of the employee, the employee's current weekly salary, and the percentage increase expressed as a decimal (for example, 0.04 for a 4 percent raise). Design the program so that it runs continuously for any number of employees using three modules. The housekeeping module prompts the user for the percent raise that will be applied to every employee, and prompts for the first employee's name. The detail loop executes continuously until the user enters "XXX" for the employee's name. The detail loop gets the employee's weekly salary, applies the raise, produces the result, and prompts for the next employee name. The end-of-job module, which executes after the user enters the sentinel value for the name, displays a message that indicates the program is complete.

9. Draw the hierarchy chart and design the logic for a program for the manager of the Jeter County softball team who wants to compute batting averages for his players. A batting average is computed as hits divided by at-bats, and is usually expressed to three decimal positions (for example, .235). Design a program that prompts the user for a player jersey number, the number of hits, and the number of at-bats, and then displays all the data, including the calculated batting average. The program accepts players continuously until 0 is entered for the jersey number. Use appropriate modules, including one that displays "End of job" after the sentinel is entered for the jersey number.

Find the Bugs

10. Your student disk contains files named DEBUG02-01.txt, DEBUG02-02.txt, and DEBUG02-03.txt. Each file starts with some comments that describe the problem. Comments are lines that begin with two slashes (//). Following the comments, each file contains pseudocode that has one or more bugs you must find and correct.

Game Zone

11. For games to hold your interest, they almost always include some random, unpredictable behavior. For example, a game in which you shoot asteroids loses some of its fun if the asteroids follow the same, predictable path each time you play. Therefore, generating random values is a key component in creating most interesting computer games. Many programming languages come with a built-in module you can use to generate random numbers. The syntax varies in each language, but it is usually something like the following:

```
myRandomNumber = random(10)
```

In this statement, `myRandomNumber` is a numeric variable you have declared and the expression `random(10)` means "call a method that generates and returns a random number between 1 and 10." By convention, in a flowchart, you would place a statement like this in a processing symbol with two vertical stripes at the edges, as shown below.

```
myRandomNumber =
random(10)
```

Create a flowchart or pseudocode that shows the logic for a program that generates a random number, then asks the user to think of a number between 1 and 10. Then display the randomly generated number so the user can see whether his or her guess was accurate. (In future chapters you will improve this game so that the user can enter a guess and the program can determine whether the user was correct.)

Up for Discussion

12. Many programming style guides are published on the Web. These guides suggest good identifiers, explain standard indentation rules, and identify style issues in specific programming languages. Find style guides for at least two languages (for example, C++, Java, Visual Basic, or C#) and list any differences you notice.

13. In this chapter, you learned the term *mnemonic*, which is a memory device like the sentence "Every good boy does fine." Another popular mnemonic is "May I have a large container of coffee?" What is its meaning? Have you learned other mnemonics as you have studied various subjects? Describe at least five other mnemonics that people use for remembering lists of items.

14. What advantages are there to requiring variables to have a data type?

15. Would you prefer to write a large program by yourself, or work on a team in which each programmer produces one or more modules? Why?

16. Extreme programming is a system for rapidly developing software. One of its tenets is that all production code is written by two programmers sitting at one machine. Is this a good idea? Does working this way as a programmer appeal to you? Why or why not?

CHAPTER 3

Understanding Structure

In this chapter, you will learn about:

- ◎ The features of unstructured spaghetti code
- ◎ The three basic structures—sequence, selection, and loop
- ◎ Using a priming input to structure a program
- ◎ The need for structure
- ◎ Recognizing structure
- ◎ Structuring and modularizing unstructured logic

Understanding Unstructured Spaghetti Code

Professional computer programs usually get far more complicated than the examples you have seen so far in Chapters 1 and 2. Imagine the number of instructions in the computer program that NASA uses to calculate the launch angle of a space shuttle, or in the program the IRS uses to audit your income tax return. Even the program that produces your paycheck at your job contains many, many instructions. Designing the logic for such a program can be a time-consuming task. When you add several thousand instructions to a program, including several hundred decisions, it is easy to create a complicated mess. The popular name for logically snarled program statements is **spaghetti code**, because the logic is as hard to follow as one noodle through a plate of spaghetti. Programs that use spaghetti code logic are **unstructured programs**; that is, they do not follow the rules of structured logic that you will learn in this chapter. **Structured programs** *do* follow those rules.

For example, suppose you start a job as a dog washer, and you receive instructions for how to wash a dog, as shown in Figure 3-1. This kind of flowchart is an example of unstructured spaghetti code. A computer program that is structured similarly might "work"—that is, it might produce correct results—but would be difficult to read and maintain, and its logic would be difficult to follow.

You might be able to follow the logic of the dog-washing procedure in Figure 3-1 for two reasons:

- You probably already know how to wash a dog.

- The flowchart contains a very limited number of steps.

However, imagine that the described process was far more complicated or that you were not familiar with the process. (For example, imagine you must wash 100 dogs concurrently while applying flea and tick medication, giving them haircuts, and researching their genealogy.) Depicting more complicated logic in an unstructured way would be cumbersome. By the end of this chapter, you will understand how to make the unstructured process in Figure 3-1 clearer and less error-prone.

Software developers say that spaghetti code has a shorter life than structured code. This means that programs developed using spaghetti code exist as production programs in an organization for less time. Such programs are so difficult to alter that when improvements are required, developers often find it easier to abandon the existing program and start from scratch. Obviously, this costs more money.

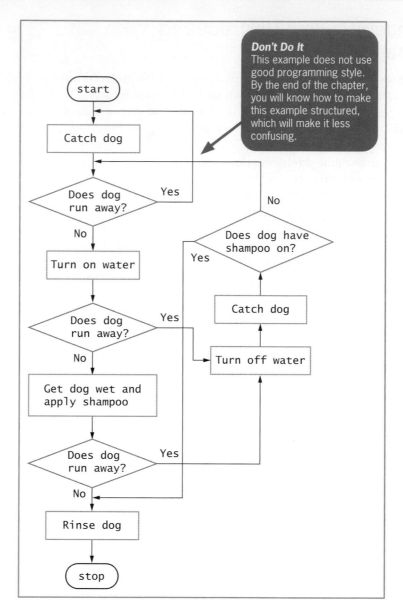

Figure 3-1   Spaghetti code logic for washing a dog

TWO TRUTHS & A LIE

Understanding Unstructured Spaghetti Code

1. The popular name for logically snarled program statements is spaghetti code.

2. Programs written using spaghetti code cannot produce correct results.

3. Programs written using spaghetti code are more difficult to follow than other programs.

The false statement is #2. Programs written using spaghetti code can produce correct results, but they are more difficult to understand and maintain than programs that use structured techniques.

Understanding the Three Basic Structures

In the mid-1960s, mathematicians proved that any program, no matter how complicated, can be constructed using one or more of only three structures. A **structure** is a basic unit of programming logic; each structure is one of the following:

- sequence
- selection
- loop

With these three structures alone, you can diagram any task, from doubling a number to performing brain surgery. You can diagram each structure with a specific configuration of flowchart symbols.

The first of these three basic structures is a sequence, as shown in Figure 3-2. With a **sequence structure**, you perform an action or task, and then you perform the next action, in order. A sequence can contain any number of tasks, but there is no option to branch off and skip any of the tasks. (In other words, a flowchart that describes a sequence structure never contains a decision symbol, and pseudocode that describes a sequence structure never contains an if or a while.) Once you start a series of actions in a sequence, you must continue step by step until the sequence ends.

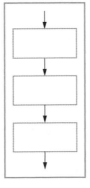

Figure 3-2
Sequence structure

As an example, driving directions often are listed as a sequence. For example, to tell a friend how to get to your house from school, you might provide the following sequence, in which one step follows the other and no steps can be skipped:

```
go north on First Avenue for 3 miles
turn left on Washington Boulevard
go west on Washington for 2 miles
stop at 634 Washington
```

The second of the three structures is a **selection structure** or **decision structure**, as shown in Figure 3-3. With this structure, you ask a question and, depending on the answer, you take one of two courses of action. Then, no matter which path you follow, you continue with the next task. (In other words, a flowchart that describes a selection structure must begin with a decision symbol, and the branches of the decision must join at the bottom of the structure. Pseudocode that describes a selection structure must start with if and end with endif.)

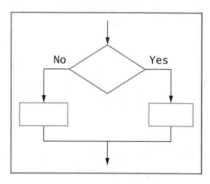

Figure 3-3 Selection structure

Some people call the selection structure an **if-then-else** because it fits the following statement:

```
if someCondition is true then
    do oneProcess
else
    do theOtherProcess
```

For example, you might provide part of the directions to your house as follows:

```
if traffic is backed up on Washington Boulevard then
    continue for 1 block on First Avenue and turn left on
    Adams Lane
else
    turn left on Washington Boulevard
```

Similarly, a payroll program might include a statement such as:

```
if hoursWorked is more than 40 then
    calculate regularPay and overtimePay
else
    calculate regularPay
```

The previous examples can also be called **dual-alternative ifs** (or **dual-alternative selections**), because they contain two alternatives—the action taken when the tested condition is true and the action taken when it is false. Note that it is perfectly correct for one branch of the selection to be a "do nothing" branch. In each of the following examples, an action is taken only when the tested condition is true:

```
if it is raining then
    take an umbrella
```

```
if employee participates in
the dental plan then
    deduct $40 from employee
    gross pay
```

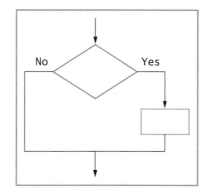

The previous examples are **single-alternative ifs** (or **single-alternative selections**); a diagram of their structure is shown in Figure 3-4. In these cases, you do not take any special action if it is not raining or if the employee does not belong to the dental plan. The

Figure 3-4 Single-alternative selection structure

case in which nothing is done is often called the **null case**.

The third of the three basic structures, shown in Figure 3-5, is a loop. In a **loop structure**, you continue to repeat actions while a condition remains true. The action or actions that occur within the loop are known as the **loop body**. In the most common type of loop, a condition is evaluated; if the answer is true, you

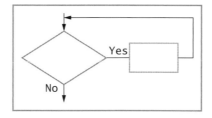

Figure 3-5 Loop structure

execute the loop body and evaluate the condition again. If the condition is still true, you execute the loop body again and then reevaluate the original condition. This continues until the condition becomes false, and then you exit the structure. (In other words, a flowchart that describes a loop structure always begins with a decision symbol that has a branch that returns to a spot prior to the decision. Pseudocode that describes a loop starts with `while` and ends with `endwhile`.) You may hear programmers refer to looping as **repetition** or **iteration**.

Sometimes you must ask a negative question to execute a loop body. The most common example is to repeat a loop while a sentinel condition has *not* been met.

Some programmers call this structure a **while...do**, or more simply, a **while loop**, because it fits the following statement:

```
while testCondition continues to be true
    do someProcess
```

When you provide directions to your house, part of the directions might be:

```
while the address of the house you are passing remains
below 634
        travel forward to the next house and look at the address
```

You encounter examples of looping every day, as in each of the following:

```
while you continue to be hungry
        take another bite of food and see if you still feel
        hungry
```

```
while unread pages remain in the reading assignment
        read another unread page and see if there are more pages
```

All logic problems can be solved using only these three structures—sequence, selection, and loop. The three structures can be combined in an infinite number of ways. For example, you can have a sequence of tasks followed by a selection, or a loop followed by a sequence. Attaching structures end to end is called **stacking structures**. For example, Figure 3-6 shows a structured flowchart achieved by stacking structures, and shows pseudocode that might follow that flowchart logic.

> Whether you are drawing a flowchart or writing pseudocode, you can use either of the following pairs to represent decision outcomes: Yes and No or true and false. This book follows the convention of using Yes and No in flowchart diagrams and true and false in pseudocode.

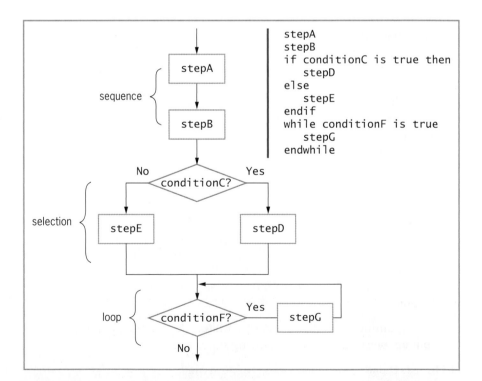

Figure 3-6 Structured flowchart and pseudocode with three stacked structures

The pseudocode in Figure 3-6 shows two **end-structure statements**—`endif` and `endwhile`. You can use an `endif` statement to clearly show where the actions that depend on a decision end. The instruction that follows `if` occurs when its tested condition is true, the instruction that follows `else` occurs when the tested condition is false, and any instructions that follow `endif` occur in either case—instructions after the `endif` are not dependent on the `if` statement at all. In other words, statements beyond the `endif` statement are "outside" the decision structure. Similarly, you use an `endwhile` statement to show where a loop structure ends. In Figure 3-6, while `conditionF` continues to be true, `stepG` continues to execute. If any statements followed the `endwhile` statement, they would be outside of, and not a part of, the loop. (You first saw the `endwhile` statement in Chapter 2.)

Besides stacking structures, you can replace any individual tasks or steps in a structured flowchart diagram or pseudocode segment with additional structures. In other words, any sequence, selection, or loop can contain other sequences, selections, or loops. For example, you can have a sequence of three tasks on one side of a selection, as shown in Figure 3-7. Placing a structure within another structure is called **nesting structures**.

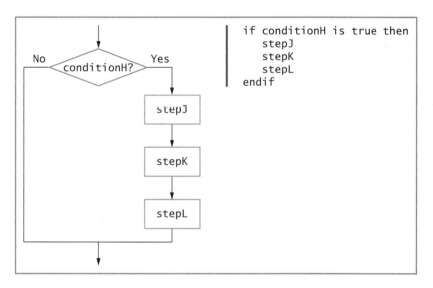

Figure 3-7 Flowchart and pseudocode showing nested structures—a sequence nested within a selection

In the pseudocode for the logic shown in Figure 3-7, the indentation shows that all three statements (`stepJ`, `stepK`, and `stepL`) must execute if `conditionH` is true. The three statements constitute a **block**, or a group of statements that executes as a single unit.

In place of one of the steps in the sequence in Figure 3-7, you can insert a selection. In Figure 3-8, the process named `stepK` has been replaced with a loop structure that begins with a test of the condition named `conditionM`.

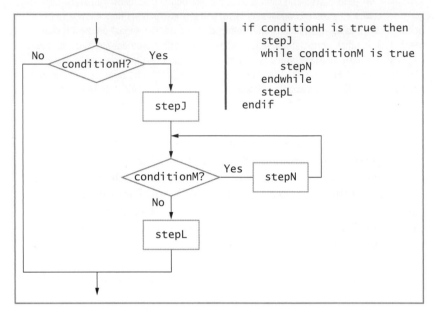

if conditionH is true then
    stepJ
    while conditionM is true
        stepN
    endwhile
    stepL
endif

Figure 3-8 Flowchart and pseudocode showing nested structures—a loop nested within a sequence, nested within a selection

When you nest structures, the statements that start and end a structure are always on the same level and always in pairs. Structures cannot overlap. For example, if you have an `if` that contains a `while`, then the `endwhile` statement will come before the `endif`. On the other hand, if you have a `while` that contains an `if`, then the `endif` statement will come before the `endwhile`.

In the pseudocode shown in Figure 3-8, notice that `if` and `endif` are vertically aligned. This shows that they are all "on the same level." Similarly, `stepJ`, `while`, `endwhile`, and `stepL` are aligned, and they are evenly indented. In the flowchart in Figure 3-8, you could draw a vertical line through the symbols containing `stepJ`, the entry and exit points of the `while` loop, and `stepL`. The flowchart and the pseudocode represent exactly the same logic.

There is no limit to the number of levels you can create when you nest and stack structures. For example, Figure 3-9 shows logic that has been made more complicated by replacing `stepN` with a selection. The structure that performs `stepP` or `stepQ` based on the outcome of `conditionO` is nested within the loop that is controlled by `conditionO`. In the pseudocode in Figure 3-9, notice how the `if`, `else`, and `endif` that describe the condition selection are aligned with each other and within the `while` structure that is controlled by `conditionM`. As before, the indentation used in the pseudocode reflects the logic laid out graphically in the flowchart.

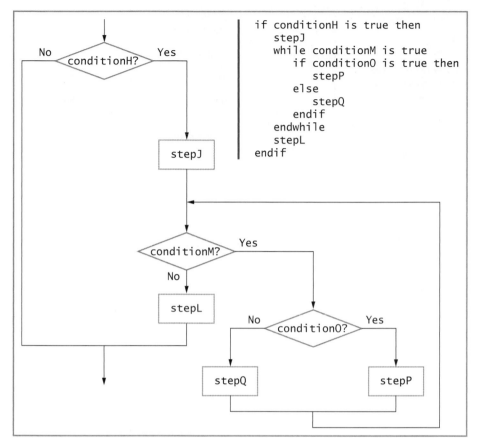

```
if conditionH is true then
    stepJ
    while conditionM is true
        if conditionO is true then
            stepP
        else
            stepQ
        endif
    endwhile
    stepL
endif
```

Figure 3-9   Flowchart and pseudocode for loop within selection within sequence within selection

Many of the preceding examples are generic so that you can focus on the relationships of the shapes without worrying what they do. Keep in mind that generic instructions like **stepA** and generic conditions like **conditionC** can stand for anything. For example, Figure 3-10 shows the process of buying and planting flowers outdoors in the spring after the danger of frost is over. The flowchart and pseudocode structures are identical to the ones in Figure 3-9. In the exercises at the end of this chapter, you will be asked to develop more scenarios that fit the same pattern.

The possible combinations of logical structures are endless, but each segment of a structured program is a sequence, a selection, or a loop. The three structures are shown together in Figure 3-11. Notice that each structure has one entry and one exit point. One structure can attach to another only at one of these points.

Try to imagine physically picking up any of the three structures using the entry and exit "handles." These are the spots at which you could connect a structure to any of the others. Similarly, any complete structure, from its entry point to its exit point, can be inserted within the process symbol of any other structure.

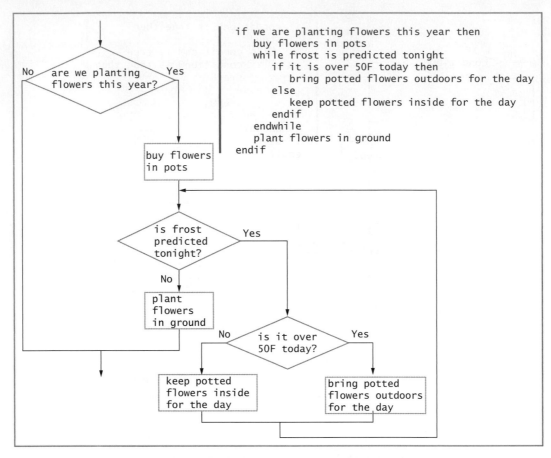

Figure 3-10   The process of buying and planting flowers in the spring

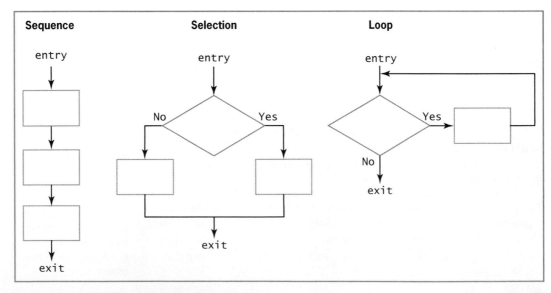

Figure 3-11   The three structures

In summary, a structured program has the following characteristics:

- A structured program includes only combinations of the three basic structures—sequence, selection, and loop. Any structured program might contain one, two, or all three types of structures.

Watch the video
*Understanding
Structure.*

103

- Each of the structures has a single entry point and a single exit point.

- Structures can be stacked or connected to one another only at their entry or exit points.

- Any structure can be nested within another structure.

 A structured program is never *required* to contain examples of all three structures. For example, many simple programs contain only a sequence of several tasks that execute from start to finish without any needed selections or loops. As another example, a program might display a series of numbers, looping to do so, but never making any decisions about the numbers.

TWO TRUTHS & A LIE

Understanding the Three Basic Structures

1. Each structure in structured programming is a sequence, selection, or loop.

2. All logic problems can be solved using only these three structures—sequence, selection, and loop.

3. The three structures cannot be combined in a single program.

The false statement is #3. The three structures can be stacked or nested in an infinite number of ways.

Using a Priming Input to Structure a Program

Recall the number-doubling program discussed in Chapter 2; Figure 3-12 shows a similar program. The program inputs a number and checks for the end-of-file condition. If it is not the end of file, then the number is doubled, the answer is displayed, and the next number is input.

Is the program represented by Figure 3-12 structured? At first, it might be hard to tell. The three allowed structures were illustrated in Figure 3-11, and the flowchart in Figure 3-12 does not look exactly like any of those three shapes.

104

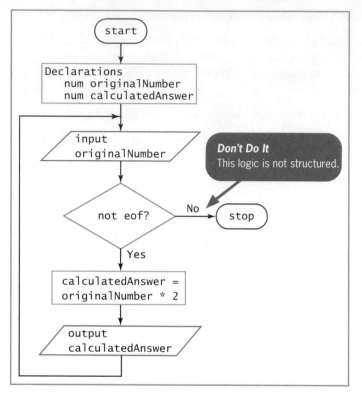

Figure 3-12 Unstructured flowchart of a number-doubling program

 Recall from Chapter 1 that this book uses **eof** to represent a generic end-of-data condition when the exact tested parameters are not important to the discussion. In this example, the test is for **not eof**, because processing will continue while it is true that the end of the data has not been reached.

However, because you may stack and nest structures while retaining overall structure, it might be difficult to determine whether a flowchart as a whole is structured. It is easiest to analyze the flowchart in Figure 3-12 one step at a time. The beginning of the flowchart looks like Figure 3-13. Is this portion of the flowchart structured? Yes, it is a sequence of two events.

Adding the next piece of the flowchart looks like Figure 3-14. The sequence is finished; either a selection or a loop is starting. You might not know which one, but you do know the sequence is not continuing, because sequences cannot contain questions. With a

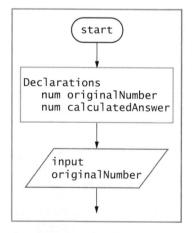

Figure 3-13 Beginning of a number-doubling flowchart

sequence, each task or step must follow without any opportunity to branch off. So, which type of structure starts with the question in Figure 3-14? Is it a selection or a loop?

Selection and loop structures differ as follows:

- In a selection structure, the logic goes in one of two directions after the question, and then the flow comes back together; the question is not asked a second time within the structure.

- In a loop, if the answer to the question results in the loop being entered and the loop statements executing, then the logic returns to the question that started the loop. When the body of a loop executes, the question that controls the loop is always asked again.

Figure 3-14 Number-doubling flowchart continued

If the number-doubling problem in the original Figure 3-12 is not eof (that is, if the end-of-file condition is not met), then some math is performed, an answer is output, a new number is obtained, and the logic returns to the eof question. In other words, while the answer to the eof question continues to be *No*, a body of statements continues to execute. Therefore, the eof question starts a structure that is more like a loop than a selection.

The number-doubling problem *does* contain a loop, but it is not a structured loop. In a structured loop, the rules are:

1. You ask a question.

2. If the answer indicates you should execute the loop body, then you do so.

3. If you execute the loop body, then you must go right back to repeat the question.

The flowchart in Figure 3-12 asks a question. If the answer is *No* (that is, while it is true that the eof condition has not been met), then the program performs two tasks in the loop body: it does the arithmetic and it displays the results. Doing two things is acceptable because two tasks with no possible branching constitute a sequence, and it is fine to nest a structure within another structure. However, when the sequence ends, the logic does not flow right back to the loop-controlling question. Instead, it goes *above* the question to get another number. For the loop in Figure 3-12 to be a structured loop, the logic must return to the eof question when the embedded sequence ends.

The flowchart in Figure 3-15 shows the flow of logic returning to the eof question immediately after the sequence. Figure 3-15 shows a structured flowchart, but the flowchart has one major flaw—it does not do the job of continuously doubling different numbers.

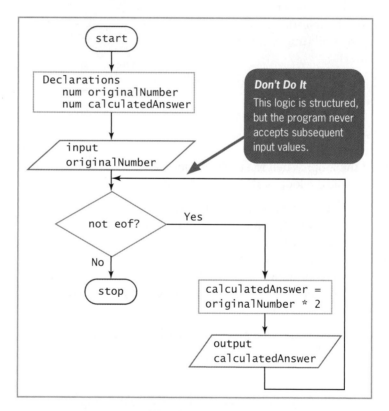

Figure 3-15   Structured, but nonfunctional, flowchart of number-doubling problem

Follow the flowchart in Figure 3-15 through a typical program run, assuming the eof condition is an input value of 0. Suppose when the program starts, the user enters a 9 for the value of originalNumber. That is not eof, so the number is multiplied by 2, and 18 is displayed as the value of calculatedAnswer. Then the question eof? is asked again. It cannot be eof because a new value representing the sentinel

(ending) value cannot be entered. The logic never returns to the
`input originalNumber` task, so the value of `originalNumber` never
changes. Therefore, 9 doubles again and the answer 18 is displayed
again. It is still not `eof`, so the same steps are repeated. This goes on
forever, with the answer 18 being output repeatedly. The program
logic shown in Figure 3-15 is structured, but it does not work as
intended. Conversely, the program in Figure 3-16 works, but it is not
structured!

The loop in
Figure 3-16 is
not structured
because after
the tasks exe-
cute within a structured
loop, the flow of logic
must return directly to the
loop-controlling question.
In Figure 3-16, the logic
does not return to this
question; instead, it goes
"too high" outside the
loop to repeat the `input`
`originalNumber` task.

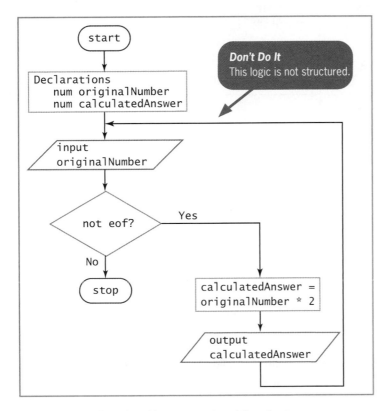

Figure 3-16   Functional but unstructured flowchart

How can the number-doubling problem be both structured and work
as intended? Often, for a program to be structured, you must add
something extra. In this case, it is a priming input step. A **priming**
input or **priming read** is an added statement that gets the first input
value in a program. For example, if a program will receive 100
data values as input, you input the first value in a statement that is
separate from the other 99. You must do this to keep the program
structured.

Consider the solution in Figure 3-17; it is structured *and* it
does what it is supposed to do. It contains a shaded, additional

input originalNumber statement. The program logic illustrated in Figure 3-17 contains a sequence and a loop. The loop contains another sequence.

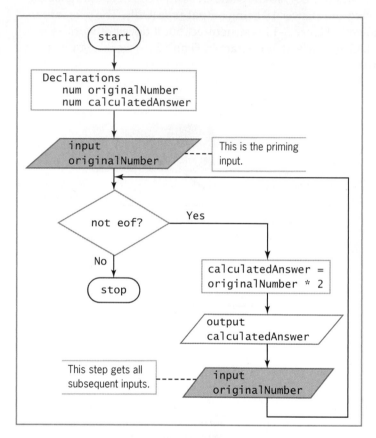

Figure 3-17   Functional, structured flowchart and pseudocode for the number-doubling problem

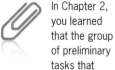

In Chapter 2, you learned that the group of preliminary tasks that sets the stage for the main work of a program is called the housekeeping section. The priming read is an example of a housekeeping task.

The additional input originalNumber step shown in Figure 3-17 is typical in structured programs. The first of the two input steps is the priming input. The term *priming* comes from the fact that the read is first, or *primary* (it gets the process going, as in "priming the pump"). The purpose of the priming input step is to control the upcoming loop that begins with the eof question. The last element within the structured loop gets the next, and all subsequent, input values. This is also typical in structured loops—the last step executed within the loop alters the condition tested in the question that begins the loop, which in this case is the eof question.

Figure 3-18 shows another way you might attempt to draw the logic for the number-doubling program. At first glance, the figure might seem to show an acceptable solution to the problem—it is structured, contains a single loop with a sequence of three steps within it, and appears to eliminate the need for the priming input statement. When the program starts, the eof question is asked. The answer is *No*, so the program gets an input number, doubles it, and displays it. Then, if it is still not eof, the program gets another number, doubles it, and displays it. The program continues until eof is encountered when getting input. The last time the input originalNumber statement executes, it encounters eof, but the program does not stop—instead, it calculates and displays a result one last time. Depending on the language you are using and on the type of input being used, you might receive an error message or you might output garbage. In either case, this last output is extraneous—no value should be doubled and output after the eof condition is encountered. As a general rule, an eof question should always come immediately after an input statement because the end-of-file condition will be detected at input. Therefore, the best solution to the number-doubling problem remains the one shown in Figure 3-17—the solution containing the priming input statement.

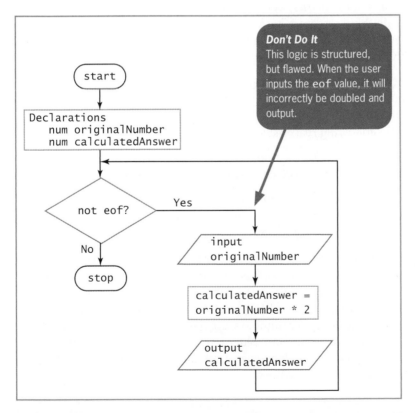

Figure 3-18 Structured but incorrect solution to the number-doubling problem

110

Understanding the Reasons for Structure

At this point, you may very well be saying, "I liked the original number-doubling program back in Figure 3-12 just fine. I could follow it. Also, the first program had one less step in it, so it was less work. Who cares if a program is structured?"

Until you have some programming experience, it is difficult to appreciate the reasons for using only the three structures—sequence, selection, and loop. However, staying with these three structures is better for the following reasons:

- *Clarity*—The number-doubling program is small. As programs get bigger, they get more confusing if they are not structured.

- *Professionalism*—All other programmers (and programming teachers you might encounter) expect your programs to be structured. It is the way things are done professionally.

- *Efficiency*—Most newer computer languages are structured languages with syntax that lets you deal efficiently with sequence, selection, and looping. Older languages, such as assembly languages, COBOL, and RPG, were developed before the principles of structured programming were discovered. However, even programs that use those older languages can be written in a structured form. Newer languages such as C#, C++, and Java enforce structure by their syntax.

In older languages, you could leave a selection or loop before it was complete by using a "go to" statement. The statement allowed the logic to "go to" any other part of the program whether it was within the same structure or not. Structured programming is sometimes called **goto-less programming.**

- *Maintenance*—You and other programmers will find it easier to modify and maintain structured programs as changes are required in the future.

- *Modularity*—Structured programs can be easily broken down into routines or modules that can be assigned to any number of programmers. The routines are then pieced back together like modular furniture at each routine's single entry or exit point. Additionally, a module often can be used in multiple programs, saving development time in the new project.

111

TWO TRUTHS & A LIE

Understanding the Reasons for Structure

1. Structured programs are clearer than unstructured programs.

2. You and other programmers will find it easier to modify and maintain structured programs as changes are required in the future.

3. Structured programs are not easily divided into parts, making them less prone to error.

The false statement is #3. Structured programs can be easily broken down into modules that can be assigned to any number of programmers.

Recognizing Structure

When you are beginning to learn about structured program design, it is difficult to detect whether a flowchart of a program's logic is structured. For example, is the flowchart segment in Figure 3-19 structured?

Yes, it is. It has a sequence and a selection structure.

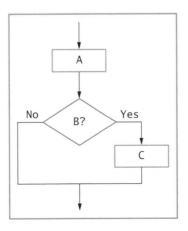

Figure 3-19 Example 1

Is the flowchart segment in Figure 3-20 structured?

Yes, it is. It has a loop, and within the loop is a selection.

Is the flowchart segment in Figure 3-21 structured?

No, it is not constructed from the three basic structures. One way to straighten out an unstructured flowchart segment is to use the "spaghetti bowl" method; that is, picture the flowchart as a bowl of spaghetti that you must untangle. Imagine you can grab one piece of pasta at the top of the bowl and start pulling. As you "pull" each symbol out of the tangled mess, you can untangle the separate paths until the entire segment is structured.

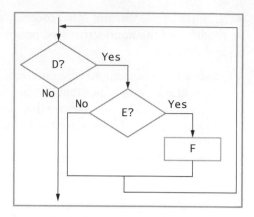

Figure 3-20   Example 2

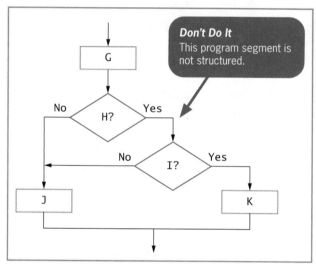

Figure 3-21   Example 3

For example, look at the diagram in Figure 3-21. If you could start pulling at the top, you would encounter a procedure box labeled G. (See Figure 3-22.) A single process like G is part of an acceptable structure—it constitutes at least the beginning of a sequence structure.

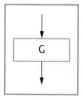

Figure 3-22   Untangling Example 3, first step

Imagine that you continue pulling symbols from the tangled segment. The next item in the flowchart is a question that tests a condition labeled H, as you can see in Figure 3-23. At this point, you know the sequence that started with G has ended. Sequences never have decisions in them, so the sequence is finished; either a selection or a loop is beginning with question H. A loop must return to the loop-controlling question at some later point. You can see from the original logic in Figure 3-21 that whether the answer to H is *Yes* or *No*, the logic never returns to H. Therefore, H begins a selection structure, not a loop structure.

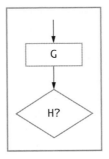

Figure 3-23 Untangling Example 3, second step

To continue detangling the logic, you would pull up on the flowline that emerges from the left side (the *No* side) of Question H. You encounter J, as shown in Figure 3-24. When you continue beyond J, you reach the end of the flowchart.

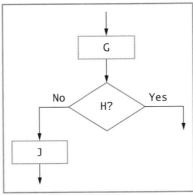

Figure 3-24 Untangling Example 3, third step

Now you can turn your attention to the *Yes* side (the right side) of the condition tested in H. When you pull up on the right side, you encounter Question I. (See Figure 3-25.)

In the original version of the flowchart in Figure 3-21, follow the line on the left side of Question I. The line emerging from the left side of selection I is attached to J, which is outside the selection structure. You might say the I-controlled selection is becoming entangled with the H-controlled selection, so you

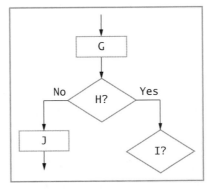

Figure 3-25 Untangling Example 3, fourth step

must untangle the structures by repeating the step that is causing the tangle. (In this example, you repeat Step J to untangle it from the other usage of J.) Continue pulling on the flowline that emerges from J until you reach the end of the program segment, as shown in Figure 3-26.

Now pull on the right side of Question I. Process K pops up, as shown in Figure 3-27; then you reach the end.

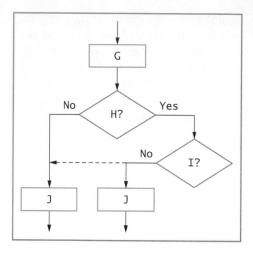

Figure 3-26 Untangling Example 3, fifth step

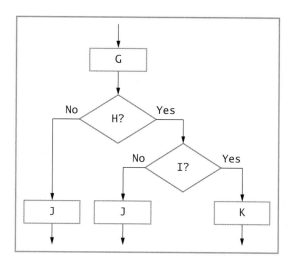

Figure 3-27 Untangling Example 3, sixth step

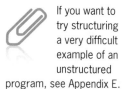

If you want to try structuring a very difficult example of an unstructured program, see Appendix E.

At this point, the untangled flowchart has three loose ends. The loose ends of Question I can be brought together to form a selection structure; then the loose ends of Question H can be brought together to form another selection structure. The result is the flowchart shown in Figure 3-28. The entire flowchart segment is structured—it has a sequence followed by a selection inside a selection.

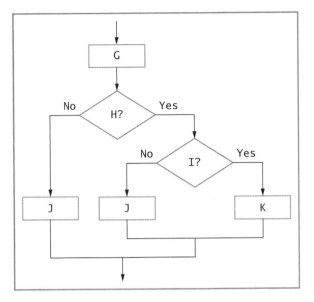

Figure 3-28 Finished flowchart and pseudocode for untangling Example 3

TWO TRUTHS & A LIE

Recognizing Structure

1. Most, but not all, sets of instructions can be expressed in a structured format.

2. When you are first learning about structured program design, it can be difficult to detect whether a flowchart of a program's logic is structured.

3. Any unstructured flowchart can be "detangled" to become structured.

The false statement is #1. Any set of instructions can be expressed in a structured format.

Structuring and Modularizing Unstructured Logic

Recall the dog-washing process illustrated in Figure 3-1 at the beginning of this chapter. When you look at it now, you should recognize it as an unstructured process. Can this process be reconfigured to perform precisely the same tasks in a structured way? Of course!

Figure 3-29 shows the beginning of the process. The first step, *Catch dog*, is a simple sequence.

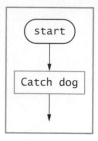

Figure 3-30 contains the next part of the process. When a question is encountered, the sequence is over, and either a loop or a selection starts. In this case, after the dog runs away, you must catch the dog and determine whether he runs away again, so a loop begins. To create a structured loop like the ones you have seen earlier in this chapter, you can repeat the *Catch dog* process and return immediately to the *Does dog run away?* question.

Figure 3-29 Washing the dog, part 1

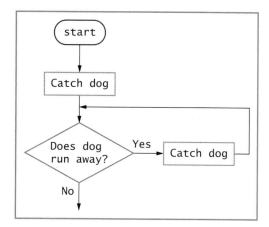

Figure 3-30   Washing the dog, part 2

In the original flowchart in Figure 3-1, you turn on the water when the dog does not run away. This step is a simple sequence, so it can correctly be added after the loop. When the water is turned on, the original logic checks to see whether the dog runs away after this new development. This starts a loop. In the original flowchart, the lines cross, creating a tangle, so you repeat as many steps as necessary to detangle the lines. After you turn off the water and catch the dog, you encounter the question *Does dog have shampoo on?* Because the logic has not yet reached the shampooing step, there is no need to ask this question; the answer at this point always will be *No*. When one of the logical paths emerging from a question can never be traveled, you can eliminate the question. Figure 3-31 shows that if the dog runs away after you turn on the water, but before you've gotten the dog wet and shampooed it, you must turn the water off, catch the dog, and return to the step that asks whether the dog runs away.

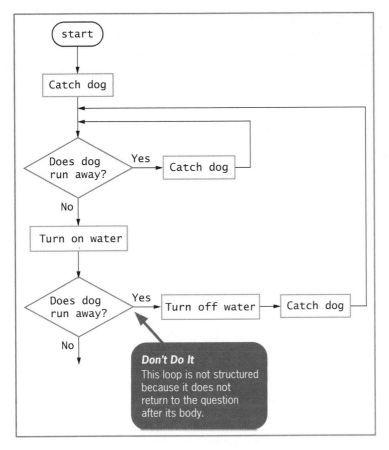

Figure 3-31   Washing the dog, part 3

The logic in Figure 3-31 is not structured because the second loop that begins with the question *Does dog run away?* does not immediately return to the loop-controlling question after its body executes. So, to make the loop structured, you can repeat the actions that occur before returning to the loop-controlling question. (See Figure 3-32.)

The flowchart segment in Figure 3-32 is structured; it contains a sequence, a loop, a sequence, and a final, larger loop. This last loop contains its own sequence, loop, and sequence.

After the dog is caught and the water is on, you wet and shampoo the dog, as shown in Figure 3-33. Then, according to the original flowchart in Figure 3-1, you once again check to see whether the dog has run away. If he has, you turn off the water and catch the dog. From this location in the logic, the answer to the *Does dog have shampoo on?* question will always be Yes; so, as before, there is no need to ask a question when there is only one possible answer. So, if the dog runs away, the last loop executes. You turn off the water, continue to catch the dog as it repeatedly escapes, and turn the water on.

When the dog is caught at last, you rinse the dog and end the program. Figure 3-33 shows both the complete flowchart and pseudocode.

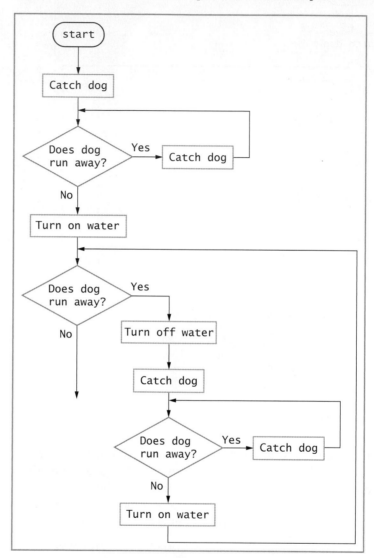

Figure 3-32 Washing the dog, part 4

The flowchart in Figure 3-33 is complete and is structured. It contains alternating sequence and loop structures.

Figure 3-33 shows three places where the sequence-loop-sequence of catching the dog and turning the water on are repeated. So, if you wanted to, you could modularize the duplicate sections so that their instruction sets are written once and contained in their own module. Figure 3-34 shows a modularized version of the program; the three module calls are shaded.

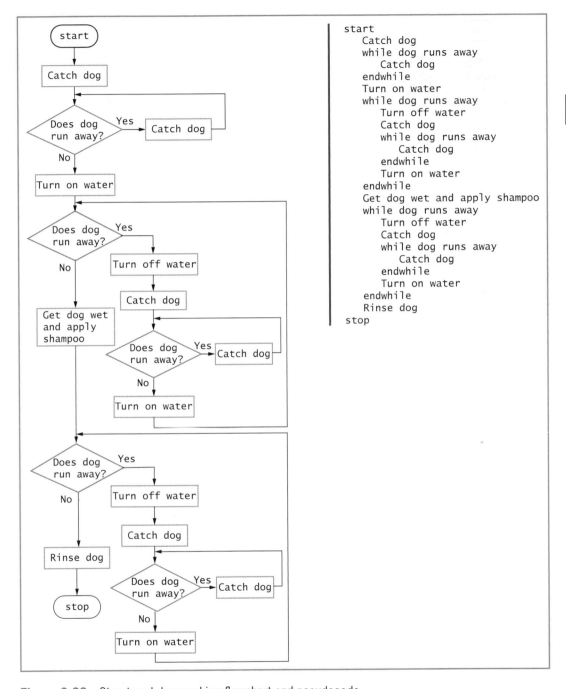

Figure 3-33 Structured dog-washing flowchart and pseudocode

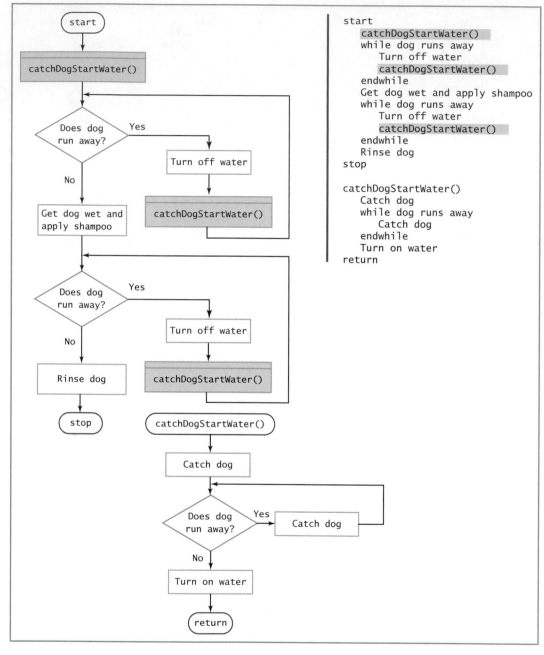

Figure 3-34   Modularized version of the dog-washing program

No matter how complicated it is, any set of steps can always be reduced to combinations of the three basic structures of sequence, selection, and loop. These structures can be nested and stacked in an infinite number of ways to describe the logic of any process and to create the logic for every computer program written in the past, present, or future.

 Watch the video *Structuring Unstructured Logic.*

 For convenience, many programming languages allow two variations of the three basic structures. The `case` structure is a variation of the selection structure and the `do` loop is a variation of the `while` loop. You can learn about these two structures in Appendix F. Even though these extra structures can be used in most programming languages, all logical problems can be solved without them.

TWO TRUTHS & A LIE

Structuring and Modularizing Unstructured Logic

1. When you encounter a question in a logical diagram, a sequence should be ending.

2. In a structured loop, the logic returns to the loop-controlling question after the loop body executes.

3. If a flowchart or pseudocode contains a question to which the answer never varies, you can eliminate the question.

The false statement is #1. When you encounter a question in a logical diagram, either a selection or a loop should start. Any structure might end before the question is encountered.

Chapter Summary

- Spaghetti code is the popular name for unstructured program statements that do not follow the rules of structured logic.

- Clearer programs can be constructed using only three basic structures: sequence, selection, and loop. These three structures can be combined in an infinite number of ways by stacking and nesting them. Each structure has one entry and one exit point; one structure can attach to another only at one of these points.

- A priming input is the statement that gets the first input value prior to starting a structured loop. The last step within the loop gets the next, and all subsequent, input values.

- Programmers use structured techniques to promote clarity, professionalism, efficiency, and modularity.

- One way to order an unstructured flowchart segment is to imagine it as a bowl of spaghetti that you must untangle.

- Any set of logical steps can be rewritten to conform to the three structures.

Key Terms

Spaghetti code is snarled, unstructured program logic.

Unstructured programs are programs that do *not* follow the rules of structured logic.

Structured programs are programs that do follow the rules of structured logic.

A **structure** is a basic unit of programming logic; each structure is a sequence, selection, or loop.

With a **sequence structure**, you perform an action or task, and then you perform the next action, in order. A sequence can contain any number of tasks, but there is no option to branch off and skip any of the tasks.

With a **selection structure** or **decision structure**, you ask a question, and, depending on the answer, you take one of two courses of action. Then, no matter which path you follow, you continue with the next task.

An **if-then-else** is another name for a selection structure.

Dual-alternative ifs (or **dual-alternative selections**) define one action to be taken when the tested condition is true and another action to be taken when it is false.

Single-alternative ifs (or **single-alternative selections**) take action on just one branch of the decision.

The **null case** is the branch of a decision in which no action is taken.

With a **loop structure**, you continue to repeat actions based on the answer to a question.

A **loop body** is the set of actions that occur within a loop.

Repetition and **iteration** are alternate names for a loop structure.

In a **while...do**, or more simply, a **while loop**, a process continues while some condition continues to be true.

Stacking structures is the act of attaching structures end to end.

End-structure statements designate the ends of pseudocode structures.

Nesting structures is the act of placing a structure within another structure.

A **block** is a group of statements that executes as a single unit.

A **priming input** or **priming read** is the statement that reads the first input data record prior to starting a structured loop.

Goto-less programming is a name to describe structured programming, because structured programmers do not use a "go to" statement.

Review Questions

1. Snarled program logic is called _____ code.

   a. snake

   b. spaghetti

   c. string

   d. gnarly

2. The three structures of structured programming are
   _____.

   a. sequence, order, and process

   b. selection, loop, and iteration

   c. sequence, selection, and loop

   d. if, else, and then

3. A sequence structure can contain _____.

   a. any number of tasks

   b. exactly three tasks

   c. no more than three tasks

   d. only one task

4. Which of the following is *not* another term for a selection structure?

   a. decision structure

   b. if-then-else structure

   c. dual-alternative if structure

   d. loop structure

5. The structure in which you ask a question, and, depending on the answer, take some action and then ask the question again, can be called all of the following except a(n) _____.

   a. iteration

   b. loop

   c. repetition

   d. if-then-else

6. Placing a structure within another structure is called _____ the structures.

   a. stacking

   b. untangling

   c. building

   d. nesting

7. Attaching structures end to end is called _____.

   a. stacking

   b. untangling

   c. building

   d. nesting

8. The statement `if age >= 65 then seniorDiscount="yes"` is an example of a _____.

   a. sequence

   b. loop

   c. dual-alternative selection

   d. single-alternative selection

9. The statement `while temperature remains below 60, leave the furnace on` is an example of a _____.

   a. sequence

   b. loop

   c. dual-alternative selection

   d. single-alternative selection

10. The statement `if age<13 then movieTicket=4.00 else movieTicket=8.50` is an example of a _____.

    a. sequence

    b. loop

    c. dual-alternative selection

    d. single-alternative selection

11. Which of the following attributes do all three basic structures share?

    a. Their flowcharts all contain exactly three processing symbols.

    b. They all have one entry and one exit point.

    c. They all contain a decision.

    d. They all begin with a process.

12. Which is true of stacking structures?

    a. Two incidences of the same structure cannot be stacked adjacently.

    b. When you stack structures, you cannot nest them in the same program.

    c. Each structure has only one point where it can be stacked on top of another.

    d. When you stack structures, the top structure must be a sequence.

13. When you input data in a loop within a program, the input statement that precedes the loop _____.

    a. is the only part of the program allowed to be unstructured

    b. cannot result in `eof`

    c. is called a priming input

    d. executes hundreds or even thousands of times in most business programs

14. A group of statements that executes as a unit is a
_____.

   a. block

   b. family

   c. chunk

   d. cohort

15. Which of the following is acceptable in a structured program?

   a. placing a sequence within the true half of a dual-alternative decision

   b. placing a decision within a loop

   c. placing a loop within one of the steps in a sequence

   d. All of these are acceptable.

16. In a selection structure, the structure-controlling question is _____.

   a. asked once at the beginning of the structure

   b. asked once at the end of the structure

   c. asked repeatedly until it is false

   d. asked repeatedly until it is true

17. In a loop, the structure-controlling question is
_____.

   a. asked exactly once

   b. never asked more than once

   c. asked before and after the loop body executes

   d. asked only if it is true, and not asked if it is false

18. Which of the following is *not* a reason for enforcing structure rules in computer programs?

   a. Structured programs are clearer to understand than unstructured ones.

   b. Other professional programmers will expect programs to be structured.

c. Structured programs usually are shorter than unstructured ones.

d. Structured programs can be broken down into modules easily.

19. Which of the following is *not* a benefit of modularizing programs?

   a. Modular programs are easier to read and understand than nonmodular ones.

   b. If you use modules, you can ignore the rules of structure.

   c. Modular components are reusable in other programs.

   d. Multiple programmers can work on different modules at the same time.

20. Which of the following is true of structured logic?

   a. You can use structured logic with newer programming languages, such as Java and C#, but not with older ones.

   b. Any task can be described using some combination of the three structures.

   c. Structured programs require that you break the code into easy-to-handle modules that each contain no more than five actions.

   d. All of these are true.

Exercises

1. In Figure 3-10, the process of buying and planting flowers in the spring was shown using the same structures as the generic example in Figure 3-9. Using exactly the same structure for the logic, create a flowchart or pseudocode that describes some other process with which you are familiar.

2. Each of the flowchart segments in Figure 3-35 is unstructured. Redraw each flowchart segment so that it does the same thing but is structured.

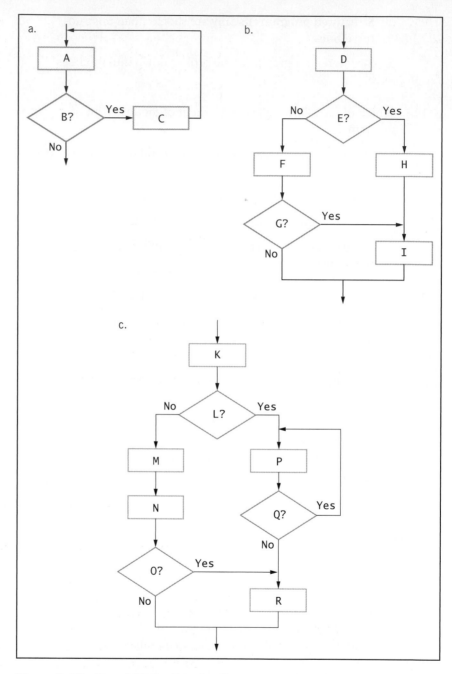

Figure 3-35 Flowcharts for Exercise 2

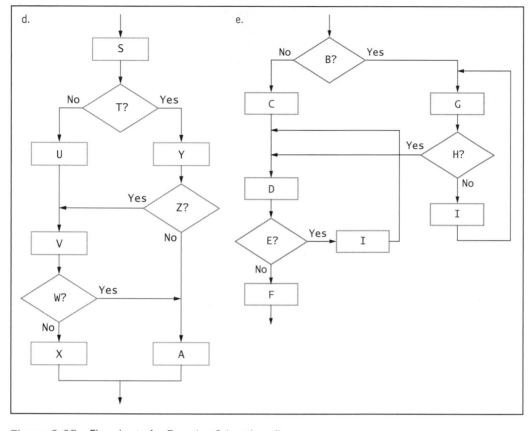

Figure 3-35 Flowcharts for Exercise 2 (continued)

3. Write pseudocode for each example (a through e) in Exercise 2, making sure your pseudocode is structured but accomplishes the same tasks as the flowchart segment.

4. Assume you have created a mechanical arm that can hold a pen. The arm can perform the following tasks:

    • Lower the pen to a piece of paper.

    • Raise the pen from the paper.

    • Move the pen 1 inch along a straight line. (If the pen is lowered, this action draws a 1-inch line from left to right; if the pen is raised, this action just repositions the pen 1 inch to the right.)

    • Turn 90 degrees to the right.

    • Draw a circle that is 1 inch in diameter.

Draw a structured flowchart or write structured pseudocode describing the logic that would cause the arm to draw or write the following. Have a fellow student act as the mechanical arm and carry out your instructions.

a. a 1-inch square

b. a 2-inch by 1-inch rectangle

c. a string of three beads

d. a short word (for example, "cat"). Do not reveal the word to your partner until the exercise is over.

5. Assume you have created a mechanical robot that can perform the following tasks:

- Stand up.

- Sit down.

- Turn left 90 degrees.

- Turn right 90 degrees.

- Take a step.

Additionally, the robot can determine the answer to one test condition:

- Am I touching something?

Place two chairs 20 feet apart, directly facing each other. Draw a structured flowchart or write pseudocode describing the logic that would allow the robot to start from a sitting position in one chair, cross the room, and end up sitting in the other chair. Have a fellow student act as the robot and carry out your instructions.

6. Looking up a word in a dictionary can be a complicated process. For example, assume you want to look up "logic." You might open the dictionary to a random page and see "juice." You know this word comes alphabetically before "logic," so you flip forward and see "lamb." That is still not far enough, so you flip forward and see "monkey." You have gone too far, so you flip back, and so on. Draw a structured flowchart or write pseudocode that describes the process of looking up a word in a dictionary. Pick a word at random and have a fellow student attempt to carry out your instructions.

7. Draw a structured flowchart or write structured pseudocode describing your preparation to go to work or school in the morning. Include at least two decisions and two loops.

8. Draw a structured flowchart or write structured pseudocode describing your preparation to go to bed at night. Include at least two decisions and two loops.

9. Draw a structured flowchart or write structured pseudocode describing how your paycheck is calculated. Include at least two decisions.

10. Draw a structured flowchart or write structured pseudocode describing the steps a retail store employee should follow to process a customer purchase. Include at least two decisions.

 ## Find the Bugs

11. Your student disk contains files named DEBUG03-01.txt, DEBUG03-02.txt, and DEBUG03-03.txt. Each file starts with some comments that describe the problem. Comments are lines that begin with two slashes (//). Following the comments, each file contains pseudocode that has one or more bugs you must find and correct.

 ## Game Zone

12. Choose a very simple children's game and describe its logic, using a structured flowchart or pseudocode. For example, you might try to explain Rock, Paper, Scissors; Musical Chairs; Duck, Duck, Goose; the card game War; or the elimination game Eenie, Meenie, Minie, Moe.

13. Choose a television game show such as *Deal or No Deal* or *Jeopardy!* and describe its rules using a structured flowchart or pseudocode.

14. Choose a sport such as baseball or football and describe the actions in one limited play period (such as an at-bat in baseball or a possession in football) using a structured flowchart or pseudocode.

Up for Discussion

15. Find more information about one of the following people and explain why he or she is important to structured programming: Edsger Dijkstra, Corrado Bohm, Giuseppe Jacopini, and Grace Hopper.

16. Computer programs can contain structures within structures and stacked structures, creating very large programs. Computers can also perform millions of arithmetic calculations in an hour. How can we possibly know the results are correct?

17. Develop a checklist of rules you can use to help you determine whether a flowchart or pseudocode segment is structured.

CHAPTER 4

Making Decisions

In this chapter, you will learn about:

- ◎ Evaluating Boolean expressions to make comparisons
- ◎ The relational comparison operators
- ◎ AND logic
- ◎ OR logic
- ◎ Making selections within ranges
- ◎ Precedence when combining AND and OR operators

Evaluating Boolean Expressions to Make Comparisons

Mathematician George Boole (1815–1864) approached logic more simply than his predecessors did, by expressing logical selections with common algebraic symbols. He is considered the founder of mathematical logic, and Boolean (true/false) expressions are named for him.

The reason people frequently think computers are smart lies in the computer program's ability to make decisions. A medical diagnosis program that can decide if your symptoms fit various disease profiles seems quite intelligent, as does a program that can offer different potential vacation routes based on your destination.

Every decision you make in a computer program involves evaluating a **Boolean expression**—an expression whose value can be only true or false. True/false evaluation is "natural" from a computer's standpoint because computer circuitry consists of two-state on-off switches, often represented by 1 or 0. Every computer decision yields a true-or-false, yes-or-no, 1-or-0 result. A Boolean expression is used in every selection structure. The selection structure is not new to you—it's one of the basic structures you learned about in Chapter 3. See Figures 4-1 and 4-2.

This book follows the convention that the two logical paths emerging from a decision are drawn to the right and left of a diamond in a flowchart. Some programmers draw one of the flowlines emerging from the bottom of the diamond. The exact format of the diagram is not as important as the idea that one logical path flows into a selection, and two possible outcomes emerge.

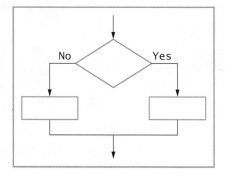

Figure 4-1   The dual-alternative selection structure

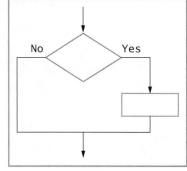

Figure 4-2   The single-alternative selection structure

In Chapter 3 you learned that you can refer to the structure in Figure 4-1 as a dual-alternative, or binary, selection because an action is associated with each of two possible outcomes: depending on the answer to the question represented by the diamond, the logical flow proceeds either to the left branch of the structure or to the right. The choices are mutually exclusive; that is, the logic can flow only to one of the two alternatives, never to both.

You can call a single-alternative decision (or selection) a *single-sided decision*. Similarly, a dual-alternative decision is a *double-sided decision* (or selection).

The flowchart segment in Figure 4-2 represents a single-alternative selection in which action is required for only one outcome of the question. You call this form of the selection structure an **if-then**, because no alternative or "else" action is necessary.

Figure 4-3 shows the flowchart and pseudocode for an interactive program that computes pay for employees. The program displays the weekly pay for each employee at the same hourly rate ($10.00) and assumes there are no payroll deductions. The mainline logic calls housekeeping(), detailLoop(), and finish() modules. The detailLoop() module contains a typical if-then-else decision that determines whether an employee has worked more than a standard workweek (40 hours), and pays one and one-half times the employee's usual hourly rate for hours worked in excess of 40 per week.

Throughout this book, many examples are presented in both flowchart and pseudocode form. When you analyze a solution, you might find it easier to concentrate on just one of the two design tools at first. When you understand how the program works using one tool (for example, the flowchart), you can confirm that the solution is identical using the other tool.

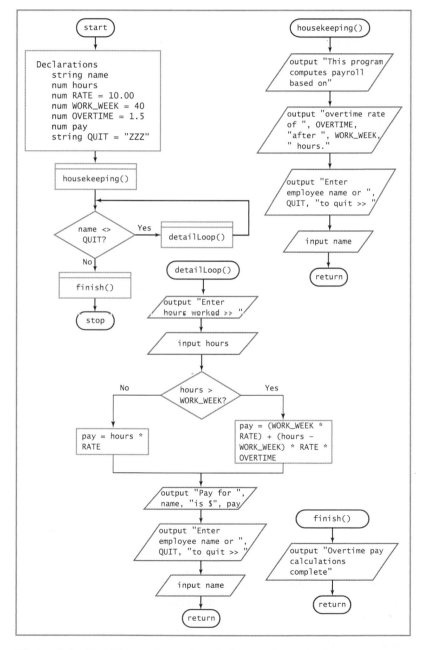

Figure 4-3 Flowchart and pseudocode for overtime payroll program

```
start
    Declarations
        string name
        num hours
        num RATE = 10.00
        num WORK_WEEK = 40
        num OVERTIME = 1.5
        num pay
        string QUIT = "ZZZ"
    housekeeping()
    while name <> QUIT
        detailLoop()
    endwhile
    finish()
stop

housekeeping()
    output "This program computes payroll based on"
    output "overtime rate of ", OVERTIME, "after ", WORK_WEEK, " hours."
    output "Enter employee name or ", QUIT, "to quit >> "
    input name
return

detailLoop()
    output "Enter hours worked >> "
    input hours
    if hours > WORK_WEEK then
        pay = (WORK_WEEK * RATE) + (hours - WORK_WEEK) * RATE * OVERTIME
    else
        pay = hours * RATE
    endif
    output "Pay for ", name, "is $", pay
    output "Enter employee name or ", QUIT, "to quit >> "
    input name
return

finish()
    output "Overtime pay calculations complete"
return
```

Figure 4-3   Flowchart and pseudocode for overtime payroll program (continued)

In the detailLoop() module of the program in Figure 4-3, the longer overtime calculation is the **then clause** of the decision—the part of the decision that holds the action or actions that execute when the tested condition in the decision is true. The shorter calculation, which calculates pay by multiplying hours by RATE, constitutes the **else clause** of the decision—the part that executes only when the tested condition in the decision is false.

Figure 4-4 shows a typical execution of the program in a command-line environment. Data values are entered for three employees. The first two employees do not work more than 40 hours, so their pay is displayed simply as hours times $10.00. The third employee, however, has worked one hour of overtime, and so makes $15 for the last hour instead of just $10.

Watch the video *Boolean Expressions and Decisions*.

Figure 4-4 Typical execution of the overtime payroll program in Figure 4-3

TWO TRUTHS & A LIE

Evaluating Boolean Expressions to Make Comparisons

1. The then clause is the part of a decision that executes when a tested condition in a decision is true.

2. The else clause is the part of a decision that executes when a tested condition in a decision is true.

3. A Boolean expression is one whose value is true or false.

The false statement is #2. The else clause is the part of a decision that executes when a tested condition in a decision is false.

Using Relational Comparison Operators

Table 4-1 describes the six **relational comparison operators** supported by all modern programming languages. Each of these operators is binary—that is, each requires two operands. When you construct an expression using two operands and one of the operators

In Chapter 2 you learned that the assignment operator is also a binary operator.

138

described in Table 4-1, the expression evaluates to true or false based on the operands' values. Usually, both operands in a comparison must be the same data type; that is, you can compare numeric values to other numeric values, and text strings to other strings.

The term "relational comparison operators" is somewhat redundant. You can also call these operators **relational operators** or **comparison operators**.

When an operator is formed using two keystrokes, you never insert a space between them.

Some programming languages allow you to compare a character to a number. If you do, then a single character's numeric code value is used in the comparison. Appendix A contains more information on coding systems.

Operator	Name	Discussion
=	Equivalency operator	Evaluates as true when its operands are equivalent. Many languages use a double equal sign (==) to avoid confusion with the assignment operator.
>	Greater-than operator	Evaluates as true when the left operand is greater than the right operand.
<	Less-than operator	Evaluates as true when the left operand is less than the right operand.
>=	Greater-than or equal-to operator	Evaluates as true when the left operand is greater than or equivalent to the right operand.
<=	Less-than or equal-to operator	Evaluates as true when the left operand is less than or equivalent to the right operand.
<>	Not-equal-to operator	Evaluates as true when its operands are not equivalent. Some languages use an exclamation point followed by an equal sign to indicate not equal to (!=). Because the not-equal-to operator differs in the common programming languages, this book will most often spell out "is not equal to" in flowcharts and pseudocode.

Table 4-1   Relational comparison operators

In any Boolean expression, the two values compared can be either variables or constants. For example, the expression currentTotal = 100? compares a variable, currentTotal, to a numeric constant, 100. Depending on the `currentTotal` value, the expression is true or false. In the expression `currentTotal = previousTotal?`, both values are variables, and the result is also true or false depending on the values stored in each of the two variables. Although it's legal, you would never use expressions in which you compare two constants—for example, `20 = 20?` or `30 = 40?`. Such expressions are **trivial expressions** because each will always evaluate to the same result: true for `20 = 20?` and false for `30 = 40?`.

Any decision can be made using combinations of just three types of comparisons: equal, greater than, and less than. You never need the three additional comparisons (greater than or equal, less than or equal, or not equal), but using them often makes decisions more convenient. For example, assume you need to issue a 10 percent discount to any customer whose age is 65 or greater, and charge full price to other customers. You can use the greater-than-or-equal-to symbol to write the logic as follows:

```
if customerAge >= 65 then
    discount = 0.10
else
    discount = 0
endif
```

As an alternative, if the >= operator did not exist, you could express the same logic by writing:

```
if customerAge < 65 then
    discount = 0
else
    discount = 0.10
endif
```

In any decision for which a >= b is true, then a < b is false. Conversely, if a >= b is false, then a < b is true. By rephrasing the question and swapping the actions taken based on the outcome, you can make the same decision in multiple ways. The clearest route is often to ask a question so the positive or true outcome results in the action that was your motivation for making the test. When your company policy is to "provide a discount for those who are 65 and older," the phrase "greater than or equal to" comes to mind, so it is the most natural to use. Conversely, if your policy is to "provide no discount for those under 65," then it is more natural to use the "less than" syntax. Either way, the same people receive a discount.

Comparing two amounts to decide if they are *not* equal to each other is the most confusing of all the comparisons. Using "not equal to" in decisions involves thinking in double negatives, which can make

When you write pseudocode or draw a flowchart for your own use, you can indicate relationships in any way you prefer. For example, to indicate equivalency, you can use "=", "==", or spell out "is equal to". When you take a class or work in an organization, you might be required to use a specific format for consistency.

Usually, string variables are not considered to be equal unless they are identical, including the spacing and whether they appear in uppercase or lowercase. For example, "black pen" is *not* equal to "blackpen", "BLACK PEN", or "Black Pen".

139

you prone to include logical errors in your programs. For example, consider the flowchart segment in Figure 4-5.

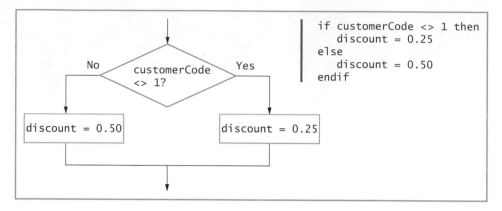

Figure 4-5 Using a negative comparison

In Figure 4-5, if the value of customerCode *is* equal to 1, the logical flow follows the false branch of the selection. If customerCode <> 1 is true, discount is 0.25; if customerCode <> 1 is not true, it means customerCode *is* 1, and discount is 0.50. Even saying the phrase "if the customer code is not equal to one is not true" is awkward.

Figure 4-6 shows the same decision, this time asked in a positive way. Making the decision if customerCode *is* 1 then discount = 0.50 is clearer than trying to determine what customerCode is *not*.

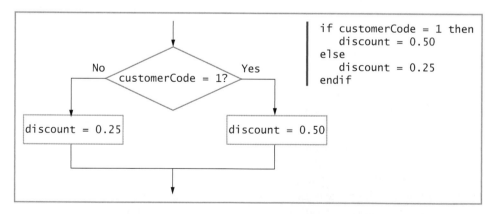

Figure 4-6 Using the positive equivalent of the negative comparison in Figure 4-5

Although negative comparisons can be awkward to use, your meaning is sometimes clearest when using them. Frequently, this occurs when you use an if without an else, taking action only when some comparison is false. An example would be: if customerZipCode is not equal to LOCAL_ZIP_CODE then add deliveryCharge to total.

Avoiding a Common Error with Relational Operators

A common error that occurs when you use relational operators is using the wrong one and missing the boundary or limit required for a selection. If you use > to make a selection when you should have used >=, all the cases that are = will go unselected. Unfortunately, those who request programs do not always speak as precisely as a computer. If, for example, your boss says, "Write a program that selects all employees over 65," does she mean to include employees who are 65 or not? In other words, is the comparison age > 65 or age >= 65? Although the phrase "over 65" indicates "greater than 65," people do not always say what they mean, and the best course of action is to double-check the intended meaning with the person who requested the program—for example, the end user, your supervisor, or your instructor. Similar phrases that can cause misunderstandings are "no more than," "at least," and "not under."

TWO TRUTHS & A LIE

Using Relational Comparison Operators

1. Usually, you can compare only values that are of the same data type.

2. A Boolean expression is defined as one that decides whether two values are equal.

3. In any Boolean expression, the two values compared can be either variables or constants.

The false statement is #2. Although deciding whether two values are equal is a Boolean expression, so is deciding whether one is greater than or less than another. A Boolean expression is one that results in a true or false value.

Understanding AND Logic

Often, you need more than one selection structure to determine whether an action should take place. When you ask multiple questions before an outcome is determined, you create a **compound condition**. For example, suppose you work for a cell phone company that charges customers as follows:

- The basic monthly service bill is $30.

- An additional $20 is billed to customers who make more than 100 calls that last for a total of more than 500 minutes.

You first learned about nesting structures in Chapter 3. You can always stack and nest any of the basic structures.

The logic needed for this billing program includes an **AND decision**—a decision in which two conditions must be true for an action to take place. In this case, both a minimum number of calls must be made *and* a minimum number of minutes must be used before the customer is charged the additional amount. An AND decision can be constructed using a **nested decision**, or a **nested if**—that is, a decision "inside of" another decision. The flowchart and pseudocode for the program that determines the charges for customers is shown in Figure 4-7.

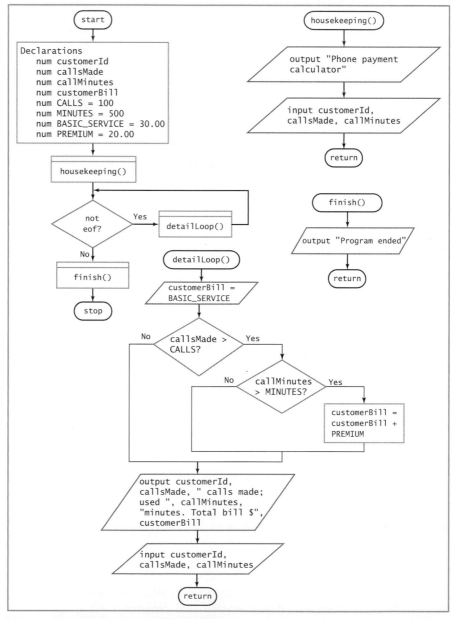

Figure 4-7   Flowchart and pseudocode for cell phone billing program

```
start
   Declarations
      num customerId
      num callsMade
      num callMinutes
      num customerBill
      num CALLS = 100
      num MINUTES = 500
      num BASIC_SERVICE = 30.00
      num PREMIUM = 20.00
   housekeeping()
   while not eof
      detailLoop()
   endwhile
   finish()
stop

housekeeping()
   output "Phone payment calculator"
   input customerId, callsMade, callMinutes
return

detailLoop()
   customerBill = BASIC_SERVICE
   if callsMade > CALLS then
      if callMinutes > MINUTES then
         customerBill = customerBill + PREMIUM
      endif
   endif
   output customerId, callsMade, " calls made; used ",
      callMinutes, " minutes. Total bill $", customerBill
   input customerId, callsMade, callMinutes
return

finish()
   output "Program ended"
return
```

Figure 4-7 Flowchart and pseudocode for cell phone billing program (continued)

In the cell phone billing program, the customer data is retrieved from a file. This eliminates the need for prompts and keeps the program shorter so you can concentrate on the decision-making process. If this was an interactive program, you would use a prompt before each input statement. Chapter 7 covers file processing and explains a few additional steps you can take when working with files.

A series of nested if statements is also called a **cascading if statement**.

Most languages allow you to use a variation of the decision structure called the *case structure* when you must nest a series of decisions about a single variable. Appendix F contains information about the case structure.

In Figure 4-7, the appropriate variables and constants are declared, and then the `housekeeping()` module displays an introductory heading and gets the first set of input data. After control returns to the mainline logic, the `eof` condition is tested, and if it is not `eof`, the `detailLoop()` module executes. In the `detailLoop()` module, the customer's bill is set to the standard fee, and then the nested decision executes. In the nested `if` structure in Figure 4-7, the expression `callsMade > CALLS` is evaluated first. If this expression is true, only then is the second Boolean expression (`callMinutes > MINUTES`) evaluated. If that expression is also true, then the $20 premium is added to the customer's bill. If neither of the tested conditions is true, the customer's bill value is never altered, retaining the initially assigned value of $30.

Nesting AND Decisions for Efficiency

When you nest decisions because the resulting action requires that two conditions be true, you must decide which of the two decisions to make first. Logically, either selection in an AND decision can come first. However, when there are two selections, you often can improve your program's performance by correctly choosing which selection to make first.

For example, Figure 4-8 shows two ways to design the nested decision structure that assigns a premium to customer bills if they make more than 100 cell phone calls and use more than 500 minutes in a billing period. The program can ask about calls made first, eliminate customers who have not made more than the minimum, and ask about the minutes used only for customers who "pass" the minimum calls test. Or, you could ask about the minutes first, eliminate those who do not qualify, and ask about the number of calls only for customers who "pass" the minutes test. Either way, only customers who exceed both limits must pay the premium. Does it make a difference which question is asked first? As far as the result goes, no. Either way, the same customers pay the premium—those who qualify on the basis of both criteria. As far as program efficiency goes, however, it *might* make a difference which question is asked first.

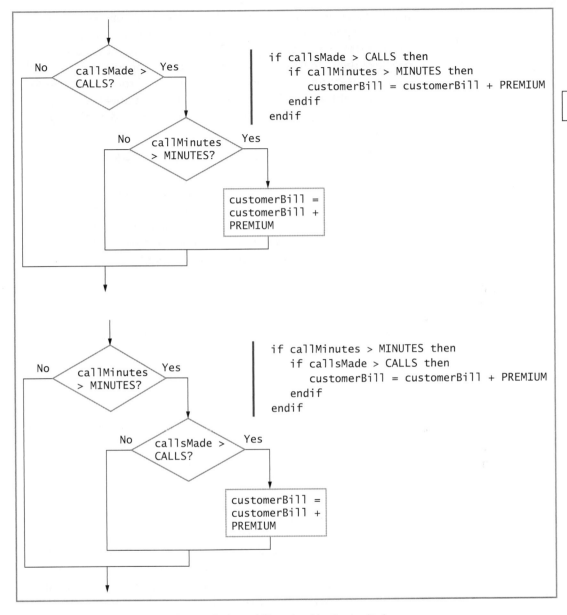

Figure 4-8   Two ways to produce cell phone bills using identical criteria

Assume you know that out of 1000 cell phone customers, about 90 percent, or 900, make more than 100 calls in a billing period. Assume you also know that only about half the 1000 customers, or 500, use more than 500 minutes of call time.

If you use the logic shown first in Figure 4-8, and you need to produce 1000 phone bills, the first question, `callsMade > CALLS?`, will execute 1000 times. For approximately 90 percent of the customers, or 900 of them, the answer is `true`, so 100 customers are eliminated from the premium assignment, and 900 proceed to the next question about the minutes used. Only about half the customers use more than 500 minutes, so 450 of the 900 pay the premium, and it takes 1900 questions to identify them.

Using the alternate logic shown second in Figure 4-8, the first question, `callMinutes > MINUTES?`, will also be asked 1000 times—once for each customer. Because only about half the customers use the high number of minutes, only 500 will "pass" this test and proceed to the question for number of calls made. Then, about 90 percent of the 500, or 450 customers, will pass the second test and be billed the premium amount. It takes 1500 questions to identify the 450 premium-paying customers.

Whether you use the first or second decision order in Figure 4-8, the same 450 employees who satisfy both criteria pay the premium. The difference is that when you ask about the number of calls first, the program must ask 400 more questions than when you ask about the minutes used first.

The 400-question difference between the first and second set of decisions doesn't take much time on most computers. But it does take *some* time, and if a corporation has hundreds of thousands of customers instead of only 1000, or if many such decisions have to be made within a program, performance time can be significantly improved by asking questions in the more efficient order.

Watch the video *Writing Efficient Nested Selections.*

Often, when you must make nested decisions, you have no idea which event is more likely to occur; in that case, you can legitimately ask either question first. However, if you do know the probabilities of the conditions, or can make a reasonable guess, the general rule is: *In an AND decision, first ask the question that is less likely to be true.* This eliminates as many instances of the second decision as possible, which speeds up processing time.

Using the AND Operator

Most programming languages allow you to ask two or more questions in a single comparison by using a **conditional AND operator**, or more simply, an **AND operator** that joins decisions in a single statement. For example, if you want to bill an extra amount to cell phone customers who make more than 100 calls that total more than 500 minutes in a billing period, you can use nested decisions, as shown in the previous section, or you can include both decisions in a single statement by writing the following question:

```
callsMade > CALLS AND callMinutes > MINUTES?
```

When you use one or more AND operators to combine two or more Boolean expressions, each Boolean expression must be true for the entire expression to be evaluated as true. For example, if you ask, "Are you a native-born U.S. citizen and are you at least 35 years old?", the answer to both parts of the question must be "yes" before the response can be a single, summarizing "yes." If either part of the expression is false, then the entire expression is false.

One tool that can help you understand the AND operator is a truth table. **Truth tables** are diagrams used in mathematics and logic to help describe the truth of an entire expression based on the truth of its parts. Table 4-2 shows a truth table that lists all the possibilities with an AND decision. As the table shows, for any two expressions x and y, the expression x AND y is true only if both x and y are individually true. If either x or y alone is false, or if both are false, then the expression x AND y is false.

The conditional AND operator in Java, C++, and C# consists of two ampersands, with no spaces between them (&&). In Visual Basic, you use the word **And**.

x	y	x AND y
True	True	True
True	False	False
False	True	False
False	False	False

Table 4-2 Truth table for the AND operator

If the programming language you use allows an AND operator, you must realize that the question you place first (to the left of the operator) is the one that will be asked first, and cases that are eliminated based on the first question will not proceed to the second question. In other words, each part of an expression that uses an AND operator is evaluated only as far as necessary to determine whether the entire expression is true or false. This feature is called **short-circuit evaluation**. The computer can ask only one question at a time; even when your pseudocode looks like the first example in Figure 4-9, the computer will execute the logic shown in the second example.

You are never required to use the AND operator because using nested if statements can always achieve the same result, but using the AND operator often makes your code more concise, less error-prone, and easier to understand.

Using an AND operator does not eliminate your responsibility for determining which condition to test first. Even when you use an AND operator, the computer makes decisions one at a time, and makes them in the order you ask them. If the first question in an AND expression evaluates to false, then the entire expression is false, and the second question is not even tested.

148

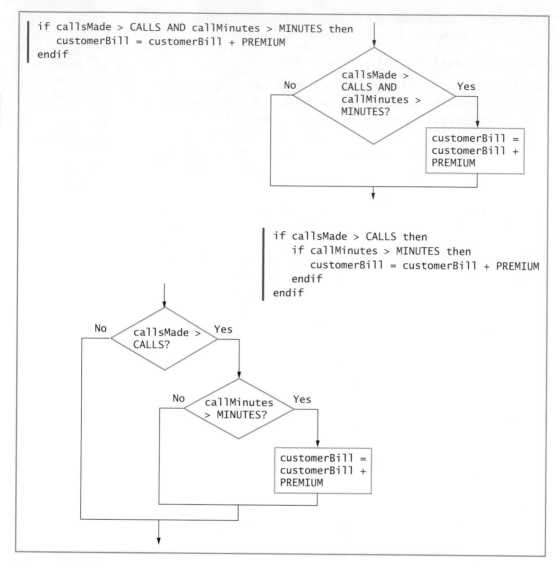

```
if callsMade > CALLS AND callMinutes > MINUTES then
    customerBill = customerBill + PREMIUM
endif
```

```
if callsMade > CALLS then
    if callMinutes > MINUTES then
        customerBill = customerBill + PREMIUM
    endif
endif
```

Figure 4-9   Using an AND operator and the logic behind it

Avoiding Common Errors in an AND Selection

When you need to satisfy two or more criteria to initiate an event in a
program, you must make sure that the second decision is made entirely
within the first decision. For example, if a program's objective is to add
a $20 premium to the bill of cell phone customers who exceed 100 calls
and 500 minutes in a billing period, then the program segment shown
in Figure 4-10 contains three different types of logic errors.

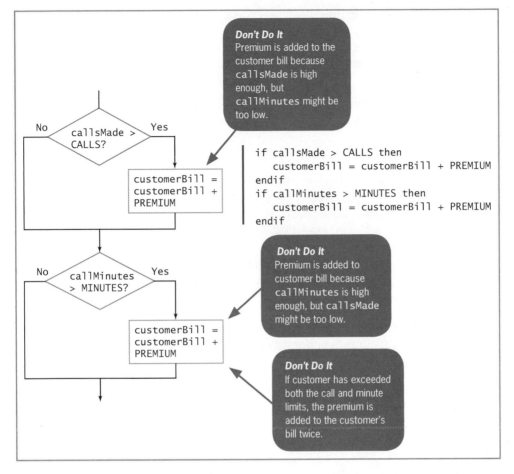

if callsMade > CALLS then
    customerBill = customerBill + PREMIUM
endif
if callMinutes > MINUTES then
    customerBill = customerBill + PREMIUM
endif

Figure 4-10 Incorrect logic to add a $20 premium to the bills of cell phone customers who meet two criteria

The logic in Figure 4-10 shows that $20 is added to the bill of a customer who makes too many calls. This customer should not necessarily be billed extra—the customer's minutes might be below the cutoff for the $20 premium. In addition, a customer who has made few calls is not eliminated from the second question. Instead, all customers are subjected to the minutes question, and some are assigned the premium even though they might not have passed the criterion for number of calls made. Additionally, any customer who passes both tests has the premium added to his bill twice. For many reasons, the logic shown in Figure 4-10 is *not* correct for this problem.

When you use the AND operator in most languages, you must provide a complete Boolean expression on each side of the operator. In other words, callMinutes > 100 AND callMinutes < 200 would be a valid expression to find callMinutes between 100 and 200. However, callMinutes > 100 AND < 200 would not be valid because what follows the AND operator (< 200) is not a complete Boolean expression.

To override the default precedence of the AND operator over the OR operator, or simply for clarity, you can surround each Boolean expression in a compound expression with its own set of parentheses. Use this format if it is clearer to you. For example, you might write the following:

```
if (callMinutes > MINUTES) AND (callsMade > CALLS)
    customerBill = customerBill + PREMIUM
endif
```

TWO TRUTHS & A LIE

Understanding AND Logic

1. When you nest decisions because the resulting action requires that two conditions be true, either decision logically can be made first and the same selections will occur.

2. When two selections are required for an action to take place, you often can improve your program's performance by appropriately choosing which selection to make first.

3. To improve efficiency in a nested selection in which two conditions must be true for some action to occur, you should first ask the question that is more likely to be true.

The false statement is # 3. For efficiency in a nested selection, you should first ask the question that is less likely to be true.

Understanding OR Logic

Sometimes you want to take action when one *or* the other of two conditions is true. This is called an **OR decision** because either one condition *or* some other condition must be met in order for an event to take place. If someone asks, "Are you free for dinner Friday or Saturday?", only one of the two conditions has to be true for the answer to the whole question to be "yes"; only if the answers to both halves of the question are false is the value of the entire expression false.

For example, suppose you want to add $20 to the bills of cell phone customers who either make more than 100 calls or use more than 500 minutes. Figure 4-11 shows the altered `detailLoop()` module of the billing program that accomplishes this objective.

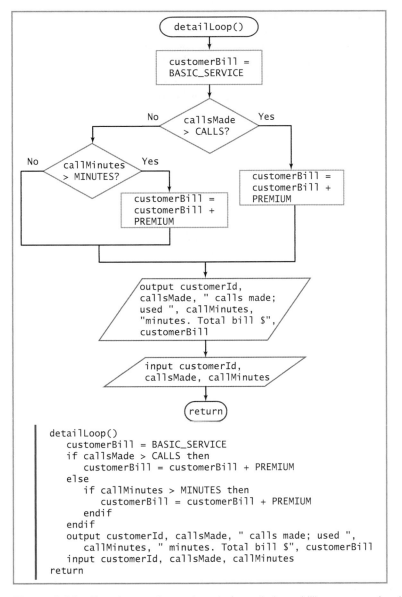

```
detailLoop()
    customerBill = BASIC_SERVICE
    if callsMade > CALLS then
        customerBill = customerBill + PREMIUM
    else
        if callMinutes > MINUTES then
            customerBill = customerBill + PREMIUM
        endif
    endif
    output customerId, callsMade, " calls made; used ",
        callMinutes, " minutes. Total bill $", customerBill
    input customerId, callsMade, callMinutes
return
```

Figure 4-11 Flowchart and pseudocode for cell phone billing program in which a customer must meet one or both of two criteria to be billed a premium

The `detailLoop()` in the program in Figure 4-11 asks the question `callsMade > CALLS?`, and if the result is true, the extra amount is added to the customer's bill. Because just making too many calls (more than 100) is enough for the customer to incur the premium, there is no need for further questioning. If the customer has not made more than 100 calls, only then does the program need to ask whether `callMinutes > MINUTES` is true. If the customer did not make over 100 calls, but used more than 500 minutes nevertheless, then the premium amount is added to the customer's bill.

Writing OR Decisions for Efficiency

As with an AND selection, when you use an OR selection, you can choose to ask either question first. For example, you can add an extra $20 to the bills of customers who meet one or the other of two criteria using the logic in either part of Figure 4-12.

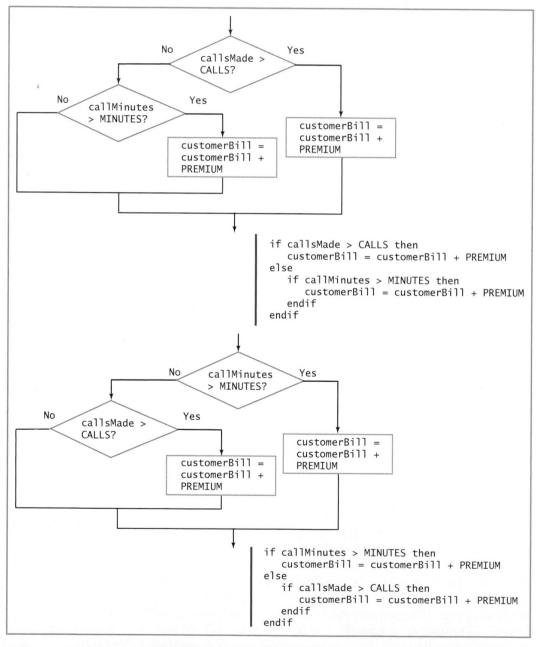

```
if callsMade > CALLS then
    customerBill = customerBill + PREMIUM
else
    if callMinutes > MINUTES then
        customerBill = customerBill + PREMIUM
    endif
endif
```

```
if callMinutes > MINUTES then
    customerBill = customerBill + PREMIUM
else
    if callsMade > CALLS then
        customerBill = customerBill + PREMIUM
    endif
endif
```

Figure 4-12 Two ways to assign a premium to bills of customers who meet one of two criteria

You might have guessed that one of these selections is superior to the other when you have some background information about the relative likelihood of each condition you are testing. For example, assume you know that out of 1000 cell phone customers, about 90 percent, or 900, make more than 100 calls in a billing period. Assume you also know that only about half the 1000 customers, or 500, use more than 500 minutes of call time.

When you use the logic shown in the first half of Figure 4-12, you first ask about the calls made. For 900 customers the answer is true, and you add the premium to their bills. Only about 100 sets of customer data continue to the next question regarding the call minutes, where about 50 percent of the 100, or 50, are billed the extra amount. In the end, you have made 1100 decisions to correctly add premium amounts for 950 customers.

If you use the OR logic in the second half of Figure 4-12, you ask about minutes used first—1000 times, once each for 1000 customers. The result is true for 50 percent, or 500 customers, whose bill is increased. For the other 500 customers, you ask about the number of calls made. For 90 percent of the 500, the result is true, so premiums are added for 450 additional people. In the end, the same 950 customers are billed an extra $20—but after executing 1500 decisions, 400 more decisions than when using the first decision logic.

The general rule is: *In an OR decision, first ask the question that is more likely to be true*. This approach eliminates as many executions of the second decision as possible, and the time it takes to process all the data is decreased. As with the AND situation, in an OR situation, it is more efficient to eliminate as many extra decisions as possible.

Using the OR Operator

If you need to take action when either one or the other of two conditions is met, you can use two separate, nested selection structures, as in the previous examples. However, most programming languages allow you to ask two or more questions in a single comparison by using a **conditional OR operator** (or simply the **OR operator**). For example, you can ask the following question:

```
callsMade > CALLS OR callMinutes > MINUTES
```

When you use the logical OR operator, only one of the listed conditions must be met for the resulting action to take place. Table 4-3 shows the truth table for the OR operator. As you can see in the table, the entire expression x OR y is false only when x and y each are false individually.

C#, C++, C, and Java use the symbol || as the logical OR operator. In Visual Basic, the operator is Or.

As with the AND operator, most programming languages require a complete Boolean expression on each side of the OR operator.

x	y	x OR y
True	True	True
True	False	True
False	True	True
False	False	False

Table 4-3   Truth table for the OR operator

If the programming language you use supports the OR operator, you still must realize that the question you place first is the question that will be asked first, and cases that pass the test of the first question will not proceed to the second question. As with the AND operator, this feature is called short-circuiting. The computer can ask only one question at a time; even when you write code, as shown at the top of Figure 4-13, the computer will execute the logic shown at the bottom.

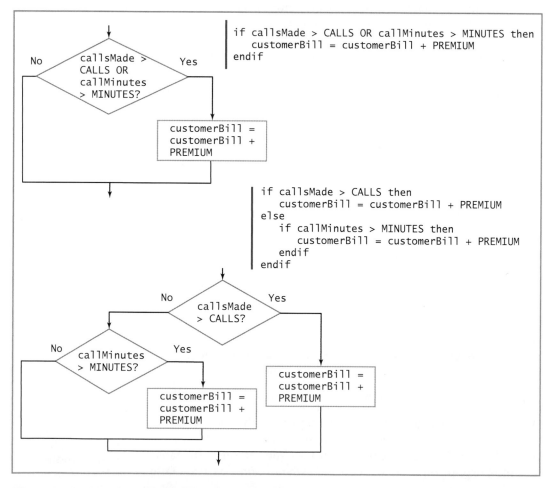

Figure 4-13   Using an OR operator and the logic behind it

Avoiding Common Errors in an OR Selection

You might have noticed that the assignment statement `customerBill = customerBill + PREMIUM` appears twice in the decision-making processes in Figures 4-12 and 4-13. When you create a flowchart, the temptation is to draw the logic to look like Figure 4-14. Logically, you might argue that the flowchart in Figure 4-14 is correct because the correct customers are billed the extra $20. However, this flowchart is not structured. The second question is not a self-contained structure with one entry and exit point; instead, the flowline "breaks out" of the inner selection structure to join the true side of the outer selection structure.

 If you do not understand why the flowchart segment in Figure 4-14 is unstructured, review Chapter 3.

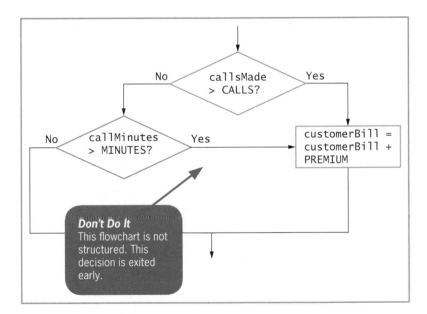

Figure 4-14 Unstructured flowchart for determining customer cell phone bill

An additional source of error that is specific to the OR selection stems from a problem with language and the way people use it more casually than computers do. When your boss wants to add an extra amount to bills of cell phone customers who have made more than 100 calls or used more than 500 minutes, she is likely to say, "Add $20 to the bill of anyone who makes more than 100 calls and to anyone who has used more than 500 minutes." Her request contains the word "and" between two types of people—those who made many calls and those who used many minutes—placing the emphasis on the people. However, each decision you make is about the added $20 for a single customer who has met one criterion *or* the other *or* both. In other words, the OR condition is between each customer's attributes, and not between different customers. Instead of the manager's previous statement, it would be clearer if she said, "Add $20 to the bill of anyone who has made more than 100 calls or has used more than 500 minutes," but you can't count on people to speak like computers. As a programmer, you have the job of clarifying what really is being requested. Often, a casual request for A *and* B logically means a request for A *or* B.

The way we casually use English can cause another type of error when you are required to find whether a value falls between two other values. For example, a movie theater manager might say, "Provide a discount to patrons who are under 13 years old and to those who are over 64 years old; otherwise, charge the full price." Because the manager has used the word "and" in the request, you might be tempted to create the decision shown in Figure 4-15; however, this logic will not provide a discounted price for any movie patron. You must remember that every time the decision is made in Figure 4-15, it is made for a single movie patron. If `patronAge` contains a value lower than 13, then it cannot possibly contain a value over 64. Similarly, if it contains a value over 64, there is no way it can contain a lesser value. Therefore, no value could be stored in `patronAge` for which both parts of the AND question could be true—and the price will never be set to the discounted price for any patron. Figure 4-16 shows the correct logic.

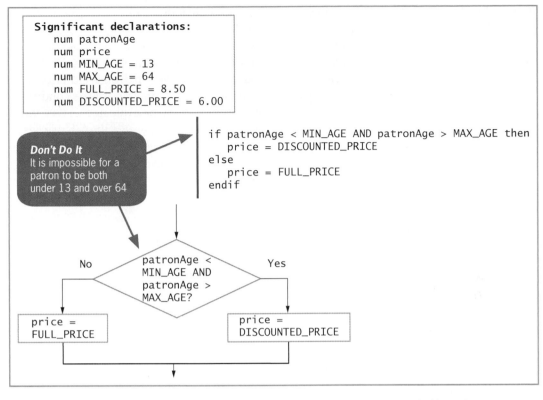

Figure 4-15 Incorrect logic that attempts to provide a discount for young and old movie patrons

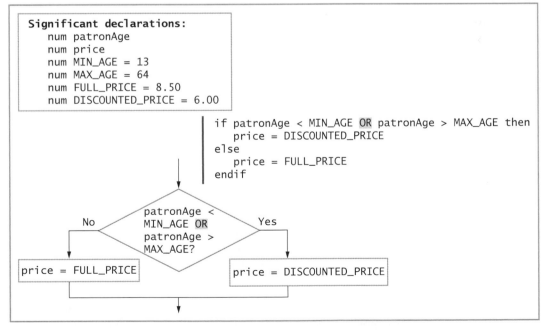

Figure 4-16 Correct logic that provides a discount for young and old movie patrons

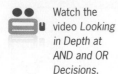

A similar error can occur in your logic if the theater manager says something like, "Don't give a discount—that is, charge full price—if a patron is over 12 or under 65." Because the word "or" appears in the request, you might plan your logic to resemble Figure 4-17. No patron ever receives a discount, because every patron is either over 12 or under 65. Remember, in an OR decision, only one of the conditions needs to be true for the entire expression to be evaluated as true. So, for example, because a patron who is 10 is under 65, the full price is charged, and because a patron who is 70 is over 12, the full price also is charged. Figure 4-18 shows the correct logic for this decision.

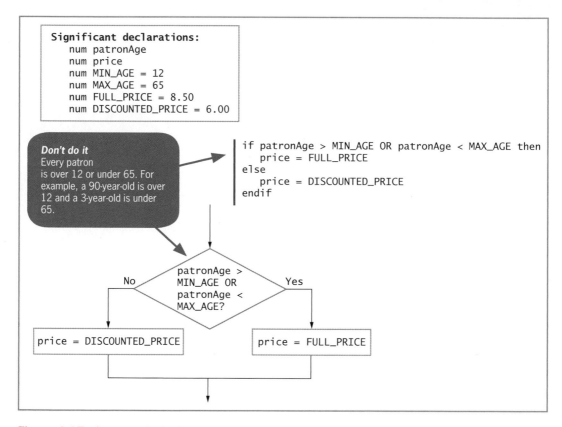

Figure 4-17   Incorrect logic that attempts to charge full price for patrons whose age is over 12 and under 65

Besides AND and OR operators, most languages support a NOT operator. You use the **logical NOT operator** to reverse the meaning of a Boolean expression. For example, the statement `if NOT (age < 21) output "OK"` outputs "OK" when `age` is greater than or equal to 21. The NOT operator is unary instead of binary—that is, you do not use it between two expressions, but you use it in front of a single expression. In C++, Java, and C#, the exclamation point is the symbol used for the NOT operator. In Visual Basic, the operator is Not.

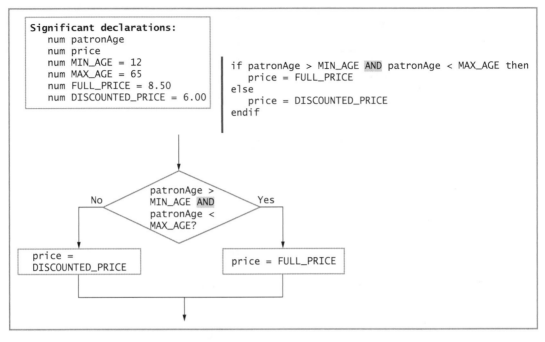

Figure 4-18   Correct logic that charges full price for patrons whose age is over 12 and under 65

TWO TRUTHS & A LIE

Understanding OR Logic

1. In an OR selection, two or more conditions must be met in order for an event to take place.

2. When you use an OR selection, you can choose to ask either question first and still achieve a usable program.

3. The general rule is: In an OR decision, first ask the question that is more likely to be true.

The false statement is #1. In an OR selection, only one of two conditions must be met in order for an event to take place.

Making Selections within Ranges

You often need to make selections based on a variable falling within a range of values. For example, suppose your company provides various customer discounts based on the number of items ordered, as shown in Figure 4-19.

Items Ordered	Discount Rate (%)
0 to 10	0
11 to 24	10
25 to 50	15
51 or more	20

Figure 4-19   Discount rates based on items ordered

When you write the program that determines a discount rate based on the number of items, you could make hundreds of decisions, such as itemQuantity = 1?, itemQuantity = 2?, and so on. However, it is more convenient to find the correct discount rate by using a range check.

When you use a **range check**, you compare a variable to a series of values that mark the limiting ends of ranges. To perform a range check, make comparisons using either the lowest or highest value in each range of values. For example, to find each discount rate listed in Figure 4-19, you can use one of the following techniques:

- Make comparisons using the low ends of the ranges.

  - You can ask: Is itemQuantity less than 11? If not, is it less than 25? If not, is it less than 51? (If the value could be negative, you would also check for values less than 0 and take action if necessary.)

  - You can ask: Is itemQuantity greater than or equal to 51? If not, is it greater than or equal to 25? If not, is it greater than or equal to 11? (If the value could be negative, you would also check for values greater than or equal to 0 and take action if necessary.)

- Make comparisons using the high ends of the ranges.

  - You can ask: Is itemQuantity greater than 50? If not, is it greater than 24? If not, is it greater than 10? (If there is a maximum allowed value for itemQuantity, you would also check for values greater than that limit and take action if necessary.

  - You can ask: Is itemQuantity less than or equal to 10? If not, is it less than or equal to 24? If not, is it less than or equal to 50? (If there is a maximum allowed value for itemQuantity, you would also check for values less than or equal to that limit and take action if necessary.

Figure 4-20 shows the flowchart and pseudocode that represent the logic for a program that determines the correct discount for each order quantity. In the decision-making process, itemsOrdered is compared to the high end of the lowest-range group (RANGE1). If itemsOrdered is less than or equal to that value, then you know the correct discount, DISCOUNT1; if not, you continue checking. If itemsOrdered is less than or equal to the high end of the next range (RANGE2), then the customer's discount is DISCOUNT2; if not, you continue checking, and the customer's discount eventually is set to DISCOUNT3 or DISCOUNT4.

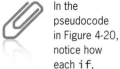 In the pseudocode in Figure 4-20, notice how each if, else, and endif group aligns vertically.

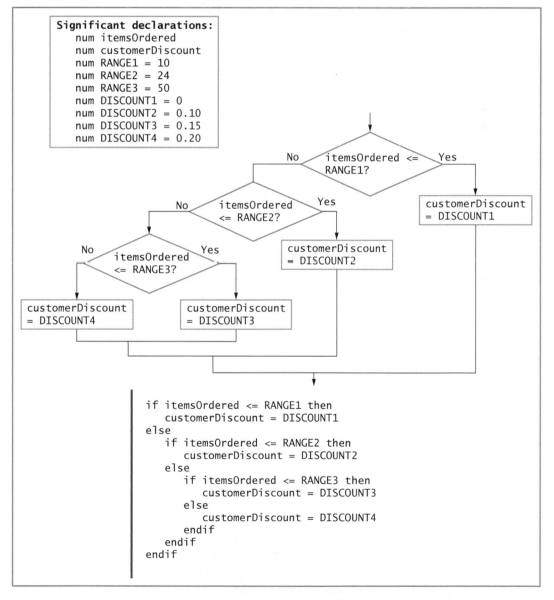

Figure 4-20 Flowchart and pseudocode of logic that selects correct discount based on items

In computer memory, a percent sign (%) is not stored with a value that represents a percentage. Instead, the mathematical equivalent is stored. For example, 15% is stored as 0.15.

For example, consider an order for 30 items. The expression itemsOrdered <= RANGE1 evaluates as false, so the else clause of the decision executes. There, itemsOrdered <= RANGE2 also evaluates to false, so its else clause executes. The expression itemsOrdered <= RANGE3 is true, so customerDiscount becomes DISCOUNT3, which is 0.15. Walk through the logic with other values for itemsOrdered and verify for yourself that the correct discount is applied each time.

Avoiding Common Errors When Using Range Checks

When new programmers perform range checks, they are prone to including logic that has too many decisions, entailing more work than is necessary.

Figure 4-21 shows a program segment that contains a range check in which the programmer has asked one question too many—the shaded question in the figure. If you know that itemsOrdered is not less than or equal to RANGE1, not less than or equal to RANGE2, and not less than or equal to RANGE3, then itemsOrdered must be greater than RANGE3. Asking whether itemsOrdered is greater than RANGE3 is a waste of time; no customer order can ever travel the logical path on the far left of the flowchart. You might say such a path is a **dead** or **unreachable path,** and that the statements written there constitute dead or unreachable code. Although a program that contains such logic will execute and assign the correct discount to customers who order more than 50 items, providing such a path is inefficient.

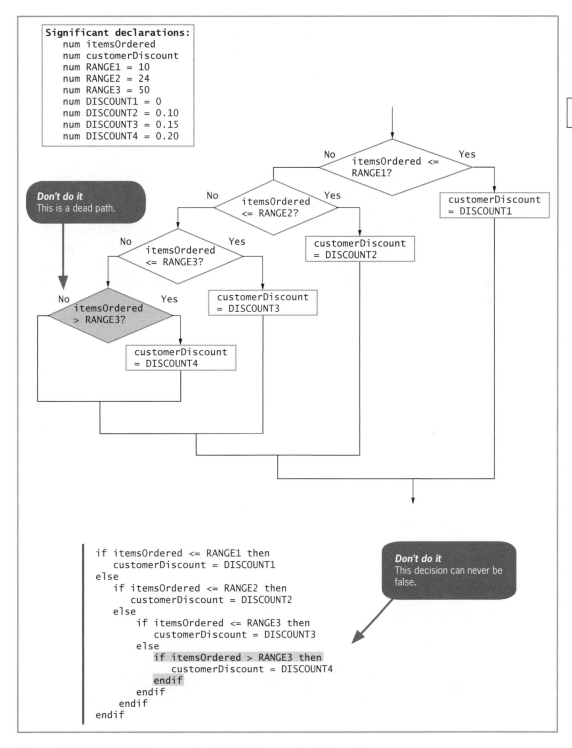

Significant declarations:
```
num itemsOrdered
num customerDiscount
num RANGE1 = 10
num RANGE2 = 24
num RANGE3 = 50
num DISCOUNT1 = 0
num DISCOUNT2 = 0.10
num DISCOUNT3 = 0.15
num DISCOUNT4 = 0.20
```

Don't do it
This is a dead path.

Don't do it
This decision can never be false.

```
if itemsOrdered <= RANGE1 then
   customerDiscount = DISCOUNT1
else
   if itemsOrdered <= RANGE2 then
      customerDiscount = DISCOUNT2
   else
      if itemsOrdered <= RANGE3 then
         customerDiscount = DISCOUNT3
      else
         if itemsOrdered > RANGE3 then
            customerDiscount = DISCOUNT4
         endif
      endif
   endif
endif
```

Figure 4-21   Inefficient range selection including unreachable path

When you ask questions of human beings, you sometimes ask a question to which you already know the answer. For example, a good trial lawyer seldom asks a question in court if the answer will be a surprise. With computer logic, however, such questions are an inefficient waste of time.

Beginning programmers sometimes justify their use of unnecessary questions as "just making really sure." Such caution is unnecessary when writing computer logic.

In Figure 4-21, it is easier to see the useless path in the flowchart than in the pseudocode representation of the same logic. However, anytime you use an `if` without an `else`, you are doing nothing when the question's answer is false.

Another error that programmers make when writing the logic to perform a range check also involves asking unnecessary questions. You should never ask a question if there is only one possible answer or outcome. Figure 4-22 shows an inefficient range selection that asks two unneeded questions. In the figure, if `itemsOrdered` is less than or equal to RANGE1, `customerDiscount` is set to DISCOUNT1. If `itemsOrdered` is not less than or equal to RANGE1, then it must be greater than RANGE1, so the next decision (shaded in the figure) does not have to check for values greater than RANGE1. The computer logic will never execute the shaded decision unless `itemsOrdered` is already greater than RANGE1—that is, unless it follows the `false` branch of the first selection. If you use the logic in Figure 4-22, you are wasting computer time asking a question that has previously been answered. The same logic applies to the second shaded decision in Figure 4-22.

TWO TRUTHS & A LIE

Making Selections within Ranges

1. When you perform a range check, you compare a variable to every value in a series of ranges.

2. You can perform a range check by making comparisons using the lowest value in each range of values you are using.

3. You can perform a range check by making comparisons using the highest value in each range of values you are using.

The false statement is #1. When you use a range check, you compare a variable to a series of values that represents the ends of ranges. Depending on your logic, you can use either the high or low end of each range.

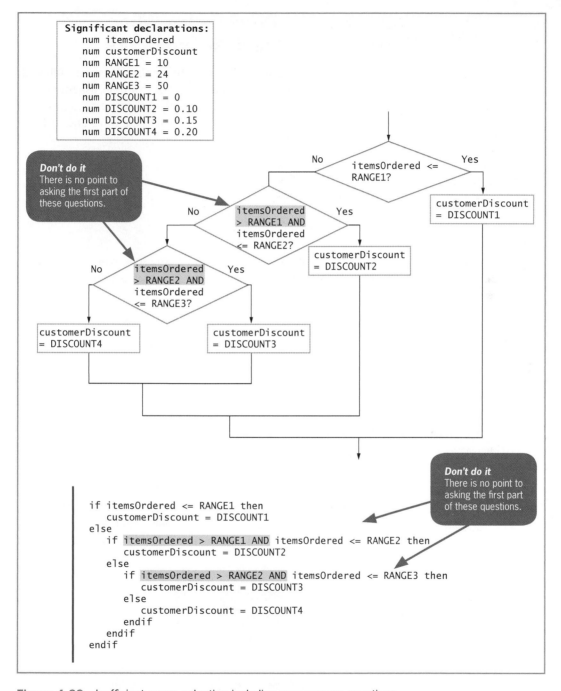

Significant declarations:
```
num itemsOrdered
num customerDiscount
num RANGE1 = 10
num RANGE2 = 24
num RANGE3 = 50
num DISCOUNT1 = 0
num DISCOUNT2 = 0.10
num DISCOUNT3 = 0.15
num DISCOUNT4 = 0.20
```

Don't do it
There is no point to asking the first part of these questions.

itemsOrdered <= RANGE1?

No — Yes

customerDiscount = DISCOUNT1

No — itemsOrdered > RANGE1 AND itemsOrdered <= RANGE2? — Yes

customerDiscount = DISCOUNT2

No — itemsOrdered > RANGE2 AND itemsOrdered <= RANGE3? — Yes

customerDiscount = DISCOUNT4

customerDiscount = DISCOUNT3

Don't do it
There is no point to asking the first part of these questions.

```
if itemsOrdered <= RANGE1 then
   customerDiscount = DISCOUNT1
else
   if itemsOrdered > RANGE1 AND itemsOrdered <= RANGE2 then
      customerDiscount = DISCOUNT2
   else
      if itemsOrdered > RANGE2 AND itemsOrdered <= RANGE3 then
         customerDiscount = DISCOUNT3
      else
         customerDiscount = DISCOUNT4
      endif
   endif
endif
```

Figure 4-22 Inefficient range selection including unnecessary questions

Understanding Precedence When Combining AND and OR Operators

Most programming languages allow you to combine as many AND and OR operators in an expression as you need. For example, assume you need to achieve a score of at least 75 on each of three tests to pass a course. You can declare a constant MIN_SCORE equal to 75 and test the multiple conditions with a statement like the following:

```
if score1 >= MIN_SCORE AND score2 >= MIN_SCORE AND
score3 >= MIN_SCORE then
    classGrade = "Pass"
else
    classGrade = "Fail"
endif
```

On the other hand, if you are enrolled in a course in which you need to pass only one of three tests to pass the course, then the logic is as follows:

```
if score1 >= MIN_SCORE OR score2 >= MIN_SCORE OR score3 >=
MIN_SCORE then
    classGrade = "Pass"
else
    classGrade = "Fail"
endif
```

The logic becomes more complicated when you combine AND and OR operators within the same statement. When you do, the AND operators take **precedence**, meaning their Boolean values are evaluated first.

For example, consider a program that determines whether a movie theater patron can purchase a discounted ticket. Assume discounts are allowed for children and senior citizens who attend "G"-rated movies. The following code looks reasonable, but it produces incorrect results because the expression that contains the AND operator (see shading) evaluates before the one that contains the OR operator.

Don't Do It
The AND evaluates first, which is not the intention.

```
if age <= 12 OR age >= 65 AND rating = "G" then
    output "Discount applies"
endif
```

For example, assume a movie patron is 10 years old and the movie rating is "R". The patron should not receive a discount (or be allowed

In Chapter 2 you learned that in every programming language, multiplication has precedence over addition in an arithmetic statement. That is, the value of 2 + 3 * 4 is 14 because the multiplication occurs before the addition. Similarly, in every programming language, AND has precedence over OR because computer circuitry treats the AND operator as multiplication and the OR operator as addition.

to see the movie!). However, within the `if` statement, the part of the expression that contains the `AND`, `age >= 65 AND rating = "G"`, is evaluated first. For a 10-year-old and an "R"-rated movie, the question is false (on both counts), so the entire `if` statement becomes the equivalent of the following:

```
if age <= 12 OR aFalseExpression then
    output "Discount applies"
endif
```

Because the patron is 10, `age <= 12` is `true`, so the original `if` statement becomes the equivalent of:

```
if aTrueExpression OR aFalseExpression then
    output "Discount applies"
endif
```

The combination `true OR false` evaluates as `true`. Therefore, the string `"Discount applies"` prints when it should not.

Many programming languages allow you to use parentheses to correct the logic and force the `OR` expression to be evaluated first, as shown in the following pseudocode.

```
if (age <= 12 OR age >= 65) AND rating = "G" then
    output "Discount applies"
endif
```

With the added parentheses, if the patron's `age` is 12 or under `OR` the `age` is 65 or over, the expression is evaluated as:

```
if aTrueExpression AND rating = "G" then
    output "Discount applies"
endif
```

When the age value qualifies a patron for a discount, then the rating value must also be acceptable before the discount applies. This was the original intention.

You can use the following techniques to avoid confusion when mixing `AND` and `OR` operators:

- You can use parentheses to override the default order of operations, as in the movie discount example.

- You can use parentheses for clarity even though they do not change what the order of operations would be without them. For example, if a customer should be between 12 and 19 or have a school ID to receive a high school discount, you can use the expression `(age > 12 AND age < 19) OR validId = "Yes"`, even though the evaluation would be the same without the parentheses.

- You can use nesting if statements instead of using AND and OR operators. With the flowchart and pseudocode shown in Figure 4-23, it is clear which movie patrons receive the discount. In the flowchart, you can see that the OR is nested entirely within the Yes branch of the rating = "G"? selection. Similarly, in the pseudocode in Figure 4-23, you can see by the alignment that if the rating is not "G", the logic proceeds directly to the last endif statement, bypassing any checking of age at all.

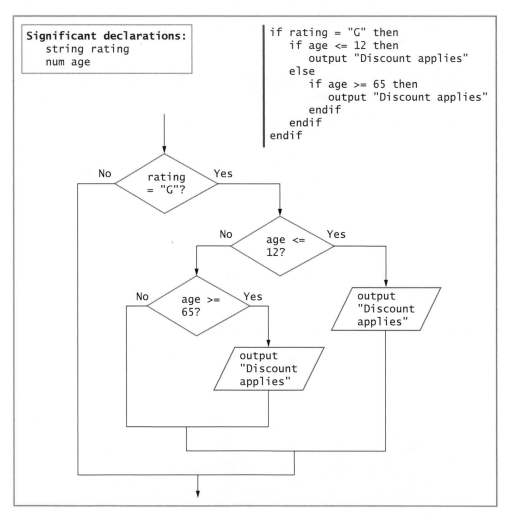

Figure 4-23   Nested decisions that determine movie patron discount

TWO TRUTHS & A LIE

Understanding Precedence When Combining AND and OR Operators

1. Most programming languages allow you to combine as many AND and OR operators in an expression as you need.

2. When you combine AND and OR operators, the OR operators take precedence, meaning their Boolean values are evaluated first.

3. You can always avoid the confusion of mixing AND and OR decisions by nesting if statements instead of using AND and OR operators.

The false statement is #2. When you combine AND and OR operators, the AND operators take precedence, meaning the Boolean values of their expressions are evaluated first.

Chapter Summary

- Every decision you make in a computer program involves evaluating a Boolean expression. You can use if-then-else or if-then structures to choose between two possible outcomes. You use if-then-else structures when action is required whether the selection is true or false. Use if-then structures when there is only one outcome for the question for which action is required.

- You can use relational comparison operators to compare two operands of the same type. The standard comparison operators are =, >, <, >=, <=, and <>.

- In an AND decision, two conditions must be true for a resulting action to take place. An AND decision requires a nested decision, or a nested if. In an AND decision, it is most efficient to first ask the question that is less likely to be true. Most programming languages allow you to ask two or more questions in a single comparison by using a conditional AND operator.

- In an OR decision, at least one of two conditions must be true for a resulting action to take place. In an OR decision, first ask the question that is more likely to be true. Most programming languages allow you to ask two or more questions in a single comparison by using a conditional OR operator.

- To perform a range check, make comparisons with either the lowest or highest value in each range of values you are using. Common errors that occur when programmers perform range checks include asking unnecessary and previously answered questions.

- When you combine AND and OR operators in an expression, the AND operators take precedence, meaning their Boolean values are evaluated first.

Key Terms

A **Boolean expression** is one that represents only one of two states, usually expressed as true or false.

In an **if-then** decision structure, action is taken only when the Boolean expression in the decision is true.

A **then clause** of a decision holds the action that results when the Boolean expression in the decision is true.

The **else clause** of a decision holds the action or actions that execute only when the Boolean expression in the decision is false.

Relational comparison operators are the symbols that express Boolean comparisons. Examples include =, >, <, >=, <=, and <>. These operators are also called **relational operators** or **comparison operators**.

A **trivial expression** is one that always evaluates to the same value.

A **compound condition** is constructed when you need to ask multiple questions before determining an outcome.

With an **AND decision**, two conditions must both be true for an action to take place.

A **nested decision**, or a **nested if**, is a decision "inside of" another decision.

A series of nested if statements can also be called a **cascading if statement**.

A **conditional AND operator** (or, more simply, an **AND operator**) is a symbol that you use to combine decisions so that two (or more) conditions must be true for an action to occur.

Truth tables are diagrams used in mathematics and logic to help describe the truth of an entire expression based on the truth of its parts.

Short-circuit evaluation is a logical feature in which expressions in each part of a larger expression are evaluated only as far as necessary to determine the final outcome.

An **OR decision** contains two (or more) decisions; if at least one condition is met, the resulting action takes place.

A **conditional OR operator** (or, more simply, an **OR operator**) is a symbol that you use to combine decisions when any one condition can be true for an action to occur.

The **logical NOT operator** is a symbol that reverses the meaning of a Boolean expression.

When you use a **range check**, you compare a variable to a series of values that marks the limiting ends of ranges.

A **dead** or **unreachable path** is a logical path that can never be traveled.

When an operator has **precedence**, it is evaluated before others.

Review Questions

1. The selection statement `if quantity > 100 then discountRate = RATE` is an example of a _____.

   a. dual-alternative selection

   b. single-alternative selection

   c. structured loop

   d. all of these

2. The selection statement `if dayOfWeek = "Sunday" then price = LOWER_PRICE else price = HIGHER_PRICE` is an example of a _____.

   a. dual-alternative selection

   b. single-alternative selection

   c. unary selection

   d. all of the above

3. All selection statements must have _____.

    a. a **then** clause

    b. an **else** clause

    c. both of these

    d. none of these

4. An expression like **amount < 10** is a(n) _____ expression.

    a. Gregorian

    b. Edwardian

    c. Machiavellian

    d. Boolean

5. Usually, you compare only variables that have the same _____.

    a. type

    b. size

    c. name

    d. value

6. Symbols such as > and < are known as _____ operators.

    a. arithmetic

    b. sequential

    c. relational comparison

    d. scripting accuracy

7. If you could use only three relational comparison operators, you could get by with _____.

    a. greater than, less than, and greater than or equal to

    b. equal to, less than, and greater than

    c. less than, less than or equal to, and not equal to

    d. equal to, not equal to, and less than

8. If a > b is false, then which of the following is always true?

    a. a <= b

    b. a < b

    c. a = b

    d. a >= b

9. Usually, the most difficult comparison operator to work with is _____.

    a. equal to

    b. greater than

    c. less than

    d. not equal to

10. Which of the lettered choices is equivalent to the following decision?

```
if x > 10 then
    if y > 10 then
        output "X"
    endif
endif
```

    a. if x > 10 OR y > 10 then output "X"

    b. if x > 10 AND x > y then output "X"

    c. if y > x then output "X"

    d. if x > 10 AND y > 10 then output "X"

11. The Midwest Sales region of Acme Computer Company consists of five states—Illinois, Indiana, Iowa, Missouri, and Wisconsin. About 50 percent of the regional customers reside in Illinois, 20 percent in Indiana, and 10 percent in each of the other three states. Suppose you have input records containing Acme customer data, including state of residence. To most efficiently select and display all customers who live in the Midwest Sales region, you would ask first about residency in _____.

    a. Illinois

    b. Indiana

    c. either Iowa, Missouri, or Wisconsin—it does not matter which one of these three is first

    d. any of the five states—it does not matter which one is first

12. The Boffo Balloon Company makes helium balloons. Large balloons cost $13.00 a dozen, medium-sized balloons cost $11.00 a dozen, and small balloons cost $8.60 a dozen. About 60 percent of the company's sales are of the smallest balloons, 30 percent are medium, and large balloons constitute only 10 percent of sales. Customer order records include customer information, quantity ordered, and size. To write a program that makes the most efficient determination of an order's price based on size ordered, you should ask first whether the size is _____ .

   a. large

   b. medium

   c. small

   d. It does not matter.

13. The Boffo Balloon Company makes helium balloons in three sizes, 12 colors, and with a choice of 40 imprinted sayings. As a promotion, the company is offering a 25 percent discount on orders of large, red "Happy Valentine's Day" balloons. To most efficiently select the orders to which a discount applies, you would use _____ .

   a. nested if statements using OR logic

   b. nested if statements using AND logic

   c. three completely separate unnested if statements

   d. Not enough information is given.

14. In the following pseudocode, what percentage raise will an employee in Department 5 receive?

```
if department < 3 then
   raise = SMALL_RAISE
else
   if department < 5 then
      raise = MEDIUM_RAISE
   else
      raise = BIG_RAISE
   endif
endif
```

   a. SMALL_RAISE

   b. MEDIUM_RAISE

   c. BIG_RAISE

   d. impossible to tell

15. In the following pseudocode, what percentage raise will an employee in Department 8 receive?

```
if department < 5 then
   raise = SMALL_RAISE
else
   if department < 14 then
      raise = MEDIUM_RAISE
   else
      if department < 9
         raise = BIG_RAISE
      endif
   endif
endif
```

   a. SMALL_RAISE

   b. MEDIUM_RAISE

   c. BIG_RAISE

   d. impossible to tell

16. In the following pseudocode, what percentage raise will an employee in Department 10 receive?

```
if department < 2 then
   raise = SMALL_RAISE
else
   if department < 6 then
      raise = MEDIUM_RAISE
   else
      if department < 10
         raise = BIG_RAISE
      endif
   endif
endif
```

   a. SMALL_RAISE

   b. MEDIUM_RAISE

   c. BIG_RAISE

   d. impossible to tell

17. When you use a range check, you compare a variable to the _____ value in the range.

   a. lowest

   b. middle

   c. highest

   d. lowest or highest

18. If sales = 100, rate = 0.10, and expenses = 50, which of the following expressions is true?

    a. `sales >= expenses AND rate < 1`

    b. `sales < 200 OR expenses < 100`

    c. `expenses = rate OR sales = rate`

    d. two of the above

19. If a is true, b is true, and c is false, which of the following expressions is true?

    a. `a OR b AND c`

    b. `a AND b AND c`

    c. `a AND b OR c`

    d. two of the above

20. If d is true, e is false, and f is false, which of the following expressions is true?

    a. `e OR f AND d`

    b. `f AND d OR e`

    c. `d OR e AND f`

    d. two of the above

Exercises

1. Assume the following variables contain the values shown:

   ```
   numberRed = 100    numberBlue = 200  numberGreen = 300
   wordRed = "Wagon" wordBlue = "Sky"   wordGreen = "Grass"
   ```

   For each of the following Boolean expressions, decide whether the statement is true, false, or illegal.

   a. `numberRed = numberBlue?`

   b. `numberBlue > numberGreen?`

   c. `numberGreen < numberRed?`

   d. `numberBlue = wordBlue?`

   e. `numberGreen = "Green"?`

   f. `wordRed = "Red"?`

   g. `wordBlue = "Blue"?`

   h. `numberRed <= numberGreen?`

   i. `numberBlue >= 200?`

   j. `numberGreen >= numberRed + numberBlue?`

   k. `numberRed > numberBlue AND numberBlue < numberGreen?`

   l. `numberRed = 100 OR numberRed > numberBlue?`

   m. `numberGreen < 10 OR numberBlue > 10?`

   n. `numberBlue = 30 AND numberGreen = 300 OR numberRed = 200?`

2. Chocolate Delights Candy Company manufactures several types of candy. Design a flowchart or pseudocode for the following:

   a. A program that accepts a candy name (for example, "chocolate-covered blueberries"), price per pound, and number of pounds sold in the average month, and displays the item's data only if it is a best-selling item. Best-selling items are those that sell more than 2000 pounds per month.

   b. A program that accepts candy data continuously until a sentinel value is entered and displays a list of high-priced, best-selling items. Best-selling items are defined in Exercise 2a. High-priced items are those that sell for $10 per pound or more.

3. Pastoral College is a small college in the Midwest. Design a flowchart or pseudocode for the following:

   a. A program that accepts a student's data as follows: ID number, first and last name, major field of study, and grade point average. Display a student's data if the student's grade point average is below 2.0.

   b. A program that continuously accepts students' data until a sentinel value is entered and displays a list of all students whose grade point averages are below 2.0.

   c. A program for the Literary Honor Society that continuously reads student data and displays every student who is an English major with a grade point average of 3.5 or higher.

4. The Summerville Telephone Company charges 10 cents per minute for all calls outside the customer's area code that last over 20 minutes. All other calls are 13 cents per minute. Design a flowchart or pseudocode for the following:

   a. A program that accepts the following data about one phone call: customer area code (three digits), customer phone number (seven digits), called area code (three digits), called number (seven digits), and call time in minutes (four digits). Display the calling number, called number, and price for the call.

   b. A program that continuously accepts data about phone calls until a sentinel value is entered, and displays all the details only about calls that cost over $10.

   c. A program that continuously accepts data about phone calls until a sentinel value is entered, and displays details only about calls placed from the 212 area code to the 704 area code that last over 20 minutes.

   d. A program that prompts the user for a three-digit area code from which to select phone calls. Then the program continuously accepts phone call data until a sentinel value is entered, and displays data only for phone calls placed to or from the specified area code.

5. The Drive-Rite Insurance Company provides automobile insurance policies for drivers. Design a flowchart or pseudo-code for the following:

a. A program that accepts insurance policy data, including a policy number; customer last name; customer first name; age; premium due month, day, and year; and number of driver accidents in the last three years. If an entered policy number is not between 1000 and 9999 inclusive, set the policy number to 0. If the month is not between 1 and 12 inclusive, or the day is not correct for the month (for example, not between 1 and 31 for January or 1 and 29 for February), set the month, day, and year to 0. Display the policy data after any revisions have been made.

b. A program that continuously accepts policy holders' data until a sentinel value has been entered, and displays the data for any policy holder over 35 years old.

c. A program that accepts policy holders' data and displays the data for any policy holder who is at least 21 years old.

d. A program that accepts policy holders' data and displays the data for any policy holder no more than 30 years old.

e. A program that accepts policy holders' data and displays the data for any policy holder whose premium is due no later than March 15 any year.

f. A program that accepts policy holders' data and displays the data for any policy holder whose premium is due up to and including January 1, 2012.

g. A program that accepts policy holders' data and displays the data for any policy holder whose premium is due by April 27, 2011.

h. A program that accepts policy holders' data and displays the data for any policy holder who has a policy number between 1000 and 4000 inclusive, whose policy comes due in April or May of any year, and who has had fewer than three accidents.

6. The Barking Lot is a dog day care center. Design a flowchart or pseudocode for the following:

    a. A program that accepts data for an ID number of a dog's owner, and the name, breed, age, and weight of the dog. Display a bill containing all the input data as well as the weekly day care fee, which is $55 for dogs under 15 pounds, $75 for dogs from 15 to 30 pounds inclusive, $105 for dogs from 31 to 80 pounds inclusive, and $125 for dogs over 80 pounds.

    b. A program that continuously accepts dogs' data until a sentinel value is entered, and displays billing data for each dog.

    c. A program that continuously accepts dogs' data until a sentinel value is entered, and displays billing data for dog owners who owe more than $100.

7. Rick Hammer is a carpenter who wants an application to compute the price of any desk a customer orders, based on the following: desk length and width in inches, type of wood, and number of drawers. The price is computed as follows:

    • The minimum charge for all desks is $200.

    • If the surface (length * width) is over 750 square inches, add $50.

    • If the wood is mahogany, add $150; for oak, add $125. No charge is added for pine.

    • For every drawer in the desk, there is an additional $30 charge.

Design a flowchart or pseudocode for the following:

    a. A program that accepts data for an order number, customer name, length and width of the desk ordered, type of wood, and number of drawers. Display all the entered data and the final price for the desk.

    b. A program that continuously accepts desk order data and displays all the relevant information for oak desks that are over 36 inches long and have at least one drawer.

8. Black Dot Printing is attempting to organize carpools to save energy. Each input record contains an employee's name and town of residence. Ten percent of the company's employees live in Wonder Lake; 30 percent live in the adjacent town of Woodstock. Black Dot wants to encourage employees who live in either town to drive to work together. Design a flowchart or pseudocode for the following:

    a. A program that accepts an employee's data and displays it with a message that indicates whether the employee is a candidate for the carpool.

    b. A program that continuously accepts employee data until a sentinel value is entered, and displays a list of all employees who are carpool candidates.

9. Diana Lee, a supervisor in a manufacturing company, wants to know which employees have increased their production this year over last year. These employees will receive certificates of commendation and bonuses. Design a flowchart or pseudocode for the following:

    a. A program that continuously accepts each worker's first and last names, this year's number of units produced, and last year's number of units produced. Display each employee with a message indicating whether the employee's production has increased over last year's production.

    b. A program that accepts each worker's data and displays the name and a bonus amount. The bonuses will be distributed as follows:

        If this year's production is greater than last year's production and this year's production is:

        • 1000 units or fewer, the bonus is $25.

        • 1001 to 3000 units, the bonus is $50.

        • 3001 to 6000 units, the bonus is $100.

        • 6001 units and up, the bonus is $200.

    c. Modify Exercise 9b to reflect the following new facts, and have the program execute as efficiently as possible:

        • Thirty percent of employees have greater production rates this year than last year.

        • Sixty percent of employees produce over 6000 units per year; 20 percent produce 3001 to 6000; 15 percent produce 1001 to 3000 units; and only 5 percent produce fewer than 1001.

Find the Bugs

10. Your student disk contains files named DEBUG04-01.txt, DEBUG04-02.txt, and DEBUG04-03.txt. Each file starts with some comments that describe the problem. Comments are lines that begin with two slashes (//). Following the comments, each file contains pseudocode that has one or more bugs you must find and correct.

Game Zone

11. In Chapter 2, you learned that many programming languages allow you to generate a random number between 1 and a limiting value named LIMIT by using a statement similar to randomNumber = random(LIMIT). Create the logic for a guessing game in which the application generates a random number and the player tries to guess it. Display a message indicating whether the player's guess was correct, too high, or too low. (After you finish Chapter 5, you will be able to modify the application so that the user can continue to guess until the correct answer is entered.)

12. Create a lottery game application. Generate three random numbers, each between 0 and 9. Allow the user to guess three numbers. Compare each of the user's guesses to the three random numbers and display a message that includes the user's

Matching Numbers	Award ($)
Any one matching	10
Two matching	100
Three matching, not in order	1000
Three matching in exact order	1,000,000
No matches	0

guess, the randomly determined three digits, and the amount of money the user has won, as follows:

Make certain that your application accommodates repeating digits. For example, if a user guesses 1, 2, and 3, and the randomly generated digits are 1, 1, and 1, do not give the user credit for three correct guesses—just one.

Up for Discussion

13. Computer programs can be used to make decisions about your insurability as well as the rates you will be charged for health and life insurance policies. For example, certain pre-existing conditions may raise your insurance premiums considerably. Is it ethical for insurance companies to access your health records and then make insurance decisions about you? Explain your answer.

14. Job applications are sometimes screened by software that makes decisions about a candidate's suitability based on keywords in the applications. Is such screening fair to applicants? Explain your answer.

15. Medical facilities often have more patients waiting for organ transplants than there are available organs. Suppose you have been asked to write a computer program that selects which of several candidates should receive an available organ. What data would you want on file to be able to use in your program, and what decisions would you make based on the data? What data do you think others might use that you would choose not to use?

CHAPTER 5

Looping

In this chapter, you will learn about:

- ◎ The advantages of looping
- ◎ Using a loop control variable
- ◎ Nested loops
- ◎ Avoiding common loop mistakes
- ◎ Using a `for` loop
- ◎ Common loop applications

Understanding the Advantages of Looping

Although making decisions is what makes computers seem intelligent, it's looping that makes computer programming both efficient and worthwhile. When you use a loop, you can write one set of instructions that operates on multiple, separate sets of data.

Recall the loop structure that you learned about in Chapter 3; it looks like Figure 5-1. As long as a Boolean expression remains true, a while loop's body executes.

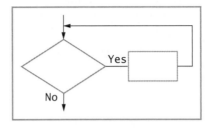

Figure 5-1 The loop structure

Using fewer instructions not only results in less time required for design and coding, but in less compile time and reduced errors.

185

You have already learned that many programs use a loop to control repetitive tasks. For example, Figure 5-2 shows the basic structure of many business programs. After some housekeeping tasks are taken care of, the detail loop repeats once for every data record that must be processed.

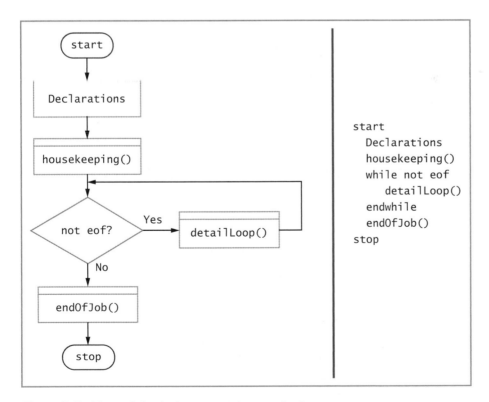

Figure 5-2 The mainline logic common to many business programs

Watch the video *A Quick Introduction to Loops*.

186

For example, Figure 5-2 might represent the mainline logic of a typical payroll program. The first employee's data would be entered in the housekeeping() module, and while the eof condition is not met, the detailLoop() module would perform such tasks as determining regular and overtime pay, and deducting taxes, insurance premiums, charitable contributions, union dues, and other items. Then, after the employee's paycheck is output, the next employee's data would be entered, and the detailLoop() module would repeat. The advantage to having a computer produce payroll checks is that all of the calculation instructions need to be written only once and can be repeated indefinitely.

TWO TRUTHS & A LIE

Understanding the Advantages of Looping

1. When you use a loop, you can write one set of instructions that operates on multiple, separate sets of data.

2. A major advantage of having a computer perform complicated tasks is the ability to repeat them.

3. A loop is a structure that branches in two logical paths before continuing.

The false statement is #3. A loop is a structure that repeats actions while some condition continues.

Using a Loop Control Variable

You can use a while loop to execute a body of statements continuously as long as some condition continues to be true. To make a while loop end correctly, you should declare a variable to control the loop's execution, and three separate actions should occur:

- The **loop control variable** is initialized before entering the loop.

- The loop control variable is tested, and if the result is true, the loop body is entered.

- The body of the loop must take some action that alters the value of the loop control variable (so that the while expression eventually evaluates as false).

When you write a loop, you must control the number of repetitions it performs; if you do not, you run the risk of creating an infinite loop. Commonly, you can control a loop's repetitions in one of two ways:

You first learned about infinite loops in Chapter 1; they are loops that do not end.

- Use a counter to create a definite, counter-controlled loop.

- Use a sentinel value to create an indefinite loop.

The body of a loop might contain any number of statements, including method calls, decisions, and other loops. Once your logic enters the body of a structured loop, the entire loop body must execute. Your program can leave a structured loop only at the comparison that tests the loop control variable.

Using a Definite Loop with a Counter

Figure 5-3 shows a loop that displays "Hello" four times. The variable count is the loop control variable. This loop is a **definite loop** because it executes a definite, predetermined number of times—in this case, four. The loop is a **counted loop** or **counter-controlled loop** because the program keeps track of the number of loop repetitions by counting them.

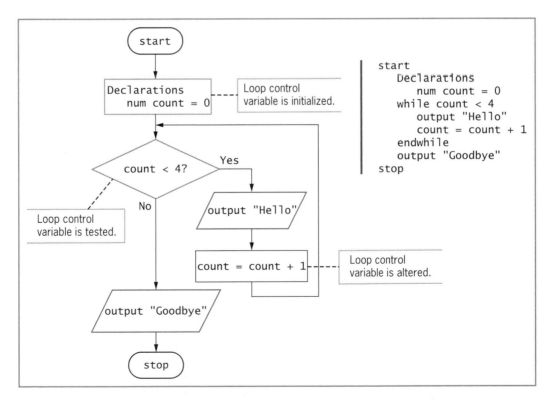

Figure 5-3 A counted while loop that outputs "Hello" four times

Watch the video *Looping*.

The loop in Figure 5-3 executes as follows:

- The loop control variable is initialized to 0.

- The `while` expression compares `count` to 4.

- The value of `count` is less than 4, and so the loop body executes. The loop body shown in Figure 5-3 consists of two statements. The first statement displays "Hello" and the second statement adds 1 to `count`.

- The next time `count` is evaluated, its value is 1, which is still less than 4, so the loop body executes again. "Hello" is displayed a second time and `count` becomes 2, "Hello" displays a third time and `count` becomes 3, then "Hello" displays a fourth time and `count` becomes 4. Now when the expression `count<4` evaluates, it is `false`, so the loop ends.

Because you so frequently need to increment a variable, many programming languages contain a shortcut operator for incrementing. You will learn about these shortcut operators when you study a programming language that uses them.

Within a correctly functioning loop's body, you can change the value of the loop control variable in a number of ways. Many loop control variable values are altered by **incrementing**, or adding to them, as in Figure 5-3. Other loops are controlled by reducing, or **decrementing**, a variable and testing whether the value remains greater than some benchmark value. For example, the loop in Figure 5-3 could be rewritten so that `count` is initialized to 4, and reduced by 1 on each pass through the loop. The loop should then continue while `count` remains greater than 0. Loops are also controlled by adding or subtracting values other than 1. For example, to display company profits at five-year intervals for the next 50 years, you would want to add 5 to a loop control variable during each iteration.

The looping logic shown in Figure 5-3 uses a counter. A **counter** is any numeric variable you use to count the number of times an event has occurred. In everyday life, people usually count things starting with 1. Many programmers prefer starting their counted loops with a variable containing a 0 value for two reasons:

- In many computer applications, numbering starts with 0 because of the 0-and-1 nature of computer circuitry.

- When you learn about arrays in Chapter 6, you will discover that array manipulation naturally lends itself to 0-based loops.

Using an Indefinite Loop with a Sentinel Value

Often, the value of a loop control variable is not altered by arithmetic, but instead is altered by user input. For example, perhaps you want to continue performing some task while the user indicates a desire to continue. In that case, you do not know when you write the program whether the loop will be executed two times, 200 times, or not at all. This type of loop is an **indefinite loop**.

Consider an interactive program that displays "Hello" repeatedly as long as the user wants to continue. The loop is indefinite because each time the program executes, the loop might be performed a different number of times. The program appears in Figure 5-4.

The program shown in Figure 5-4 continues to display "Hello" while the user's response is Y. If the user enters anything other than Y, the program ends. The loop could also be written to display while the response is not N. In that case, a user entry of anything other than N would cause the program to continue. In Chapter 1, you learned that a value such as Y or N that stops a loop is called a sentinel value.

The first **input** statement in the application in Figure 5-4 is a priming input statement. You learned about the priming input statement in Chapter 3.

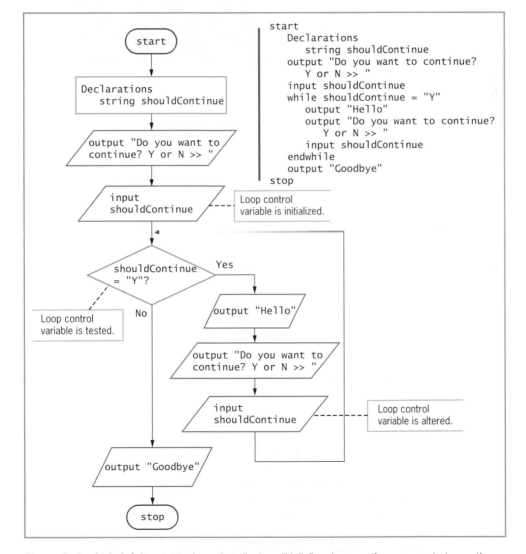

```
start
    Declarations
        string shouldContinue
    output "Do you want to continue?
        Y or N >> "
    input shouldContinue
    while shouldContinue = "Y"
        output "Hello"
        output "Do you want to continue?
            Y or N >> "
        input shouldContinue
    endwhile
    output "Goodbye"
stop
```

Figure 5-4   An indefinite `while` loop that displays "Hello" as long as the user wants to continue

190

In most programming languages, comparisons are case sensitive. If a program tests shouldContinue="Y", a user response of y will result in a false evaluation.

In the program in Figure 5-4, the loop control variable is shouldContinue. The program executes as follows:

• The loop control variable is initialized by the user's first response.

• The while expression compares the loop control variable to Y.

• If the user has entered Y, then "Hello" is output and the user is asked whether the program should continue.

• At any point, if the user enters N, the loop ends.

Figure 5-5 shows how the program might look when it is executed at the command line and in a GUI environment. The screens in Figure 5-5 show programs that perform exactly the same tasks using different environments. In each environment, the user can continue to choose to see "Hello" messages, or can choose to quit the program and display "Goodbye".

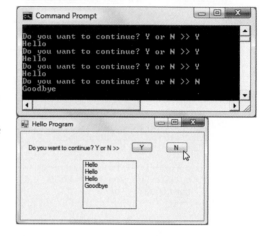

Figure 5-5   Typical executions of the program in Figure 5-4 in two environments

Understanding the Loop in a Program's Mainline Logic

The flowchart and pseudocode segments in Figure 5-4 contain three steps that should occur in every properly functioning loop:

1. You must provide a starting value for the variable that will control the loop.

2. You must test the loop control variable to determine whether the loop body executes.

3. Within the loop, you must alter the loop control variable.

In Chapter 2 you learned that the mainline logic of many business programs follows a standard outline that consists of housekeeping tasks, a loop that repeats, and finishing tasks. The three crucial steps that occur in any loop also occur in standard mainline logic. Figure 5-6 shows the flowchart for the mainline logic of the payroll program that you saw in Figure 2-8. In Figure 5-6, the three loop-controlling steps are highlighted. In this case, the three steps—initializing, testing, and altering the loop control variable—are in different modules. However, the steps all occur in the correct places, showing that the mainline logic uses a standard and correct loop.

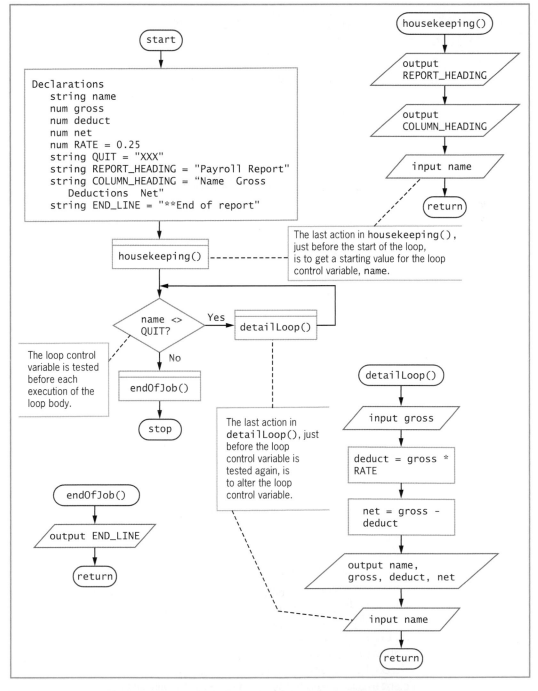

Figure 5-6 A payroll program showing how the loop control variable is used

TWO TRUTHS & A LIE

Using a Loop Control Variable

1. To make a `while` loop execute correctly, a loop control variable must be set to 0 before entering the loop.

2. To make a `while` loop execute correctly, a loop control variable should be tested before entering the loop body.

3. To make a `while` loop execute correctly, the body of the loop must take some action that alters the value of the loop control variable.

The false statement is #1. A loop control variable must be initialized, but not necessarily to 0.

Nested Loops

Program logic gets more complicated when you must use loops within loops, or **nested loops**. When one loop appears inside another, the loop that contains the other loop is called the **outer loop**, and the loop that is contained is called the **inner loop**. You need to create nested loops when the values of two (or more) variables repeat to produce every combination of values. Usually, when you create nested loops, each loop has its own loop control variable.

For example, suppose you want to write a program that produces quiz answer sheets like the ones shown in Figure 5-7. Each answer sheet has a unique heading followed by five parts with three questions in each part, and you want a fill-in-the-blank line for each question. You could write a program that uses 63 separate output statements to produce three sheets, but it is more efficient to use nested loops.

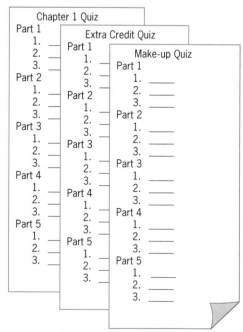

Figure 5-7 Quiz answer sheets

Figure 5-8 shows the logic for the program that produces answer sheets. Three loop control variables are declared for the program:

- `quizName` controls the `detailLoop()` module that is called from the mainline logic.

- `partCounter` controls the outer loop within the `detailLoop()` module; it keeps track of the answer sheet parts.

- `questionCounter` controls the inner loop in the `detailLoop()` module; it keeps track of the questions and answer lines within each part section on each answer sheet.

Five named constants are also declared. Three of these constants (`QUIT`, `PARTS`, and `QUESTIONS`) hold the sentinel values for each of the three loops in the program. The other two hold the text that will be output (the word "Part" that precedes each part number, and the period-space-underscore combination that forms a fill-in line for each question).

When the program starts, the `housekeeping()` module executes and the user enters the name to be output at the top of the first quiz.

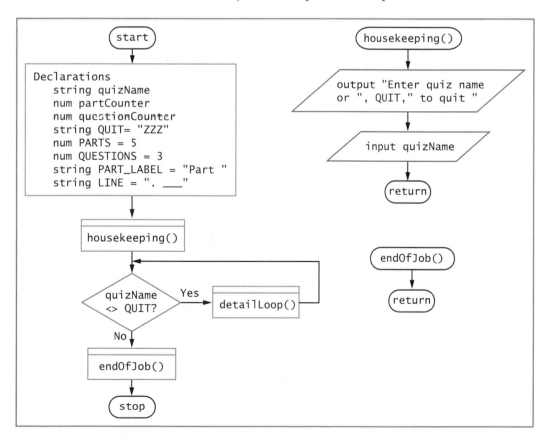

Figure 5-8 Flowchart and pseudocode for `AnswerSheet` program

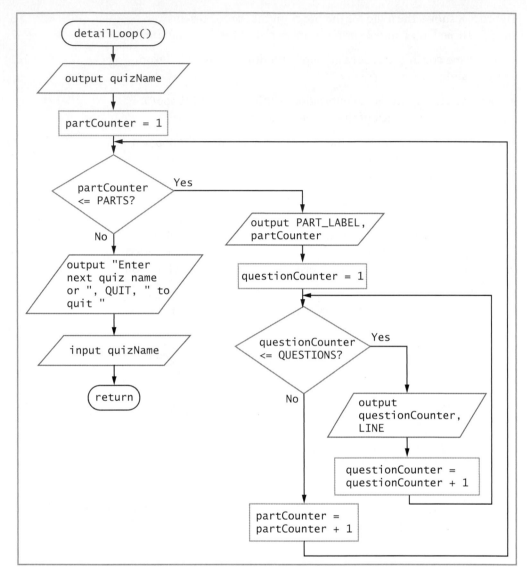

Figure 5-8   Flowchart and pseudocode for `AnswerSheet` program (continued)

If the user enters the QUIT value, the program ends immediately, but if the user enters anything else, such as "Make-up Quiz", then the detailLoop() module executes.

In the detailLoop() the quiz name is output at the top of the answer sheet. Then partCounter is initialized to 1. The partCounter variable is the loop control variable for the outer loop in this module. The outer loop continues while partCounter is less than or equal to PARTS. The last statement in the outer loop adds 1 to partCounter. In other words, the outer loop will execute when partCounter is 1, 2, 3, 4, and 5.

```
start
   Declarations
      string quizName
      num partCounter
      num questionCounter
      string QUIT = "ZZZ"
      num PARTS = 5
      num QUESTIONS = 3
      string PART_LABEL = "Part "
      string LINE = ". _____"
   housekeeping()
   while quizName <> QUIT
      detailLoop()
   endwhile
   endOfJob()
stop

housekeeping()
   output "Enter quiz name or ", QUIT, "to quit "
   input quizName
return

detailLoop()
   output quizName
   partCounter = 1
   while partCounter <= PARTS
      output PART_LABEL, partCounter
      questionCounter = 1
      while questionCounter <= QUESTIONS
         output questionCounter, LINE
         questionCounter = questionCounter + 1
      endwhile
      partCounter = partCounter + 1
   endwhile
   output "Enter next quiz name or ", QUIT, " to quit "
   input quizName
return

endOfJob()
return
```

Figure 5-8 Flowchart and pseudocode for `AnswerSheet` program (continued)

In the outer loop in the `detailLoop()` module in Figure 5-8, the word "Part" and the current `partCounter` value are output. Then the following steps execute:

- The loop control variable for the inner loop is initialized by setting `questionCounter` to 1.

- The loop control variable `questionCounter` is evaluated by comparing it to `QUESTIONS`, and while `questionCounter` does not exceed `QUESTIONS`, the loop body executes: the value of `questionCounter` is output, followed by a period and a fill-in-the-blank line.

 In Figure 5-8, some output would be sent to one output device, such as a monitor. Other output would be sent to another output device, such as a printer. The statements needed to send output to separate devices differs among languages. Chapter 7 provides more details.

 The `endOfJob()` module is included in the program in Figure 5-8, even though it contains no statements, so that the mainline logic contains all the parts you have learned. An empty module that acts as a placeholder is called a **stub**.

 In the program in Figure 5-8, it is important that `questionCounter` is reset to 1 within the outer loop, just before entering the inner loop. If this step was omitted, Part 1 would contain questions 1, 2, and 3, but subsequent parts would be empty.

Watch the video
Nested Loops.

- At the end of the loop body, the loop control variable is altered by adding 1 to `questionCounter` and the `questionCounter` comparison is made again.

In other words, when `partCounter` is 1, the part heading is output and underscore lines are output for questions 1, 2, and 3. Then `partCounter` becomes 2, the part heading is output, and underscore lines are created for another set of questions 1, 2, and 3. Then `partCounter` in turn becomes 3, 4, and 5, and three underscore lines are created for each part.

TWO TRUTHS & A LIE

Nested Loops

1. When one loop is nested inside another, the loop that contains the other loop is called the outer loop.

2. You need to create nested loops when the values of two (or more) variables repeat to produce every combination of values.

3. The number of times a loop executes always depends on a constant.

The false statement is #3. The number of times a loop executes can depend on a constant or a value that varies.

Avoiding Common Loop Mistakes

The mistakes programmers most often make with loops are:

- Neglecting to initialize the loop control variable

- Neglecting to alter the loop control variable

- Using the wrong comparison with the loop control variable

- Including statements inside the loop that belong outside the loop

The following sections explain these common mistakes in more detail.

Mistake: Neglecting to Initialize the Loop Control Variable

It is always a mistake to fail to initialize a loop's control variable. For example, consider the program in Figure 5-9. It prompts the user for a name, and while the name continues not to be the sentinel value "ZZZ", it outputs a greeting that uses the name and asks for the next name. This program works correctly.

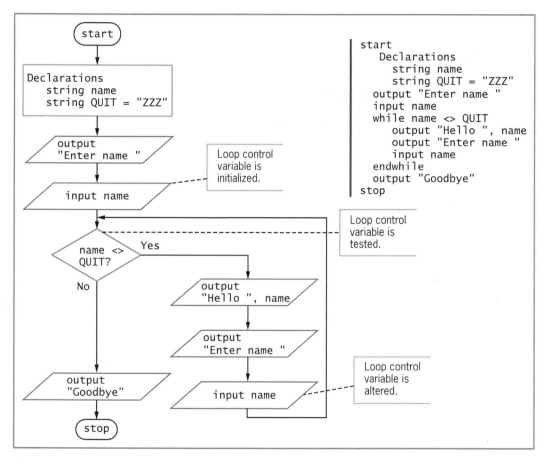

Figure 5-9 Correct logic for greeting program

Figure 5-10 shows an incorrect program in which the loop control variable is not assigned a starting value. If the `name` variable is not set to a starting value, then when the `eof` condition is tested, there is no way to predict whether or not it will be true. That's because if the user does not enter a value for name, the garbage value originally held by that variable might or might not be "ZZZ". So, one of two scenarios follows:

- Most likely, the uninitialized value of name is not "ZZZ", so the first greeting output will include garbage—for example, "Hello 12BGr5".

- By a remote chance, the uninitialized value of name *is* "ZZZ", so the program ends immediately before the user can enter any names.

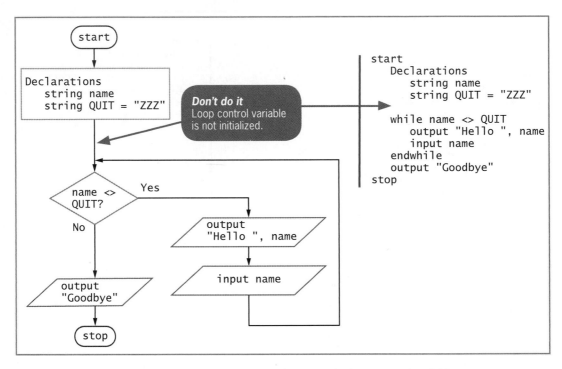

Figure 5-10   Incorrect logic for greeting program because the loop control variable initialization is missing

Mistake: Neglecting to Alter the Loop Control Variable

Different sorts of errors will occur if you fail to alter a loop control variable within the loop. For example, in the program in Figure 5-9 that accepts and displays names, you create such an error if you don't accept names within the loop. Figure 5-11 shows the resulting incorrect logic.

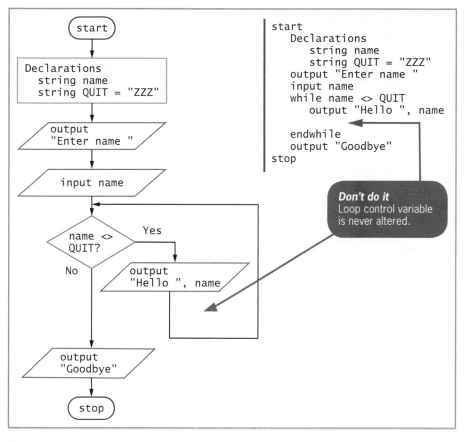

Figure 5-11   Incorrect logic for greeting program because the loop control variable is not altered

If you remove the `input name` instruction from the end of the loop in the program, no name is ever entered after the first one. For example, assume that when the program starts, the user enters "Fred". The name will be compared to the sentinel value, and the loop will be entered. After a greeting is output for Fred, no new name is entered, so when the logic returns to the loop-controlling question, the `name` will still not be "ZZZ", and greetings for Fred will continue to be output infinitely. It is always incorrect to create a loop that cannot terminate.

Mistake: Using the Wrong Comparison with the Loop Control Variable

Programmers must be careful to use the correct comparison in the statement that controls a loop. A comparison is correct only when the correct operands and operator are used. For example, although only one keystroke differs between the original greeting program in Figure 5-9 and the one in Figure 5-12, the original program correctly produces named greetings and the second one does not.

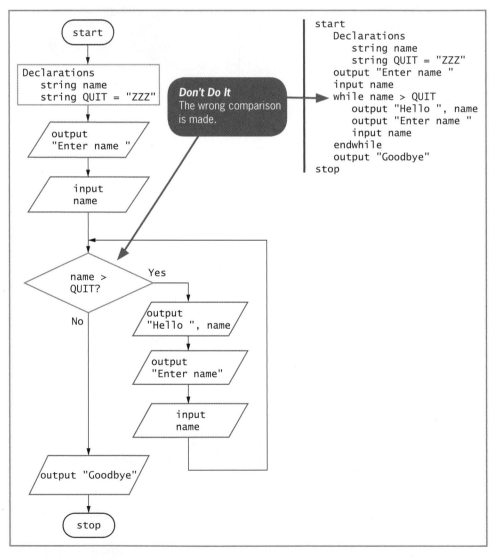

Figure 5-12 Incorrect logic for greeting program because the wrong test is made with the loop control variable

In the example in Figure 5-12, a greater-than comparison (>) is made instead of a not-equal-to (<>) comparison. Suppose that when the program executes, the user enters "Fred" as the first name. In most programming languages, when the comparison between "Fred" and "ZZZ" is made, the values are compared alphabetically. "Fred" is not greater than "ZZZ", so the loop is never entered, and the program ends.

Using the wrong comparison can have serious effects. For example, in a counted loop, if you use <= instead of < to compare a counter to a sentinel value, the program will perform one loop execution too many. If the loop displays greetings, the error might not be critical, but if such an error occurred in a loan company application, each customer might be charged a month's additional interest. If the error occurred in an airline's application, it might overbook a flight. If it occurred in a pharmacy's drug-dispensing application, each patient might receive one extra (and possibly harmful) unit of medication.

Mistake: Including Statements Inside the Loop that Belong Outside the Loop

Suppose that you want to write a program for a store manager who wants to discount every item he sells by 30 percent. The manager wants 100 new price label stickers for each item. The user enters a price, the new price is calculated, 100 stickers are printed, and the next price is entered. Figure 5-13 shows a program that performs the job, albeit somewhat inefficiently. The program is inefficient because the same value, newPrice, is calculated 100 separate times for each price that is entered.

202

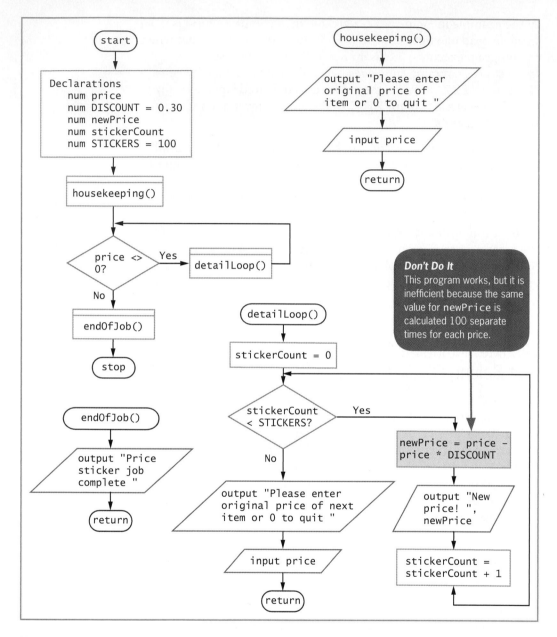

Figure 5-13 Inefficient way to produce 100 discount price stickers for differently priced items

```
start
    Declarations
        num price
        num DISCOUNT = 0.30
        num newPrice
        num stickerCount
        num STICKERS = 100
    housekeeping()
    while price <> 0
        detailLoop()
    endwhile
    endOfJob()
stop

housekeeping()
    output "Please enter original price of item or 0 to quit "
    input price
return

detailLoop()
    stickerCount = 0
    while stickerCount < STICKERS
        newPrice = price - price * DISCOUNT
        output "New price! ", newPrice
        stickerCount = stickerCount + 1
    endwhile
    output "Please enter original price of
        next item or 0 to quit "
    input price
return

endOfJob()
    output "Price sticker job complete"
return
```

Don't Do It
This program works, but it is inefficient because the same value for newPrice is calculated 100 separate times for each price.

Figure 5-13 Inefficient way to produce 100 discount price stickers for differently priced items (continued)

Figure 5-14 shows the same program, in which the newPrice value that is output on the sticker is calculated only once per new price; the calculation has been moved to a better location. The programs in Figures 5-13 and 5-14 do the same thing. However, the one in Figure 5-14 does it more efficiently. As you become more proficient at programming, you will recognize many opportunities to perform the same tasks in alternate, more elegant, and more efficient ways.

When you describe people or events as "elegant," you mean they possess a refined gracefulness. Similarly, programmers use the term "elegant" to describe programs that are well designed and easy to understand and maintain.

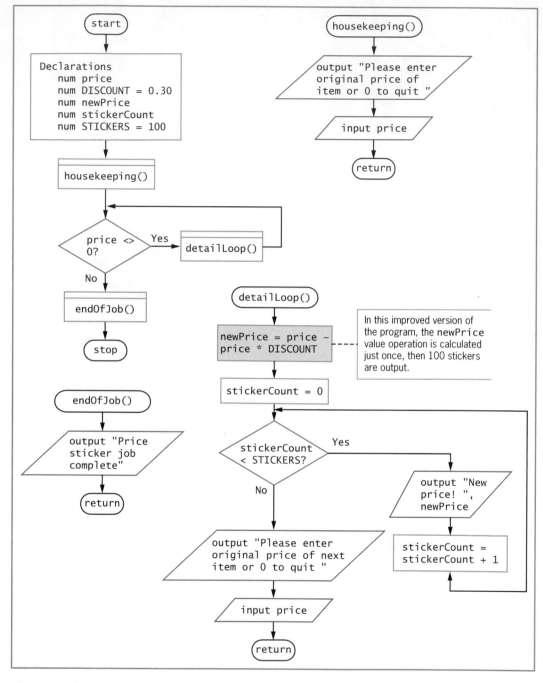

Figure 5-14   Improved discount sticker-making program

```
start
    Declarations
        num price
        num DISCOUNT = 0.30
        num newPrice
        num stickerCount
        num STICKERS = 100
    housekeeping()
    while price <> 0
        detailLoop()
    endwhile
    endOfJob()
stop

housekeeping()
    output "Please enter original price of item or 0 to quit "
    input price
return

detailLoop()
    newPrice = price - price * DISCOUNT
    stickerCount = 0
    while stickerCount < STICKERS
        output "New price! ", newPrice
        stickerCount = stickerCount + 1
    endwhile
output "Please enter original price of next item or 0 to quit "
input price
return

endOfJob()
    output "Price sticker job complete"
return
```

> In this improved version of the program, the newPrice value operation is calculated just once, then 100 stickers are output.

Figure 5-14 Improved discount sticker-making program (continued)

TWO TRUTHS & A LIE

Avoiding Common Loop Mistakes

1. In a loop, neglecting to initialize the loop control variable is a mistake.

2. In a loop, neglecting to alter the loop control variable is a mistake.

3. In a loop, it is a mistake to compare the loop control variable using >= or <=.

The false statement is #3. Many loops are created correctly using <= or >=.

Using a for Loop

Every high-level computer programming language contains a `while` statement that you can use to code any loop, including both indefinite and definite loops. In addition to the `while` statement, most computer languages support a `for` statement. You usually use the **for statement**, or **for loop**, with definite loops—those that will loop a specific number of times—when you know exactly how many times the loop will repeat. The `for` statement provides you with three actions in one compact statement. In a `for` statement, a loop control variable is:

- Initialized

- Evaluated

- Incremented

The `for` statement sometimes takes the form:

```
for loopControlVariable = initialValue to
   finalValue step stepValue
       do something
endfor
```

For example, to display "Hello" four times, you can write either of the sets of statements in Figure 5-15.

```
count = 0                          for count = 0 to 3 step 1
while count <= 3                       output "Hello"
    output "Hello"                 endfor
    count = count + 1
endwhile
```

Figure 5-15　Comparable `while` and `for` statements that each output "Hello" four times

The code segments in Figure 5-15 each accomplish the same tasks:

- The variable `count` is initialized to 0.

- The `count` variable is compared to the limit value 3; while `count` is less than or equal to 3, the loop body executes.

- As the last statement in the loop execution, the value of `count` increases by 1. After the increase, the comparison to the limit value is made again.

The for loop simply expresses the same logic in a more compact form. The amount by which a for loop control variable changes is often called a **step value**. The step value can be positive or negative; that is, it can increment or decrement. You never are required to use a for statement for any loop; a while statement can always be used instead. However, when a loop's execution is based on a loop control variable progressing from a known starting value to a known ending value in equal steps, the for loop provides you with a convenient shorthand. It is easy for others to read, and because the loop control variable's initialization, testing, and alteration are all performed in one location, you are less likely to leave out one of these crucial elements.

The programmer doesn't need to know the starting value, ending value, or step value for the loop control variable when the program is written; only the application must know those values while the program is running. For example, any of the values might be entered by the user, or might be the result of a calculation.

207

In Java, C++, and C#, a for loop that displays 20 values might look similar to the following:

```
for(count = 0; count < 20; count++)
{
    output count
}
```

The three actions (initialization, comparison, and altering of the loop control variable) all take place within a set of parentheses that follows the keyword **for** and are separated by semicolons. The expression **count++** adds 1 to **count**. The block of statements that depends on the loop sits between a pair of curly braces.

The for loop is particularly useful when processing arrays. You will learn about arrays in Chapter 6.

Both the while loop and the for loop are examples of *pretest loops*. That means the loop control variable is tested before each iteration. Most languages allow you to use a variation of the looping structure known as a *posttest loop*, which tests the loop control variable after each iteration. Appendix F contains information about posttest loops.

TWO TRUTHS & A LIE

Using a for Loop

1. The for statement provides you with three actions in one compact statement: initializing, evaluating, and incrementing.

2. A for statement body always executes at least one time.

3. In most programming languages, you can provide a for loop with any step value.

The false statement is #2. A for statement body might not execute depending on the initial value of the loop control variable.

Common Loop Applications

Although every computer program is different, many techniques are common to a variety of applications. Loops, for example, are frequently used to accumulate totals and to validate data.

Using a Loop to Accumulate Totals

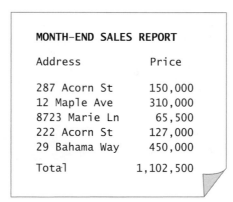

Some business reports list only totals, with no individual item details. Such reports are called **summary reports**.

Business reports often include totals. The supervisor requesting a list of employees who participate in the company dental plan is often as interested in the number of participating employees as in who they are. When you receive your telephone bill at the end of the month, you are usually more interested in the total than in the charges for the individual calls.

For example, a real estate broker might want to see a list of all properties sold in the last month as well as the total value for all the properties. A program might read sales data that includes the street address of the property sold and its selling price. The data records might be entered by a clerk as each sale is made, and stored in a file until the end of the month; then they can be used in the month-end report. Figure 5-16 shows an example of such a report.

```
MONTH-END SALES REPORT

Address          Price

287 Acorn St     150,000
12 Maple Ave     310,000
8723 Marie Ln     65,500
222 Acorn St     127,000
29 Bahama Way    450,000

Total          1,102,500
```

Figure 5-16   Month-end real estate sales report

To create the sales report, you must output the address and price for each property sold and add its value to an accumulator. An **accumulator** is a variable that you use to gather or accumulate values. An accumulator is very similar to a counter that you use to count loop iterations. However, usually you add just one to a counter, whereas you add some other value to an accumulator. If the real estate broker wants to know how many listings the company holds, you count them. When she wants to know total real estate value, you accumulate it.

To accumulate total real estate prices, you declare a numeric variable such as accumPrice and initialize it to 0. As you get each real estate transaction's data, you output it and add its value to the accumulator accumPrice, as shown shaded in Figure 5-17.

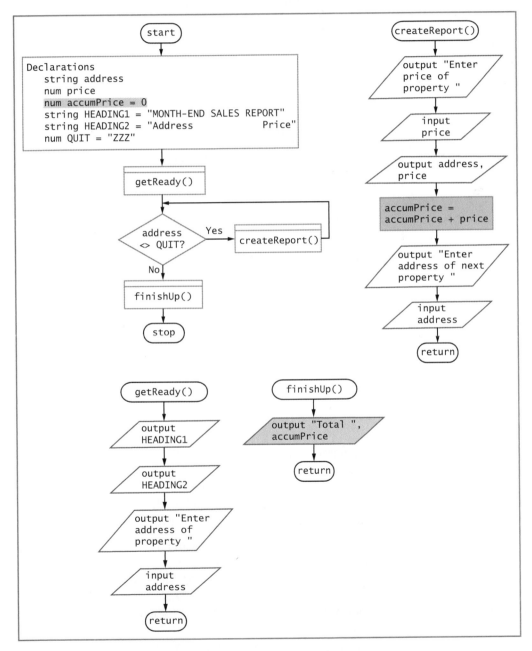

Figure 5-17 Flowchart and pseudocode for real estate sales report program

```
start
    Declarations
        string address
        num price
        num accumPrice = 0
        string HEADING1 = "MONTH-END SALES REPORT"
        string HEADING2 = "Address            Price"
        num QUIT = "ZZZ"
    getReady()
    while address <> QUIT
        createReport()
    endwhile
    finishUp()
stop

getReady()
    output HEADING1
    output HEADING2
    output "Enter address of property "
    input address
return

createReport()
    output "Enter price of property "
    input price
    output address, price
    accumPrice = accumPrice + price
    output "Enter address of next property "
    input address
return

finishUp()
    output "Total ", accumPrice
return
```

Figure 5-17   Flowchart and pseudocode for real estate sales
report program (continued)

Some
programming
languages
assign 0 to a
numeric
variable you fail to initialize explicitly, but many do
not—when you try to add
a value to an uninitialized
variable, they either issue
an error message or let
you incorrectly start with
an accumulator that holds
garbage. The safest and
clearest course of action
is to assign the value 0 to
accumulators before
using them.

After the program in Figure 5-17 gets and displays the last real estate
transaction, the user enters the sentinel value, and loop execution
ends. At that point, the accumulator will hold the grand total of all
the real estate values. The program displays the word "Total" and the
accumulated value, accumPrice. Then the program ends.

Figure 5-17 highlights the three actions you usually must take with an
accumulator:

- Accumulators are initialized to 0.

- Accumulators are altered, usually once for every data set
  processed.

- At the end of processing, accumulators are output.

After outputting the value of `accumPrice`, new programmers often want to reset it to 0. Their argument is that they are "cleaning up after themselves." Although you can take this step without harming the execution of the program, it does not serve any useful purpose. You cannot set `accumPrice` to 0 in anticipation of having it ready for the next program, or even for the next time you execute this program. Variables exist only during an execution of the program, and even if a future application happens to contain a variable named `accumPrice`, the variable will not necessarily occupy the same memory location as this one. Even if you run the same application a second time, the variables might occupy physical memory locations different from those they occupied during the first run. It is the programmer's responsibility to initialize all variables that must start with a specific value. There is no benefit to changing a variable's value when it will never be used again during the current execution.

Using a Loop to Validate Data

When you ask a user to enter data into a computer program, you have no assurance that the data will be accurate. Loops are frequently used to **validate data**; that is, to make sure it is meaningful and useful. For example, validation might ensure that a value is the correct type, or that it falls within an acceptable range.

For example, suppose part of a program you are writing asks a user to enter a number that represents his or her birth month. If the user types a number lower than 1 or greater than 12, you must take some sort of action. For example:

- You could display an error message and stop the program.

- You could choose to assign a default value for the month (for example, 1) before proceeding.

- You could reprompt the user for valid input.

If you choose this last course of action, at least two approaches could be used. You could use a selection, and if the month is invalid, you could ask the user to reenter a number, as shown in Figure 5-18.

Incorrect user entries are by far the most common source of computer errors. The programs you write will be improved if you employ **defensive programming**, which means trying to prepare for all possible errors before they occur.

Programmers employ the acronym **GIGO** for "garbage in, garbage out." It means that if your input is incorrect, your output is worthless.

212

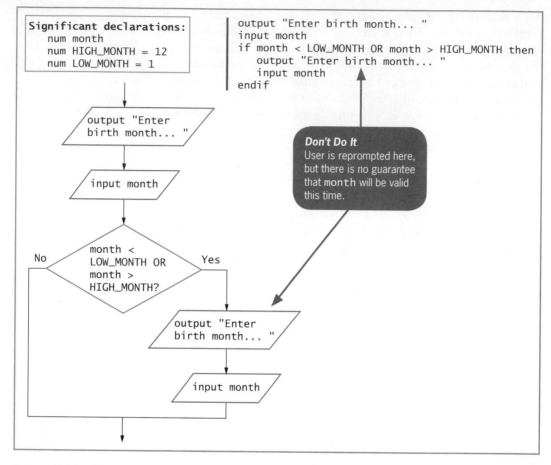

Figure 5-18 Reprompting a user once after an invalid month is entered

The problem with the logic in Figure 5-18 is that the user still might not enter valid data on the second attempt to enter a month. Of course, you could add a third decision, but you still couldn't control what the user enters.

The superior solution is to use a loop to continuously prompt a user for a month until the user enters it correctly. Figure 5-19 shows this approach.

 Just because a data item is valid does not mean that it is correct. For example, a program can determine that 5 is a valid birth month, but not that your birthday actually falls in month 5.

 Most languages provide a built-in way to check whether an entered value is numeric or not. When you rely on user input, you frequently accept each piece of input data as a string and then attempt to convert it to a number. The procedure for accomplishing numeric checks is slightly different in different programming languages.

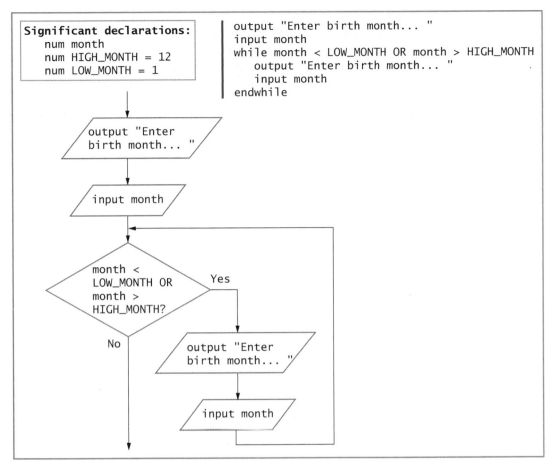

Figure 5-19 Reprompting a user continuously after an invalid month is entered

Limiting a Reprompting Loop

Reprompting a user is a good way to ensure valid data, but it can be frustrating to a user if it continues indefinitely. For example, suppose the user must enter a valid birth month, but has used another application in which January was month 0, and keeps entering 0 no matter how many times you repeat the prompt. One helpful addition to the program would be to use the limiting values as part of the prompt. In other words, instead of the statement output "Enter birth month ... ", the following statement might be more useful:

```
output "Enter birth month between ", LOW_MONTH, ", and ",
    HIGH_MONTH, " ... "
```

Still, the user might not understand the prompt or not read it carefully, so you might want to employ the tactic used in Figure 5-20, in which

Programs that frustrate users can result in lost revenue for a company. For example, if a company's Web site is difficult to navigate, users might just give up and not do business with the organization.

a count of the number of reprompts is maintained. In this example, a constant named ATTEMPTS is set to 3. While a count of the user's attempts at correct data entry remains below this limit, and the user enters invalid data, the user continues to be reprompted. If the user exceeds the limited number of allowed attempts, the loop ends. The next action depends on the application. If count equals ATTEMPTS after the data-entry loop ends, you might want to force the invalid data to a default value. **Forcing** a data item means you override incorrect data by setting the variable to a specific value. For example, you might decide that if a month value does not fall between 1 and 12, you will force the month to 0 or 99, which indicates to users that no valid value exists. In a different application, you might just choose to end the program. In an interactive, Web-based program, you might choose to have a customer service representative start a chat session with the user to offer help.

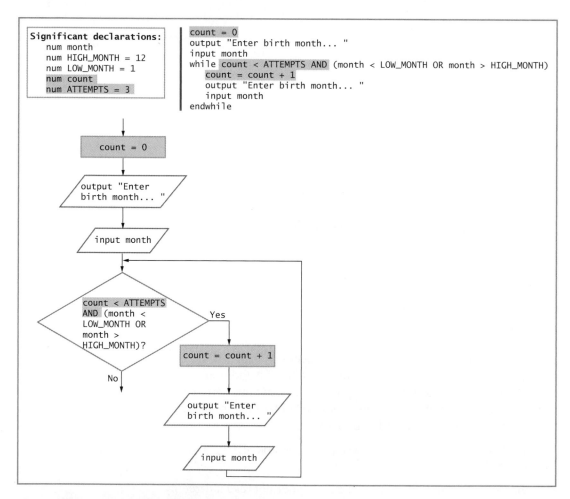

```
Significant declarations:
    num month
    num HIGH_MONTH = 12
    num LOW_MONTH = 1
    num count
    num ATTEMPTS = 3
```

```
count = 0
output "Enter birth month... "
input month
while count < ATTEMPTS AND (month < LOW_MONTH OR month > HIGH_MONTH)
    count = count + 1
    output "Enter birth month... "
    input month
endwhile
```

Figure 5-20 Limiting user reprompts

Validating a Data Type

The data you use within computer programs is varied. It stands to reason that validating data requires a variety of methods. For example, some programming languages allow you to check data items to make sure they are the correct data type. Although this technique varies from language to language, you can often make a statement like the one shown in Figure 5-21. In this program segment, isNumeric() represents a method call; it is used to check whether the entered employee salary falls within the category of numeric data. You check to ensure that a value is numeric for many reasons—an important one is that only numeric values can be used correctly in arithmetic statements. A method such as isNumeric() is most often provided with the language translator you use to write your programs. Such a method operates as a black box; in other words, you can use the method's results without understanding its internal statements.

 This book uses the data types string and num. Most programming languages provide additional, more specific data types.

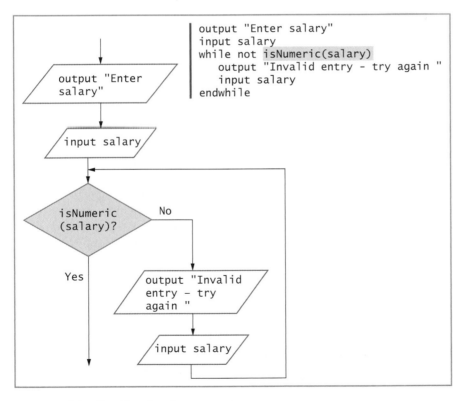

```
output "Enter salary"
input salary
while not isNumeric(salary)
    output "Invalid entry - try again "
    input salary
endwhile
```

Figure 5-21   Checking data for correct type

Besides allowing you to check whether a value is numeric, some languages contain methods such as isChar(), which checks whether a value is a character data type; isWhitespace(), which checks whether a value is a nonprinting character, such as a space or tab; and isUpper(), which checks whether a value is a capital letter.

In many languages, you accept all user data as a string of characters, and then use built-in methods to attempt to convert the characters to the correct data type for your application. When the conversion methods succeed, you have useful data; when the conversion methods fail because the user has entered the wrong data type, you can take appropriate action, such as issuing an error message, reprompting the user, or forcing the data to a default value.

Validating Reasonableness and Consistency of Data

Frequently, testing for reasonableness and consistency involves using additional data files. For example, to check that a user has entered a valid county of residence for a state, you might use a file that contains every county name within every state in the United States, and check the user's county against those contained in the file.

When you become a professional programmer, you want your programs to work correctly as a source of professional pride. On a more basic level, you do not want to be called in to work at 3 a.m. when the overnight run of your program fails because of errors you created.

Data items can be the correct type and within range, but still be incorrect. You have experienced this phenomenon yourself if anyone has ever misspelled your name or overbilled you. The data might have been the correct type—that is, alphabetic letters were used in your name—but the name itself was incorrect. Many data items cannot be checked for reasonableness; for example, the names Catherine, Katherine, and Kathryn are equally reasonable, but only one spelling is correct for a particular woman.

However, many data items can be checked for reasonableness. If you make a purchase on May 3, 2012, then the payment cannot possibly be due prior to that date. Perhaps within your organization, you cannot make more than $20.00 per hour if you work in Department 12. If your zip code is 90201, your state of residence cannot be New York. If your store's cash on hand was $3000 when it closed on Tuesday, it should not be a different value when it opens on Wednesday. If a customer's title is "Ms.", the customer's gender should be "F". Each of these examples involves comparing two data items for reasonableness or consistency. You should consider making as many such comparisons as possible when writing your own programs.

Good defensive programs try to foresee all possible inconsistencies and errors. The more accurate your data, the more useful information you will produce as output from your programs.

TWO TRUTHS & A LIE

Common Loop Applications

1. An accumulator is a variable that you use to gather or accumulate values.

2. An accumulator typically is initialized to 0.

3. An accumulator is typically reset to 0 after it is output.

The false statement is #3. There is typically no need to reset an accumulator after it is output.

Chapter Summary

- When you use a loop in a computer program, you can write one set of instructions that operates on multiple, separate sets of data.

- Three steps must occur in every loop: You must initialize a loop control variable, compare the variable to some value that controls whether the loop continues or stops, and alter the variable that controls the loop.

- When you must use loops within loops, you use nested loops. When nesting loops, you must maintain two individual loop control variables and alter each at the appropriate time.

- Common mistakes that programmers make when writing loops include neglecting to initialize the loop control variable, neglecting to alter the loop control variable, using the wrong comparison with the loop control variable, and including statements inside the loop that belong outside the loop.

- Most computer languages support a for statement or for loop that you can use with definite loops when you know how many times a loop will repeat. The for statement uses a loop control variable that it automatically initializes, evaluates, and increments.

- Loops are used in many applications—for example, to accumulate totals in business reports. Loops are also used to ensure that user data entries are valid by continuously reprompting the user.

Key Terms

A **loop control variable** is a variable that determines whether a loop will continue.

A **definite loop** is one for which the number of repetitions is a predetermined value.

A **counted loop** or **counter-controlled loop** is a loop whose repetitions are managed by a counter.

Incrementing a variable is adding a constant value to it, frequently 1.

Decrementing a variable is decreasing it by a constant value, frequently 1.

A **counter** is any numeric variable you use to count the number of times an event has occurred.

An **indefinite loop** is one for which you cannot predetermine the number of executions.

Nested loops occur when a loop structure exists within another loop structure.

An **outer loop** contains another when loops are nested.

An **inner loop** is contained within another when loops are nested.

A **stub** is a method without statements that is used as a placeholder.

A **for statement**, or **for loop**, can be used to code definite loops. The for statement contains a loop control variable that it automatically initializes, evaluates, and increments.

A **step value** is a number you use to increase a loop control variable on each pass through a loop.

A **summary report** lists only totals, without individual detail records.

An **accumulator** is a variable that you use to gather or accumulate values.

When you **validate data**, you make sure data items are meaningful and useful. For example, you ensure that values are the correct data type or that they fall within an acceptable range.

Defensive programming is a technique with which you try to prepare for all possible errors before they occur.

GIGO ("garbage in, garbage out") means that if your input is incorrect, your output is worthless.

Forcing a data item means you override incorrect data by setting it to a specific value.

Review Questions

1. The structure that allows you to write one set of instructions that operates on multiple, separate sets of data is the _____.

    a. sequence

    b. selection

    c. loop

    d. case

2. The loop that frequently appears in a program's mainline logic _____.

    a. always depends on whether a variable equals 0

    b. works correctly based on the same logic as other loops

    c. is an unstructured loop

    d. is an example of an infinite loop

3. Which of the following is *not* a step that must occur with every correctly working loop?

    a. Initialize a loop control variable before the loop starts.

    b. Set the loop control value equal to a sentinel during each iteration.

    c. Compare the loop control value to a sentinel during each iteration.

    d. Alter the loop control variable during each iteration.

4. The statements executed within a loop are known collectively as the _____.

    a. loop body

    b. loop controls

    c. sequences

    d. sentinels

5. A counter keeps track of _____.

   a. the number of times an event has occurred

   b. the number of machine cycles required by a segment of a program

   c. the number of loop structures within a program

   d. the number of times software has been revised

6. Adding 1 to a variable is also called _____ it.

   a. digesting

   b. resetting

   c. decrementing

   d. incrementing

7. Which of the following is a definite loop?

   a. a loop that executes as long as a user continues to enter valid data

   b. a loop that executes 1000 times

   c. both of the above

   d. none of the above

8. Which of the following is an indefinite loop?

   a. a loop that executes exactly 10 times

   b. a loop that follows a prompt asking a user how many repetitions to make and uses that value to control the loop

   c. both of the above

   d. none of the above

9. When you decrement a variable, you _____.

   a. set it to 0

   b. reduce it by one-tenth

   c. subtract 1 from it

   d. remove it from a program

10. When two loops are nested, the loop that is contained by the other is the _____ loop.

    a. captive

    b. unstructured

    c. inner

    d. outer

11. When loops are nested, _____.

    a. they typically share a loop control variable

    b. one must end before the other begins

    c. both must be the same type—definite or indefinite

    d. none of the above

12. Most programmers use a for loop _____.

    a. for every loop they write

    b. when a loop will not repeat

    c. when they do not know the exact number of times a loop will repeat

    d. when they know the exact number of times a loop will repeat

13. A report that lists only totals, with no details about individual records, is a(n) _____ report.

    a. accumulator

    b. final

    c. summary

    d. detailless

14. Typically, the value added to a counter variable is _____.

    a. 0

    b. 1

    c. 10

    d. 100

15. Typically, the value added to an accumulator variable is _____.

    a. 0

    b. 1

    c. the same for each iteration

    d. different in each iteration

16. After an accumulator or counter variable is displayed at the end of a program, it is best to _____.

    a. delete the variable from the program

    b. reset the variable to 0

    c. subtract 1 from the variable

    d. none of the above

17. When you _____, you make sure data items are the correct type and fall within the correct range.

    a. validate data

    b. employ offensive programming

    c. use object orientation

    d. count loop iterations

18. Overriding a user's entered value by setting it to a predetermined value is known as _____.

    a. forcing

    b. accumulating

    c. validating

    d. pushing

19. To ensure that a user's entry is the correct data type, frequently you _____.

    a. prompt the user, asking if the user is sure the type is correct

    b. use a method built into the programming language

    c. include a statement at the beginning of the program that lists the data types allowed

    d. all of the above

20. Variables might hold incorrect values even when they are _____.

    a. the correct data type

    b. within a required range

    c. coded by the programmer rather than input by a user

    d. all of the above

Exercises

1. What is output by each of the pseudocode segments in Figure 5-22?

a.
```
a = 1
b = 2
c = 5
while a < c
    a = a + 1
    b = b + c
endwhile
output a, b, c
```

b.
```
d = 4
e = 6
f = 7
while d > f
    d = d + 1
    e = e - 1
endwhile
output d, e, f
```

c.
```
g = 4
h = 6
while g < h
    g = g + 1
endwhile
output g, h
```

d.
```
j = 2
k = 5
n = 9
while j < k
    m = 6
    while m < n
        output "Goodbye"
        m = m + 1
    endwhile
    j = j + 1
endwhile
```

e.
```
j = 2
k = 5
m = 6
n = 9
while j < k
    while m < n
        output "Hello"
        m = m + 1
    endwhile
    j = j + 1
endwhile
```

f.
```
p = 2
q = 4
while p < q
    output "Adios"
    r = 1
    while r < q
        output "Adios"
        r = r + 1
    endwhile
    p = p + 1
endwhile
```

Figure 5-22 Pseudocode segments for Exercise 1

2. Design the logic for a program that outputs every number from 1 through 10.

3. Design the logic for a program that outputs every number from 1 through 10 along with its square and cube.

4. Design the logic for a program that outputs every even number from 2 through 30.

5. Design the logic for a program that outputs numbers in reverse order from 10 down to 1.

6. a. The No Interest Credit Company provides zero-interest loans to customers. Design an application that gets customer account data, including an account number, customer name, and balance due. Output the account number and name, then output the customer's projected balance each month for the next 10 months. Assume that there is no finance charge on this account, that the customer makes no new purchases, and that the customer pays off the balance with equal monthly payments, which are 10 percent of the original bill.

   b. Modify the No Interest Credit Company application so it executes continuously for any number of customers until a sentinel value is supplied for the account number.

7. a. The Some Interest Credit Company provides loans to customers at 1.5 percent interest per month. Design an application that gets customer account data, including an account number, customer name, and balance due. Output the account number and name; then output the customer's projected balance each month for the next 10 months. Assume that when the balance reaches $10 or less, the customer can pay off the account. At the beginning of every month, 1.5 percent interest is added to the balance, and then the customer makes a payment equal to 5 percent of the current balance. Assume the customer makes no new purchases.

   b. Modify the Some Interest Credit Company application so it executes continuously for any number of customers until a sentinel value is supplied for the account number.

8. Secondhand Rose Resale Shop is having a seven-day sale during which the price of any unsold item drops 10 percent each day. For example, an item that costs $10.00 on the first day costs 10 percent less, or $9.00, on the second day. On the third day, the same item is 10 percent less than $9.00, or $8.10. Design an application that allows a user to input a price until an appropriate sentinel value is entered. Output is the price of each item on each day, one through seven.

9. The Howell Bank provides savings accounts that compound interest on a yearly basis. In other words, if you deposit $100 for two years at 4 percent interest, at the end of one year you will have $104. At the end of two years, you will have the $104 plus 4 percent of that, or $108.16. Design a program that accepts an account number, the account owner's first and last names, and a balance. The program operates continuously until an appropriate sentinel value is entered for the account number. Output the projected running total balance for each account for each of the next 20 years.

10. Mr. Roper owns 20 apartment buildings. Each building contains 15 units that he rents for $800 per month each. Design the application that would output 12 payment coupons for each of the 15 apartments in each of the 20 buildings. Each coupon should contain the building number (1 through 20), the apartment number (1 through 15), the month (1 through 12), and the amount of rent due.

11. a. Design a program for the Hollywood Movie Rating Guide, in which users continuously enter a value from 0 to 4 that indicates the number of stars they are awarding to the Guide's featured movie of the week. The program executes continuously until a user enters a negative number to quit. If a user enters a star value that does not fall in the correct range, reprompt the user continuously until a correct value is entered. At the end of the program, display the average star rating for the movie.

    b. Modify the movie-rating program so that a user gets three tries to enter a valid rating. After three incorrect entries, the program issues an appropriate message and continues with a new user.

    c. Modify the movie-rating program so that the user is prompted continuously for a movie title until "ZZZZZ" is entered. Then, for each movie, continuously accept star-rating values until a negative number is entered. Display the average rating for each movie.

12. The Café Noir Coffee Shop wants some market research on its customers. When a customer places an order, a clerk asks for the customer's zip code and age. The clerk enters that data as well as the number of items the customer orders. The program operates continuously until the clerk enters a 0 for zip code at the end of the day. When the clerk enters an invalid zip code (more than 5 digits) or an invalid age (defined as less than 10 or more than 110), the program reprompts the clerk continuously.

When the clerk enters fewer than 1 or more than 12 items, the program reprompts the clerk two more times. If the clerk enters a high value on the third attempt, the program accepts the high value, but if the clerk enters a negative value on the third attempt, an error message is displayed and the order is not counted. At the end of the program, display a count of the number of items ordered by customers from the same zip code as the coffee shop (54984), and a count from other zip codes. Also display the average customer age, as well as counts of the number of items ordered by customers under 30 and by customers 30 and older.

Find the Bugs

13. Your student disk contains files named DEBUG05-01.txt, DEBUG05-02.txt, and DEBUG05-03.txt. Each file starts with some comments that describe the problem. Comments are lines that begin with two slashes (//). Following the comments, each file contains pseudocode that has one or more bugs you must find and correct.

Game Zone

14. In Chapter 2, you learned that in many programming languages you can generate a random number between 1 and a limiting value named `LIMIT` by using a statement similar to `randomNumber=random(LIMIT)`. In Chapter 4, you created the logic for a guessing game in which the application generates a random number and the player tries to guess it. Now, create the guessing game itself. After each guess, display a message indicating whether the player's guess was correct, too high, or too low. When the player eventually guesses the correct number, display a count of the number of guesses that were required.

15. Create the logic for a game that simulates rolling two dice by generating two numbers between 1 and 6 inclusive. The player chooses a number between 2 and 12 (the lowest and highest totals possible for two dice). The player then "rolls" two dice up to three times. If the number chosen by the user comes up, the user wins and the game ends. If the number does not come up within three rolls, the computer wins.

16. Create the logic for the dice game Pig, in which a player can compete with the computer. The object of the game is to be the first to score 100 points. The user and computer take turns "rolling" a pair of dice following these rules:

- On a turn, each player rolls two dice. If no 1 appears, the dice values are added to a running total for the turn, and the player can choose whether to roll again or pass the turn to the other player. When a player passes, the accumulated turn total is added to the player's game total.

- If a 1 appears on one of the dice, the player's turn total becomes 0; in other words, nothing more is added to the player's game total for that turn, and it becomes the other player's turn.

- If a 1 appears on both of the dice, not only is the player's turn over, but the player's entire accumulated total is reset to 0.

- When the computer does not roll a 1 and can choose whether to roll again, generate a random value from 1 to 2. The computer will then decide to continue when the value is 1 and decide to quit and pass the turn to the player when the value is not 1.

 Up for Discussion

17. Suppose you wrote a program that you suspect is in an infinite loop because it keeps running for several minutes with no output and without ending. What would you add to your program to help you discover the origin of the problem?

18. Suppose you know that every employee in your organization has a seven-digit ID number used for logging on to the computer system. A loop would be useful to guess every combination of seven digits in an ID. Are there any circumstances in which you should try to guess another employee's ID number?

19. If every employee in an organization had a seven-digit ID number, guessing all the possible combinations would be a relatively easy programming task. How could you alter the format of employee IDs to make them more difficult to guess?

Arrays

In this chapter, you will learn about:

◎ Arrays and how they occupy computer memory

◎ Manipulating an array to replace nested decisions

◎ Using constants with arrays

◎ Searching an array

◎ Using parallel arrays

◎ Searching an array for a range match

◎ Remaining within array bounds

◎ Using a `for` loop to process arrays

Understanding Arrays and How They Occupy Computer Memory

An **array** is a series or list of values in computer memory, all of which have the same name and data type but are differentiated with special numbers called subscripts. Usually, all the values in an array have something in common; for example, they might represent a list of employee ID numbers or a list of prices for items sold in a store. A **subscript**, also called an **index**, is a number that indicates the position of a particular item within an array.

Whenever you require multiple storage locations for physical objects, you are using a real-life counterpart of a programming array. For example, if you store important papers in a series of file folders and label each folder with a consecutive letter of the alphabet, then you are using the equivalent of an array.

When you look down the left side of a tax table to find your income level before looking to the right to find your income tax obligation, you are using an array. Similarly, if you look down the left side of a train schedule to find your station before looking to the right to find the train's arrival time, you are also using an array.

Each of these real-life arrays helps you organize real-life objects. You *could* store all your papers or mementos in one huge cardboard box, or find your tax rate or train's arrival time if both were printed randomly in one large book. However, using an organized storage and display system makes your life easier in each case. Using a programming array will accomplish the same results for your data.

 Some programmers refer to an array as a *table* or a *matrix*.

How Arrays Occupy Computer Memory

When you declare an array, you declare a structure that contains multiple data items. Each item within an array has the same name and the same data type; each separate item is one **element** of the array. Each array element occupies an area in memory next to, or contiguous to, the others. You can indicate the number of elements an array will hold—the **size of the array**—when you declare the array along with your other variables and constants. For example, you might declare an uninitialized three-element numeric array named someVals as follows:

```
num someVals[3]
```

All array elements have the same group name, but each individual element also has a unique subscript indicating how far away it is from the first element. Therefore, any array's subscripts are always

A common error by beginning programmers is to forget that array subscripts start with 0. If you assume that an array's first subscript is 1, you will always be "off by one" in your array manipulation.

 Remember that a variable can hold only one value at a time. Each array element is a single variable.

 In all languages, subscript values must be integers (whole numbers) and sequential. Some languages use 1 as the first array subscript, and some allow you to choose a starting subscript.

a sequence of integers such as 0 through 4 or 0 through 9. In most modern languages, such as Visual Basic, Java, C++, and C#, the first array element is accessed using subscript 0, and this book follows that convention.

Depending on the syntax rules of the programming language you use, you place the subscript within parentheses or square brackets following the group name. This book will use square brackets to hold array element subscripts so that you don't mistake array names for method names. Also, many newer programming languages such as C++, Java, and C# use the bracket notation.

Figure 6-1 shows an array named someVals that contains three elements, so the elements are someVals[0], someVals[1], and someVals[2]. This array's elements have been assigned values. The value stored in someVals[0] is 25; someVals[1] holds 36, and someVals[2] holds 47. The element someVals[0] is zero numbers away from the beginning of the array—in other words, it is located at the same memory address as the array. The element someVals[1] is one number away from the beginning of the array and someVals[2] is two numbers away.

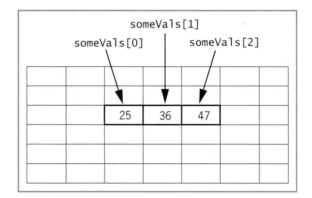

Figure 6-1 Appearance of a three-element array in computer memory

 Providing array values sometimes is called **populating the array**.

After you declare an array, you can assign values to some or all of the elements individually, as shown in the following example:

```
num someVals[3]
someVals[0] = 25
someVals[1] = 36
someVals[2] = 47
```

Alternatively, you can initialize array elements when you declare the array. Most programming languages use a statement similar to the following to declare a three-element array and assign values to it:

```
num someVals[3] = 25, 36, 47
```

When you use a list of values to initialize an array, the first value you list is assigned to the first array element, and the subsequent values are assigned in order. In other words, someVals[0] is 25, someVals[1] is 36, and someVals[2] is 47. Many programming languages allow you to initialize an array with fewer values than there are array elements declared, but no language allows you to initialize an array using more values.

After an array has been declared and appropriate values have been assigned to specific elements, you can use the elements in the same way you would use any other data item of the same type. For example, you can input values to array elements and you can output them, and if the elements are numeric, you can perform arithmetic with them.

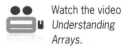

Watch the video *Understanding Arrays.*

The precise syntax used to declare an array varies. In some languages, the array size can be inferred from the size of a supplied list of initial values. For example, if you write the following, an array of four elements is created:

```
num someVals[] = 6, 8, 2, 4
```

In some languages, the brackets that indicate an array are placed following the data type, as in:

```
num[] someVals = 6, 8, 2, 4
```

Other languages require that you use terms to allocate memory or that you place the list of values between brackets. Even though the syntax used to declare arrays differs, the concepts are the same.

TWO TRUTHS & A LIE

Understanding Arrays and How They Occupy Computer Memory

1. In an array, each element has the same data type.

2. Each array element is accessed using a subscript, which can be a number or a string.

3. Array elements always occupy adjacent memory locations.

The false statement is #2. An array subscript must be a number. It can be a named constant, an unnamed constant, or a variable.

232

Manipulating an Array to Replace Nested Decisions

Consider an application requested by a Human Resources department to produce statistics on employees' claimed dependents. The department wants a report that lists the number of employees who have claimed 0, 1, 2, 3, 4, or 5 dependents. (Assume you know that no employees have more than five dependents.) For example, Figure 6-2 shows a typical report.

Without using an array, you could write the application that produces counts for the six categories of dependents (for each number of dependents, 0 through 5) by using a series of decisions. Figure 6-3 shows the pseudocode and flowchart for the decision-making part of such an application. Although this program works, its length and complexity are unnecessary once you understand how to use an array.

Dependents	Count
0	43
1	35
2	24
3	11
4	5
5	7

Figure 6-2   Typical Dependents report

In Figure 6-3, the variable dep is compared to 0. If it is 0, 1 is added to count0. If it is not 0, then dep is compared to 1. It is either added to count1 or compared to 2, and so on. Each time the application executes this decision-making process, 1 is added to one of the five variables that acts as a counter for one of the possible numbers of dependents. The dependent-counting application in Figure 6-3 works, but even with only six categories of dependents, the decision-making process is unwieldy. What if the number of dependents might be any value from 0 to 10, or 0 to 20? With either of these scenarios, the basic logic of the program would remain the same; however, you would need to declare many additional variables to hold the counts, and you would need many additional decisions.

The decision-making process in Figure 6-3 accomplishes its purpose, and the logic is correct, but the process is cumbersome and certainly not recommended. Follow the logic here so that you understand how the application works. In the next pages, you will see how to make the application more elegant.

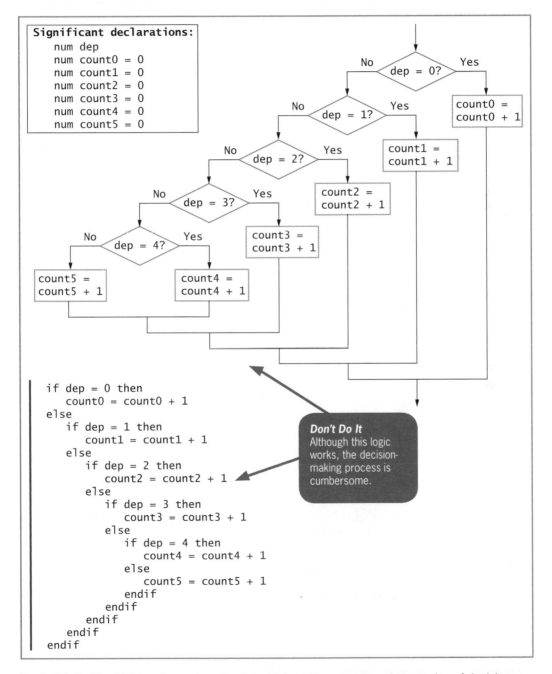

```
if dep = 0 then
    count0 = count0 + 1
else
    if dep = 1 then
        count1 = count1 + 1
    else
        if dep = 2 then
            count2 = count2 + 1
        else
            if dep = 3 then
                count3 = count3 + 1
            else
                if dep = 4 then
                    count4 = count4 + 1
                else
                    count5 = count5 + 1
                endif
            endif
        endif
    endif
endif
```

Don't Do It
Although this logic works, the decision-making process is cumbersome.

Figure 6-3 Flowchart and pseudocode of decision-making process using a series of decisions—the hard way

Using an array provides an alternate approach to this programming problem, which greatly reduces the number of statements you need. When you declare an array, you provide a group name for a number of associated variables in memory. For example, the six dependent count accumulators can be redefined as a single array named count. The individual elements become count[0], count[1], count[2], count[3], count[4], and count[5], as shown in the revised decision-making process in Figure 6-4.

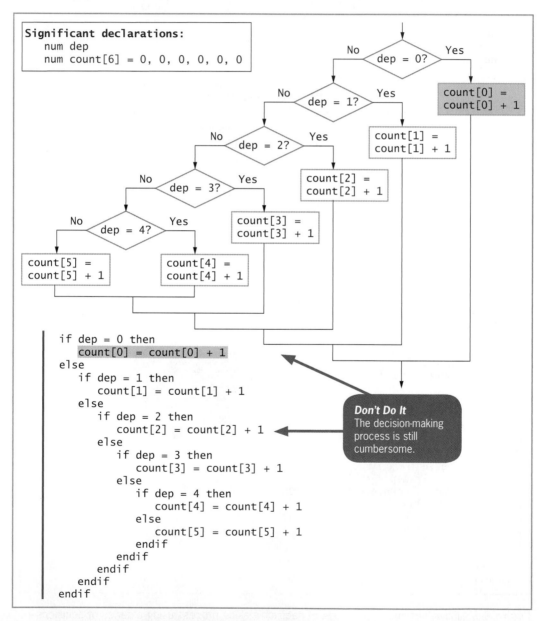

Figure 6-4   Flowchart and pseudocode of decision-making process—but still the hard way

The shaded statement in Figure 6-4 shows that when dep is 0, 1 is added to count[0]. You can see similar statements for the rest of the count elements; when dep is 1, 1 is added to count[1]; when dep is 2, 1 is added to count[2], and so on. When the dep value is 5, it means it was not 1, 2, 3, or 4, so 1 is added to count[5]. In other words, 1 is added to one of the elements of the count array instead of to an individual variable named count0, count1, count2, count3, count4, or count5. Is this version a big improvement over the original in Figure 6-3? Of course, it isn't. You still have not taken advantage of the benefits of using the array in this application.

The true benefit of using an array lies in your ability to use a variable as a subscript to the array, instead of using a literal constant such as 0 or 5. Notice in the logic in Figure 6-4 that within each decision, the value you are comparing to dep and the constant you are using as a subscript in the resulting "Yes" process are always identical. That is, when dep is 0, the subscript used to add 1 to the count array is 0; when dep is 1, the subscript used for the count array is 1, and so on. Therefore, you can just use dep as a subscript to the array. You can rewrite the decision-making process as shown in Figure 6-5.

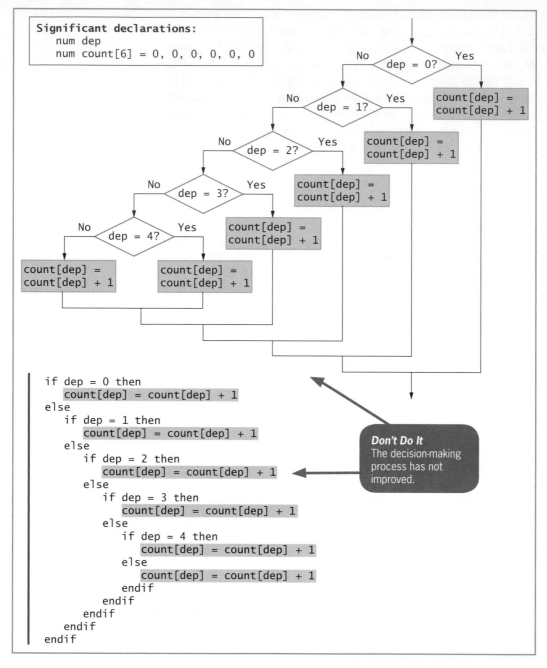

Figure 6-5 Flowchart and pseudocode of decision-making process using an array—but still a hard way

The code segment in Figure 6-5 looks no more efficient than the one in Figure 6-4. However, notice the shaded statements in Figure 6-5—the process that occurs after each decision is exactly the same. In each case, no matter what the value of dep is, you always add 1 to count[dep]. If you will always take the same action no matter what the answer to a question is, why ask the question? Instead, you can rewrite the decision-making process, as shown in Figure 6-6.

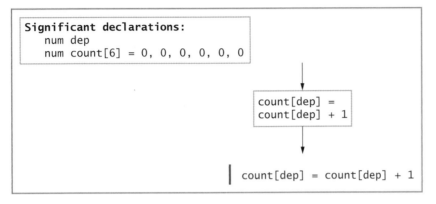

```
Significant declarations:
   num dep
   num count[6] = 0, 0, 0, 0, 0, 0
```

count[dep] =
count[dep] + 1

count[dep] = count[dep] + 1

Figure 6-6 Flowchart and pseudocode of efficient decision-making process using an array

The single statement in Figure 6-6 eliminates the *entire* decision-making process that was the original highlighted section in Figure 6-5! When dep is 2, 1 is added to count⌊2⌋; when dep is 4, 1 is added to count[4], and so on. *Now* you have a big improvement to the original process. What's more, this process does not change whether there are 20, 30, or any other number of possible categories. To use more than five accumulators, you would declare additional count elements in the array, but the categorizing logic would remain the same as it is in Figure 6-6.

Figure 6-7 shows an entire program that takes advantage of the array to produce the report that shows counts for dependent categories. Variables and constants are declared and, in the getReady() module, a first value for dep is entered into the program. In the countDependents() module, 1 is added to the appropriate element of the count array and the next value is input. The loop in the mainline logic in Figure 6-7 is an indefinite loop; it continues as long as the user does not enter the sentinel value. When data entry is complete, the finishUp() module displays the report. First, the heading is output, then dep is reset to 0, and each dep and count[dep] are output in a loop. The first output statement contains 0 (as the number of dependents) and the value stored in count[0]. Then, 1 is added to dep and the same set of instructions is used again to display the counts for each number of dependents. The loop in the finishUp() module is a definite loop; it executes precisely six times.

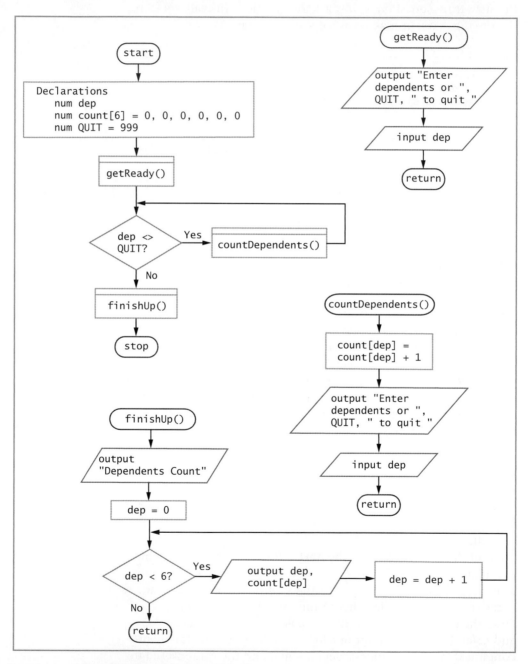

Figure 6-7   Flowchart and pseudocode for Dependents Report program

```
start
   Declarations
      num dep
      num count[6] = 0, 0, 0, 0, 0, 0
      num QUIT = 999
   getReady()
   while dep <> QUIT
      countDependents()
   endwhile
   finishUp()
stop

getReady()
   output "Enter dependents or ", QUIT, " to quit "
   input dep
return

countDependents()
   count[dep] = count[dep] + 1
   output "Enter dependents or ", QUIT, " to quit "
   input dep
return

finishUp()
   output "Dependents Count"
   dep = 0
   while dep < 6
      output dep, count[dep]
      dep = dep + 1
   endwhile
return
```

 Watch the video *Accumulating Values in an Array.*

Figure 6-7 Flowchart and pseudocode for Dependents Report program (continued)

The dependent-counting program would have *worked* when it contained a long series of decisions and output statements, but the program is easier to write when you use an array and access its values using the number of dependents as a subscript. Additionally, the new program is more efficient, easier for other programmers to understand, and easier to maintain. Arrays are never mandatory, but often they can drastically cut down on your programming time and make your logic easier to understand.

 Learning to use arrays correctly can make many programming tasks far more efficient and professional. When you understand how to use arrays, you will be able to provide elegant solutions to problems that otherwise would require tedious programming steps.

240

TWO TRUTHS & A LIE

Manipulating an Array to Replace Nested Decisions

1. You can use an array to replace a long series of decisions.

2. You realize a major benefit to using arrays when you use a numeric constant as a subscript as opposed to using a variable.

3. The process of displaying every element in a 10-element array is basically no different from displaying every element in a 100-element array.

The false statement is #2. You realize a major benefit to using arrays when you use a variable as a subscript as opposed to using a constant.

Using Constants with Arrays

In Chapter 2, you learned that named constants hold values that do not change during a program's execution. When working with arrays, you can use constants in several ways:

- To hold the size of an array

- As the array values

- As a subscript

Using a Constant as the Size of an Array

The program in Figure 6-7 still contains one minor flaw. Throughout this book you have learned to avoid "magic numbers;" that is, unnamed constants. As the totals are output in the loop at the end of the program in Figure 6-7, the array subscript is compared to the constant 6. The program can be improved if you use a named constant instead. In most programming languages you can take one of two approaches:

- You can declare a named numeric constant such as num ARRAY_SIZE = 6. Then you can use this constant every time you access the array, always making sure any subscript you use remains less than the constant value.

- In many languages, when you declare an array, a constant that represents the array size is automatically provided for each array you create. For example, in Java, after you declare an array named `count`, its size is stored in a field named `count.length`. In both C# and Visual Basic, the array size is `count.Length`. (The difference is the uppercase "L" in `Length`.)

 Besides making your code easier to modify, using a named constant makes the code easier to understand.

Using Constants as Array Element Values

Sometimes the values stored in arrays should be constants. For example, suppose you create an array that holds names for the months of the year. The first month is always "January"—the value should not change. You might create an array as follows:

```
string MONTH[12] = "January", "February", "March", "April",
    "May", "June", "July", "August", "September", "October",
    "November", "December"
```

 Recall that the convention in this book is to use all upper-case letters in constant identifiers.

Using a Constant as an Array Subscript

Occasionally you will want to use a numeric constant as a subscript to an array. For example, to display the first value in an array named `salesArray`, you might write a statement that uses an unnamed, literal constant as follows:

```
output salesArray[0]
```

You might also have occasion to use a named constant as a subscript. For example, if `salesArray` holds sales values for each of 20 branches in your company, and Indiana is state 5, you could output the value for Indiana as follows:

```
output salesArray[5]
```

However, if you declare a named constant as `num INDIANA = 5`, then you can display the same value using this statement:

```
output salesArray[INDIANA]
```

An advantage to using a named constant in this case is that the statement becomes self-documenting—anyone who reads your statement more easily understands that your intention is to display the sales value for Indiana.

TWO TRUTHS & A LIE

Using Constants with Arrays

1. If you create a named constant equal to an array size, you can use it as a subscript to the array.

2. If you create a named constant equal to an array size, you can use it as a limit against which to compare subscript values.

3. In Java, C#, and Visual Basic, when you declare an array, a constant that represents the array size is automatically provided.

The false statement is #1. If the constant is equal to the array size, then it is larger than any valid array subscript.

Searching an Array

In the dependent-counting application in this chapter, the array's subscript variable conveniently held small whole numbers—the number of dependents allowed was 0 through 5—and the dep variable directly accessed the array. Unfortunately, real life doesn't always happen in small integers. Sometimes you don't have a variable that conveniently holds an array position; sometimes you have to search through an array to find a value you need.

Consider a mail-order business in which orders come in with a customer name, address, item number, and quantity ordered. Assume the item numbers from which a customer can choose are three-digit numbers, but perhaps they are not consecutively numbered 001 through 999. Instead, over the years, items have been deleted and new items have been added to the inventory. For example, there might no longer be an item with number 105 or 129. Sometimes there might be a hundred-number gap or more between items. For example, let's say that this season you are offering only six items: 106, 108, 307, 405, 457, and 688. In an office without a computer, if a customer orders item 307, a clerical worker can tell whether the order is valid by looking down the list and verifying that 307 is on it. In a similar fashion, a computer program can use a loop to test the ordered item number against each VALID_ITEM. When you search through a list from one end to the other, you are performing a **linear search**. See Figure 6-8.

In a similar fashion, a computer program can use a loop to test the ordered item number against each VALID_ITEM. In Figure 6-8, the six valid items are shown in the shaded array declaration VALID_ITEM. (The array is declared as constant because the item numbers will never change.) You could use a series of six decisions to compare each customer order's item number to each of the six allowed values. However, a superior approach is to create an array that holds the list of valid item numbers. Then you can search through the array for an exact match to the ordered item. If you search through the entire array without finding a match for the item the customer ordered, you can take action. For example, the program in Figure 6-8 displays an error message and adds 1 to a counter of bad items.

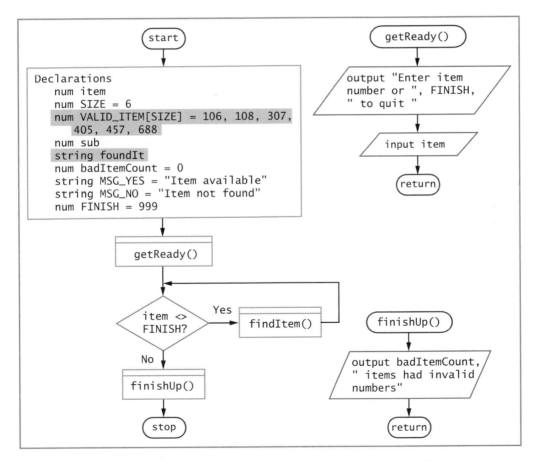

Figure 6-8 Flowchart and pseudocode for program that verifies item availability

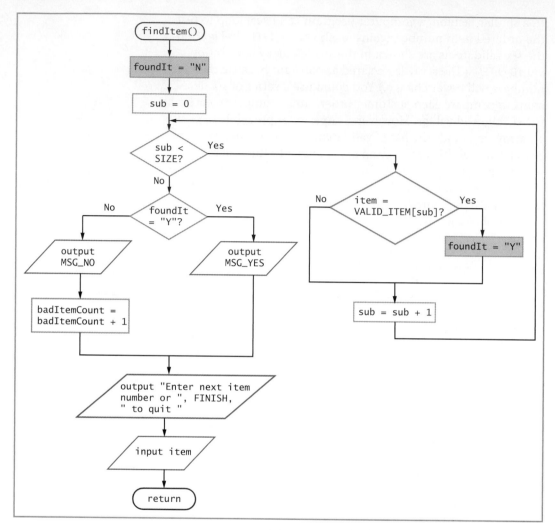

Figure 6-8 Flowchart and pseudocode for program that verifies item availability (continued)

```
start
   Declarations
      num item
      num SIZE = 6
      num VALID_ITEM[SIZE] = 106, 108, 307,
         405, 457, 688
      num sub
      string foundIt
      num badItemCount = 0
      string MSG_YES = "Item available"
      string MSG_NO = "Item not found"
      num FINISH = 999
   getReady()
   while item <> FINISH
      findItem()
   endwhile
   finishUp()
stop

getReady()
   output "Enter item number or ", FINISH, " to quit "
   input item
return

findItem()
   foundIt = "N"
   sub = 0
   while sub < SIZE
      if item = VALID_ITEM[sub] then
         foundIt = "Y"
      endif
      sub = sub + 1
   endwhile
   if foundIt = "Y" then
      output MSG_YES
   else
      output MSG_NO
      badItemCount = badItemCount + 1
   endif
   output "Enter next item number or ", FINISH, " to quit "
   input item
return

finishUp()
   output badItemCount, " items had invalid numbers"
return
```

Figure 6-8 Flowchart and pseudocode for program that verifies item availability (continued)

245

246

Instead of the string `foundIt` variable in the method in Figure 6-8, you might prefer to use a numeric variable that you set to 1 or 0. Most programming languages also support a Boolean data type that you can use for `foundIt`; when you declare a variable to be Boolean, you can set its value to true or false.

The technique for verifying that an item number exists involves setting a subscript to 0 and setting a flag variable to indicate that you have not yet determined whether the customer's order is valid. A **flag** is a variable that you set to indicate whether some event has occurred; frequently it holds a true or false value. For example, you can set a string variable named `foundIt` to "N", indicating "No". (See the first shaded statement in the `findItem()` method in Figure 6-8.) Then you compare the customer's ordered item number to the first item in the array. If the customer-ordered item matches the first item in the array, you can set the flag variable to "Y", or any other value that is not "N". (See the last shaded statement in the `findItem()` method in Figure 6-8.) If the items do not match, you increase the subscript and continue to look down the list of numbers stored in the array. If you check all six valid item numbers and the customer item matches none of them, then the flag variable `foundIt` still holds the value "N". If the flag variable is "N" after you have looked through the entire list, you can issue an error message indicating that no match was found.

TWO TRUTHS & A LIE

Searching an Array

1. Only whole numbers can be stored in arrays.

2. Only whole numbers can be used as array subscripts.

3. A flag is a variable that you set to indicate whether some event has occurred.

The false statement is #1. Whole numbers can be stored in arrays, but so can many other objects, including strings and numbers with decimal places.

Using Parallel Arrays

When you read a customer's order in a mail-order company program, you usually want to accomplish more than simply verifying the item's existence. For example, you might want to determine the price of the ordered item, multiply that price by the quantity ordered, and display the amount owed.

Suppose you have a list of item numbers and their associated prices. One array named VALID_ITEM contains six elements; each element is a valid item number. The other array also has six elements. The array is named VALID_PRICE; each element is a price of an item. Each price in the VALID_PRICE array is conveniently and purposely in the same position as the corresponding item number in the VALID_ITEM array. Two corresponding arrays such as these are **parallel arrays** because each element in one array is associated with the element in the same relative position in the other array. Figure 6-9 shows how the parallel arrays might look in computer memory.

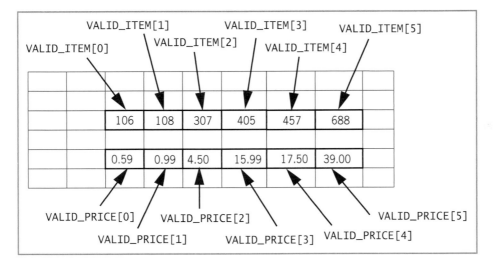

Figure 6-9   Parallel arrays in memory

When you use parallel arrays:

- Two or more arrays contain related data.

- A subscript relates the arrays. That is, elements at the same position in each array are logically related.

Figure 6-10 shows a program that declares parallel arrays. The VALID_PRICE array is shaded; each element in it corresponds to a valid item number.

When you create parallel arrays, each array can be a different data type.

248

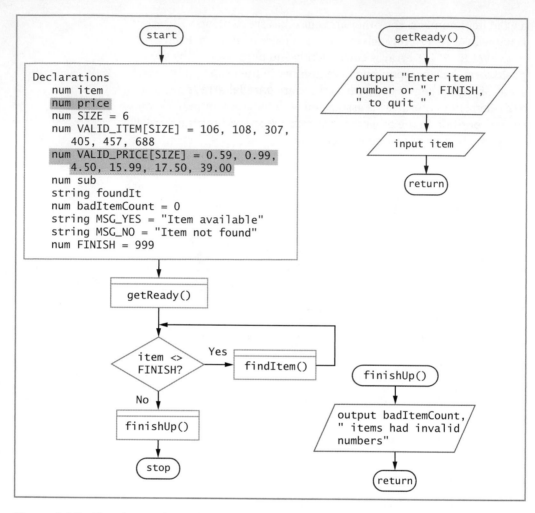

Figure 6-10   Flowchart and pseudocode of program that finds an item price using parallel arrays

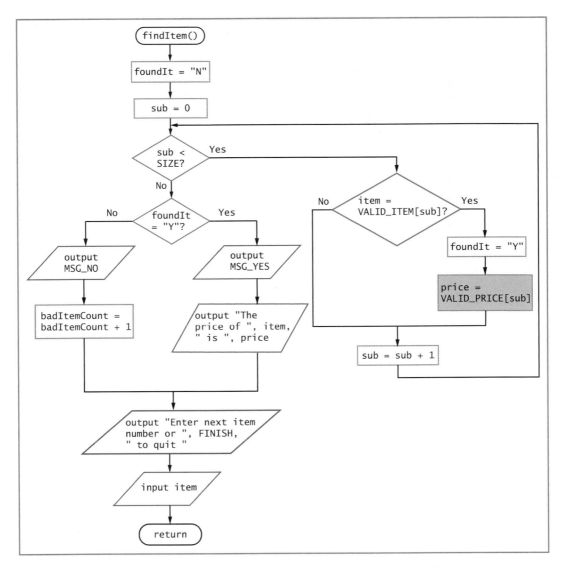

Figure 6-10 Flowchart and pseudocode of program that finds an item price using parallel arrays (continued)

```
start
    Declarations
        num item
        num price
        num SIZE = 6
        num VALID_ITEM[SIZE] = 106, 108, 307,
            405, 457, 688
        num VALID_PRICE[SIZE] = 0.59, 0.99,
            4.50, 15.99, 17.50, 39.00
        num sub
        string foundIt
        num badItemCount = 0
        string MSG_YES = "Item available"
        string MSG_NO = "Item not found"
        num FINISH = 999
    getReady()
    while item <> FINISH
        findItem()
    endwhile
    finishUp()
stop

getReady()
    output "Enter item number or ", FINISH, " to quit "
    input item
return

findItem()
    foundIt = "N"
    sub = 0
    while sub < SIZE
        if item = VALID_ITEM[sub] then
            foundIt = "Y"
            price = VALID_PRICE[sub]
        endif
        sub = sub + 1
    endwhile
    if foundIt = "Y" then
        output MSG_YES
        output "The price of ", item, " is ", price
    else
        output MSG_NO
        badItemCount = badItemCount + 1
    endif
    output "Enter next item number or ", FINISH, " to quit "
    input item
return

finishUp()
    output badItemCount, " items had invalid numbers"
return
```

Figure 6-10   Flowchart and pseudocode of program that finds an item price using parallel arrays (continued)

Some programmers object to using a cryptic variable name for a subscript, such as sub in Figure 6-10, because such names are not descriptive. These programmers would prefer a name like `priceIndex`. Others approve of short names when the variable is used only in a limited area of a program, as it is used here, to step through an array. Programmers disagree on many style issues like this one. As a programmer, it is your responsibility to find out what conventions are used among your peers in an organization.

As the program in Figure 6-10 receives a customer's order, it looks through each of the VALID_ITEM values separately by varying the subscript sub from 0 to the number of items available. When a match for the item number is found, the program pulls the corresponding parallel price out of the list of VALID_PRICE values and stores it in the price variable. (See shaded statements in Figure 6-10.)

The relationship between an item's number and its price is an **indirect relationship**. That means you don't access a price directly by knowing the item number. Instead, you determine the price by knowing an item number's position. Once you find a match for the ordered item number in the VALID_ITEM array, you know that the price of that item is in the same position in the other array, VALID_PRICE. When VALID_ITEM[sub] is the correct item, VALID_PRICE[sub] must be the correct price, so sub links the parallel arrays.

Parallel arrays are most useful when value pairs have an indirect relationship. If values in your program have a direct relationship, you probably don't need parallel arrays. For example, if items were numbered 0, 1, 2, 3, and so on consecutively, you could use the item number as a subscript to the price array instead of using a parallel array to hold item numbers. Even if the items were numbered 200, 201, 202, and so on consecutively, you could subtract a constant value (200) from each and use that as a subscript instead of using parallel arrays.

Suppose that a customer orders item 457. Walk through the logic yourself to see if you come up with the correct price per item, $17.50. Then, suppose that a customer orders item 458. Walk through the logic and see whether the appropriate "Item not found" message is displayed.

Improving Search Efficiency

The mail-order program in Figure 6-10 is still a little inefficient. If many customers order item 106 or 108, the prices are found on the first or second pass through the loop. However, the program continues searching through the item array until sub reaches the value SIZE. One way to stop the search when the item has been found and foundIt is set to "Y" is to change the loop-controlling question. Instead of simply continuing the loop while the number of comparisons does not exceed the array size, you should continue the loop while the searched item is not found *and* the number of comparisons has not exceeded the array size. Leaving a loop as soon as a match is found improves the program's efficiency. The larger the array, the more beneficial it becomes to exit the searching loop as soon as you find the desired value.

Figure 6-11 shows the improved version of the findItem() module with the altered loop-controlling question shaded.

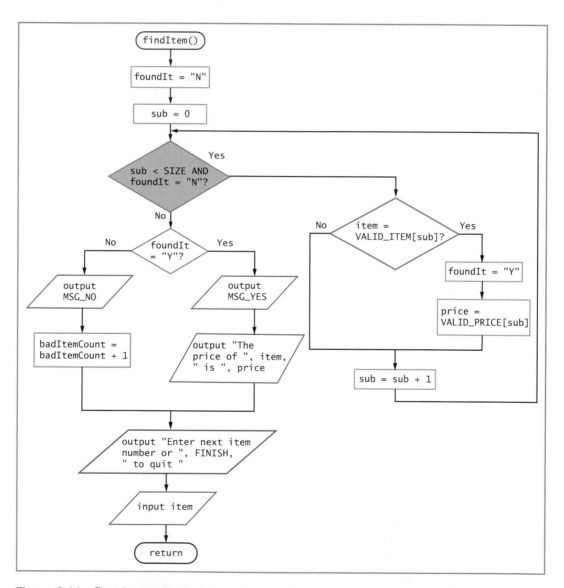

Figure 6-11   Flowchart and pseudocode of the module that finds an item price, exiting the loop as soon as it is found

Watch the video *Using Parallel Arrays*.

```
findItem()
   foundIt = "N"
   sub = 0
   while sub < SIZE AND foundIt = "N"
      if item = VALID_ITEM[sub] then
         foundIt = "Y"
         price = VALID_PRICE[sub]
      endif
      sub = sub + 1
   endwhile
   if foundIt = "Y" then
      output MSG_YES
      output "The price of ", item, " is ", price
   else
      output MSG_NO
      badItemCount = badItemCount + 1
   endif
   output "Enter next item number or ", FINISH, " to quit "
   input item
return
```

253

Figure 6-11 Flowchart and pseudocode of the module that finds an item price, exiting the loop as soon as it is found (continued)

 Notice that the price-finding program is most efficient when the most frequently ordered items are stored at the beginning of the array. Only the seldom-ordered items require loops before finding a match. Often, you can improve sort efficiency by rearranging array elements.

 As you study programming, you will learn search techniques other than a linear search. For example, a **binary search** starts looking in the middle of a sorted list, and then determines whether it should continue higher or lower.

TWO TRUTHS & A LIE

Using Parallel Arrays

1. Parallel arrays must be the same data type.

2. Parallel arrays usually contain the same number of elements.

3. You can improve the efficiency of searching through parallel arrays by using an early exit.

The false statement is #1. Parallel arrays do not need to be the same data type. For example, you might look up a name in a string array to find each person's age in a parallel numeric array.

Searching an Array for a Range Match

Customer order item numbers need to match available item numbers exactly to determine the correct price of an item. Sometimes, however, programmers want to work with ranges of values in arrays. In Chapter 4, you learned that a range of values is any series of values—for example, 1 through 5 or 20 through 30.

Suppose a company decides to offer quantity discounts when a customer orders multiple items, as shown in Figure 6-12.

Quantity	Discount %
0–8	0
9–12	10
13–25	15
26 or more	20

You want to be able to read in customer order data and determine a discount percentage based on the value in the quantity field. For example, if a customer has ordered 20 items, you want to be able to output "Your discount is 15 percent". One ill-advised approach might be to set up an array with as many elements as any customer might ever order, and store the appropriate discount for each possible number, as shown in Figure 6-13. This array is set up to contain the discount for 0 items, 1 item, 2 items, and so on. This approach has at least three drawbacks:

Figure 6-12   Discounts on orders by quantity

- It requires a very large array that uses a lot of memory.

- You must store the same value repeatedly. For example, each of the first nine elements receives the same value, 0, and each of the next four elements receives the same value, 10.

- How do you know you have enough array elements? Is a customer order quantity of 75 items enough? What if a customer orders 100 or 1000 items? No matter how many elements you place in the array, there's always a chance that a customer will order more.

```
numeric DISCOUNT[76]
  = 0, 0, 0, 0, 0, 0, 0, 0, 0,
     0.10, 0.10, 0.10, 0.10,
     0.15, 0.15, 0.15, 0.15, 0.15,
     0.15, 0.15, 0.15, 0.15, 0.15,
     0.15, 0.15, 0.15,
     0.20, 0.20, 0.20, 0.20, 0.20,
     0.20, 0.20, 0.20, 0.20, 0.20,
     0.20, 0.20, 0.20, 0.20, 0.20,
     0.20, 0.20, 0.20, 0.20, 0.20,
     0.20, 0.20, 0.20, 0.20, 0.20,
     0.20, 0.20, 0.20, 0.20, 0.20,
     0.20, 0.20, 0.20, 0.20, 0.20,
     0.20, 0.20, 0.20, 0.20, 0.20,
     0.20, 0.20, 0.20, 0.20, 0.20,
     0.20, 0.20, 0.20, 0.20, 0.20
```

Don't Do It
Although this array is usable, it is repetitious, prone to error, and difficult to use.

Figure 6-13 Usable—but inefficient—discount array

A better approach is to create two parallel arrays, each with four elements, as shown in Figure 6-14. Each

```
num DISCOUNT[4]  =    0, 0.10, 0.15, 0.20
num QUAN_LIMIT[4] = 0,    9,   13,   26
```

Figure 6-14 Parallel arrays to use for determining discount

discount rate is listed once in the DISCOUNT array, and the low end of each quantity range is listed in the QUAN_LIMIT array.

To find the correct discount for any customer's ordered quantity, you can start with the *last* quantity range limit (QUAN_LIMIT[3]). If the quantity ordered is at least that value, 26, the loop is never entered and the customer gets the highest discount rate (DISCOUNT[3], or 20 percent). If the quantity ordered is not at least QUAN_LIMIT[3]— that is, if it is less than 26—then you reduce the subscript and check to see if the quantity is at least QUAN_LIMIT[2], or 13. If so, the customer receives DISCOUNT[2], or 15 percent, and so on. Figure 6-15 shows a program that accepts a customer's quantity ordered and determines the appropriate discount rate.

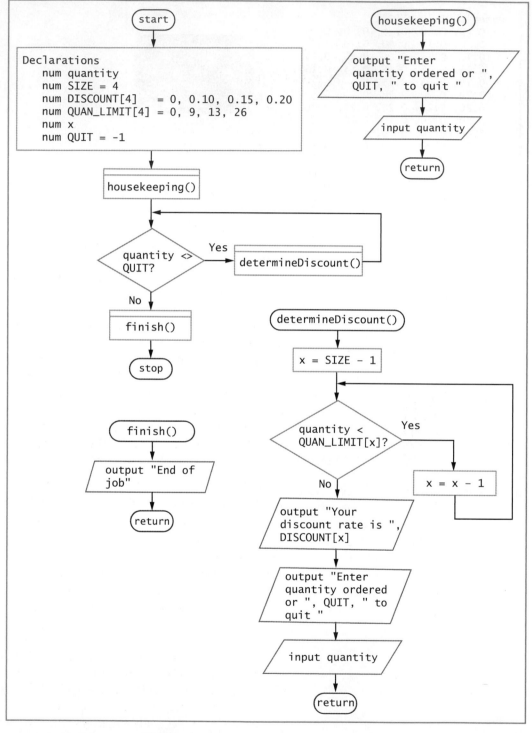

Figure 6-15　Program that determines discount rate

```
start
   Declarations
      num quantity
      num SIZE = 4
      num DISCOUNT[4] =    0, 0.10, 0.15, 0.20
      num QUAN_LIMIT[4] = 0,    9,   13,   26
      num x
      num QUIT = -1
   housekeeping()
   while quantity <> QUIT
     determineDiscount()
   endwhile
   finish()
stop

housekeeping()
   output "Enter quantity ordered or ", QUIT, " to quit "
   input quantity
return

determineDiscount()
   x = SIZE - 1
   while quantity < QUAN_LIMIT[x]
      x = x - 1
   endwhile
   output "Your discount rate is ", DISCOUNT[x]
   output "Enter quantity ordered or ", QUIT, " to quit "
   input quantity
return

finish()
   output "End of job"
return
```

Figure 6-15   Program that determines discount rate (continued)

An alternate approach to the one taken in Figure 6-15 is to store the high end of every range in an array. Then you start with the *lowest* element and check for values *less than or equal to* each array element value.

When using an array to store range limits, you use a loop to make a series of comparisons that would otherwise require many separate decisions. The program that determines customer discount rates is written using fewer instructions than would be required if you did not use an array, and modifications to your method will be easier to make in the future.

257

TWO TRUTHS & A LIE

Searching an Array for a Range Match

1. To help locate a range within which a value falls, you can store the highest value in each range in an array.

2. To help locate a range within which a value falls, you can store the lowest value in each range in an array.

3. When using an array to store range limits, you use a series of comparisons that would otherwise require many separate loop structures.

The false statement is #3. When using an array to store range limits, you use a loop to make a series of comparisons that would otherwise require many separate decisions.

Remaining within Array Bounds

Every array has a finite size. You can think of an array's size in one of two ways—either by the number of elements in the array or by the number of bytes in the array. Arrays are always composed of elements of the same data type, and elements of the same data type always occupy the same number of bytes of memory, so the number of bytes in an array is always a multiple of the number of elements in an array. For example, in Java, integers occupy 4 bytes of memory, so an array of 10 integers occupies exactly 40 bytes.

In every programming language, when you access data stored in an array, it is important to use a subscript containing a value that accesses memory occupied by the array. For example, examine the program in Figure 6-16. The method accepts a numeric value for monthNum and displays the name associated with that month.

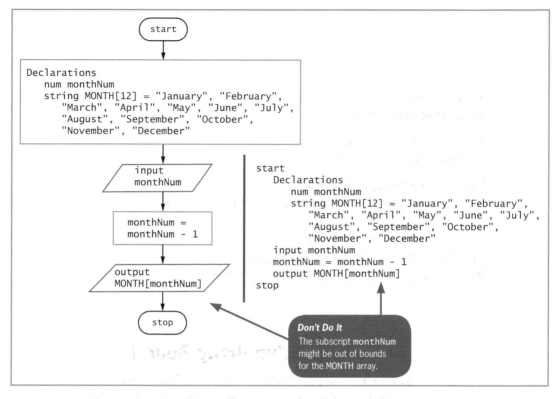

Figure 6-16 Determining the month string from user's numeric entry

In the program in Figure 6-16, notice that 1 is subtracted from monthNum when it is used as a subscript. Although most people think of January as month 1, its name occupies the location in the array with the 0 subscript. With values that seem naturally to start with 1, like month numbers, some programmers would prefer to create a 13-element array and simply never use the zero-position element. That way, each "natural" month number would be the correct value to access its data without subtracting. Other programmers dislike wasting memory by creating an extra, unused element. Although workable programs can be created with or without the extra array element, professional programmers should follow the conventions and preferences of their colleagues and managers.

The logic in Figure 6-16 makes a questionable assumption: that every number entered by the user is a valid month number. If the user enters a number that is too small or too large, one of two things will happen depending on the programming language you use. When you use a subscript value that is negative or higher than the number of elements in an array:

- Some programming languages will stop execution of the program and issue an error message.

A user might enter an invalid number, or might not enter a number at all. In Chapter 5, you learned that many languages have a built-in method with a name like `isNumeric()` that can test for such mistakes.

- Other programming languages will not issue an error message but will access a value in a memory location that is outside the area occupied by the array. That area might contain garbage, or worse, it accidentally might contain the name of an incorrect month.

Either way, a logical error occurs. When you use a subscript that is not within the range of acceptable subscripts, your subscript is said to be **out of bounds**. Users enter incorrect data frequently; a good program should be able to handle the mistake and not allow the subscript to be out of bounds.

You can improve the program in Figure 6-16 by adding a test that ensures the subscript used to access the array is within the array bounds. After you test the input value to ensure it is between 1 and 12 inclusive, you might take one of the following approaches if it is not:

- Display an error message and end the program.

- Use a default value for the month. For example, when an entered month is invalid, you might want to use a default value of December.

- Continuously reprompt the user for a new value until it is valid.

Which technique you use depends on the requirements of your program.

TWO TRUTHS & A LIE

Remaining Within Array Bounds

1. Elements in an array frequently are different data types, so calculating the amount of memory the array occupies is difficult.

2. If you attempt to access an array with a subscript that is too small, some programming languages will stop execution of the program and issue an error message.

3. If you attempt to access an array with a subscript that is too large, some programming languages access an incorrect memory location outside the array bounds.

The false statement is #1. Array elements are always the same data type, and elements of the same data type always occupy the same number of bytes of memory, so the number of bytes in an array is always a multiple of the number of elements in an array.

Using a for Loop to Process Arrays

In Chapter 5, you learned about the for loop—a loop that, in a single statement, initializes a loop control variable, compares it to a limit, and alters it. The for loop is a particularly convenient tool when working with arrays because you frequently need to process every element of an array from beginning to end. As with a while loop, when you use a for loop, you must be careful to stay within array bounds, remembering that the highest usable array subscript is one less than the size of the array. Figure 6-17 shows a for loop that correctly displays all the department names in an array declared as DEPTS. Notice that dep is incremented through one less than the number of departments because with a five-item array, the subscripts you can use are 0 through 4.

```
start
    Declarations
        num dep
        num SIZE = 5
        string DEPTS[SIZE] = "Accounting", "Personnel",
            "Technical", "Customer Service", "Marketing"
    for dep = 0 to SIZE - 1 step 1
        output DEPTS[dep]
    endfor
stop
```

Figure 6-17 Pseudocode that uses a for loop to display an array of department names

The loop in Figure 6-17 is slightly inefficient because, as it executes five times, the subtraction operation that deducts 1 from SIZE occurs each time. Five subtraction operations do not consume much computer power or time, but in a loop that processes thousands or millions of array elements, the program's efficiency would be compromised. Figure 6-18 shows a superior solution. A new constant called ARRAY_LIMIT is calculated once, then used repeatedly in the comparison operation to determine when to stop cycling through the array.

```
start
    Declarations
        num dep
        num SIZE = 5
        num ARRAY_LIMIT = SIZE - 1
        string DEPTS[SIZE] = "Accounting", "Personnel",
            "Technical", "Customer Service", "Marketing"
    for dep = 0 to ARRAY_LIMIT step 1
        output DEPTS[dep]
    endfor
stop
```

Figure 6-18 Pseudocode that uses a more efficient for loop to output department names

262

TWO TRUTHS & A LIE

Using a for Loop to Process Arrays

1.   The for loop is a particularly convenient tool when working with arrays.

2.   You frequently need to process every element of an array from beginning to end.

3.   An advantage to using a for loop to process array elements is that you don't need to be concerned about array bounds.

The false statement is #3. As with a while loop, when you use a for loop, you must be careful to stay within array bounds.

Chapter Summary

- An array is a series or list of values in computer memory, all of which have the same name and data type but are differentiated with special numbers called subscripts. Each array element occupies an area in memory next to, or contiguous to, the others.

- You often can use a variable as a subscript to an array, which allows you to replace multiple nested decisions with many fewer statements.

- Constants can be used to hold an array's size or to represent its values. Using a named constant for an array's size makes the code easier to understand and less likely to contain an error. Array values are declared as constant when they should not change during program execution.

- Searching through an array to find a value you need involves initializing a subscript, using a loop to test each array element, and setting a flag when a match is found.

- With parallel arrays, each element in one array is associated with the element in the same relative position in the other array.

- When you need to compare a value to a range of values in an array, you can store either the low- or high-end value of each range for comparison.

- When you access data stored in an array, it is important to use a subscript containing a value that accesses memory occupied by the array. When you use a subscript that is not within the defined range of acceptable subscripts, your subscript is said to be out of bounds.

- The for loop is a particularly convenient tool when working with arrays because you frequently need to process every element of an array from beginning to end.

Key Terms

An **array** is a series or list of values in computer memory, all of which have the same name but are differentiated with special numbers called subscripts.

A **subscript**, also called an **index**, is a number that indicates the position of a particular item within an array.

An **element** is a single data item in an array.

The **size of the array** is the number of elements it can hold.

Populating an array is the act of assigning values to the array elements.

A **linear search** is a search through a list from one end to the other.

A **flag** is a variable that you set to indicate whether some event has occurred.

In **parallel arrays**, each element in one array is associated with the element in the same relative position in the other array(s).

An **indirect relationship** describes the relationship between parallel arrays in which an element in the first array does not directly access its corresponding value in the second array.

A **binary search** is one that starts in the middle of a sorted list, and then determines whether it should continue higher or lower to find a target value.

Out of bounds describes an array subscript that is not within the range of acceptable subscripts for the array.

Review Questions

1. A subscript is a(n) _____.

   a. element in an array

   b. alternate name for an array

   c. number that represents the highest value stored within an array

   d. number that indicates the position of an array element

2. Each variable in an array must have the same _____ as the others.

   a. data type

   b. subscript

   c. value

   d. memory location

3. Each data item in an array is called a(n) _____.

   a. data type

   b. subscript

   c. component

   d. element

4. The subscripts of any array are always _____.

   a. integers

   b. fractions

   c. characters

   d. strings of characters

5. Suppose you have an array named number, and two of its elements are number[1] and number[4]. You know that _____.

   a. the two elements hold the same value

   b. the array holds exactly four elements

   c. there are exactly two elements between those two elements

   d. the two elements are at the same memory location

6. Suppose you want to write a program that inputs customer data and displays a summary of the number of customers who owe more than $1000 each, in each of 12 sales regions. Customer data variables include name, zipCode, balanceDue, and regionNumber. At some point during record processing, you would add 1 to an array element whose subscript would be represented by _____.

   a. name

   b. zipCode

   c. balanceDue

   d. regionNumber

7. The most useful type of subscript for manipulating arrays is a _____.

   a. numeric constant

   b. variable

   c. character

   d. filename

8. A program contains a seven-element array that holds the names of the days of the week. At the start of the program, you display the day names using a subscript named dayNum. You display the same array values again at the end of the program, where you _____ as a subscript to the array.

   a. must use dayNum

   b. can use dayNum, but can also use another variable

   c. must not use dayNum

   d. must use a numeric constant instead of a variable

9. Suppose you have declared an array as follows:
   num values[4] = 0, 0, 0, 0. Which of the following is an allowed operation?

   a. values[2] = 17

   b. input values[0]

   c. values[3] = values[0] + 10

   d. all of the above

10. Filling an array with values during a program's execution is known as _____ the array.

   a. executing

   b. colonizing

   c. populating

   d. declaring

11. Using an array can make a program _____.

   a. easier to understand

   b. illegal in some modern languages

   c. harder to maintain

   d. all of the above

12. A _____ is a variable that you set to indicate whether some event has occurred.

   a. subscript

   b. banner

   c. counter

   d. flag

13. What do you call two arrays in which each element in one array is associated with the element in the same relative position in the other array?

   a. cohesive arrays

   b. parallel arrays

   c. hidden arrays

   d. perpendicular arrays

14. In most modern programming languages, the highest subscript you should use with a 10-element array is _____.

   a. 8

   b. 9

   c. 10

   d. 11

15. Parallel arrays _____.

    a. frequently have an indirect relationship

    b. never have an indirect relationship

    c. must be the same data type

    d. must not be the same data type

16. Each element in a five-element array can hold _____ value(s).

    a. one

    b. five

    c. at least five

    d. an unlimited number of

17. After the annual dog show in which the Barkley Dog Training Academy awards points to each participant, the academy assigns a status to each dog based on the following criteria:

Points Earned	Level of Achievement
0–5	Good
6–7	Excellent
8–9	Superior
10	Unbelievable

The academy needs a program that compares a dog's points earned with the grading scale, so that each dog can receive a certificate acknowledging the appropriate level of achievement. Of the following, which set of values would be most useful for the contents of an array used in the program?

    a. 0, 6, 9, 10

    b. 5, 7, 8, 10

    c. 5, 7, 9, 10

    d. any of these

18. When you use a subscript value that is negative or higher than the number of elements in an array, _____.

    a. execution of the program stops and an error message is issued

    b. a value in a memory location that is outside the area occupied by the array will be accessed

    c. a value in a memory location that is outside the area occupied by the array will be accessed, but only if the value is the correct data type

    d. the resulting action depends on the programming language used

19. In every array, a subscript is out of bounds when it is _____.

    a. negative

    b. 0

    c. 1

    d. 999

20. You can access every element of an array using a _____.

    a. `while` loop

    b. `for` loop

    c. both of the above

    d. none of the above

Exercises

1. a. Design the logic for a program that allows a user to enter 10 numbers, then displays them in the reverse order of their entry.

    b. Modify the reverse-display program so that the user can enter up to 10 numbers until a sentinel value is entered.

2. a. Design the logic for a program that allows a user to enter 10 numbers, then displays each number and its difference from the numeric average of the numbers entered.

    b. Modify the program in Exercise 2a so that the user can enter up to 10 numbers until a sentinel value is entered.

3. a. The city of Cary is holding a special census. The city has collected data on cards that each hold the voting district and age of a citizen. The districts are numbered 1 through 22, and residents' ages range from 0 through 105. Design a program that allows a clerk to go through the cards, entering the district for each citizen until an appropriate sentinel value is entered. The output is a list of all 22 districts and the number of residents in each.

   b. Modify Exercise 3a so the clerk enters both the district and age on each card. Produce a count of the number of residents in each of the 22 districts and a count of residents in each of the following age groups: under 18, 18 through 30, 31 through 45, 46 through 64, and 65 and older.

4. a. The Midville Park District maintains five soccer teams, as shown in the table. Design a program that accepts a player's team number and displays the player's team name.

Team Number	Team Name
1	Goal Getters
2	The Force
3	Top Guns
4	Shooting Stars
5	Midfield Monsters

   b. Modify the Midville Park District program so that after the last player has been entered, the program displays a count of the number of players registered for each team.

5. a. Watson Elementary School contains 30 classrooms numbered 1 through 30. Each classroom can contain any number of students up to 35. Each student takes an achievement test at the end of the school year and receives a score from 0 through 100. Write a program that accepts data for each student in the school—student ID, classroom number, and score on the achievement test. Design a program that lists the total points scored for each of the 30 classrooms.

   b. Modify the Watson Elementary School program so that each classroom's average of the test scores is output, rather than each classroom's total.

6. The Billy Goat Fast-Food restaurant sells the following products:

Product	Price ($)
Cheeseburger	2.49
Pepsi	1.00
Chips	0.59

Design the logic for an application that allows a user to enter an ordered item continuously until a sentinel value is entered. After each item, display its price or the message "Sorry, we do not carry that" as output. After all items have been entered, display the total price for the order.

7. Design the application logic for a company that wants a report containing a breakdown of payroll by department. Input includes each employee's department number, hourly salary, and number of hours worked. The output is a list of the seven departments in the company and the total gross payroll (rate times hours) for each department. The department names are shown in the accompanying table.

Department Number	Department Name
1	Personnel
2	Marketing
3	Manufacturing
4	Computer Services
5	Sales
6	Accounting
7	Shipping

8. Design a program that computes pay for employees. Allow a user to continuously input employees' names until an appropriate sentinel value is entered. Also input each employee's hourly wage and hours worked. Compute each employee's gross pay (hours times rate), withholding tax percentage (based on the accompanying table), withholding tax amount, and net pay (gross pay minus withholding tax). Display all the results for each employee. After the last employee has been entered, display the sum of all the hours worked, the total gross payroll, the total withholding for all employees, and the total net payroll.

Weekly Gross Pay ($)	Withholding Percent (%)
0.00–200.00	10
200.01–350.00	14
350.01–500.00	18
500.01 and up	22

9. The Perfect Party Catering Company hosts events for clients. Create an application that accepts an event number, the event host's last name, and numeric month, day, and year values representing

Code	Entrée	Price per Person ($)
1	Roast beef	24.50
2	Salmon	19.00
3	Linguine	16.50
4	Chicken	18.00

the event date. The application should also accept the number of guests who will attend the event and a numeric meal code that represents the entrée the event hosts will serve. As each client's data is entered, verify that the month, day, year, and meal code are valid; if any of these is not valid, continue to prompt the user until it is. The valid meal codes are shown in the accompanying table.

Design the logic for an application that outputs each event number, host name, validated date, meal code, entrée name, number of guests, gross total price for the party, and price for the party after discount. The gross

Number of Guests	Discount ($)
1–25	0
26–50	75
51–100	125
101–250	200
251 and over	300

total price for the party is the meal price per guest times the number of guests. The final price includes a discount based on the accompanying table.

10. a. *Daily Life Magazine* wants an analysis of the demographic characteristics of its readers. The Marketing department has collected reader survey records containing the age, gender, marital status, and annual income of readers. Design an application that allows a user to enter reader data and, when data entry is complete, produces a count of readers by age groups as follows: under 20, 20–29, 30–39, 40–49, and 50 and older.

b. Modify the *Daily Life Magazine* program so that it produces a count of readers by gender within age group— that is, under-20 females, under-20 males, and so on.

c. Modify the *Daily Life Magazine* program so that it produces a count of readers by income groups as follows: under $30,000, $30,000–$49,999, $50,000–$69,999, and $70,000 and up.

272

11. Glen Ross Vacation Property Sales employs seven salespeople, as shown in the accompanying table.

ID Number	Salesperson Name
103	Darwin
104	Kratz
201	Shulstad
319	Fortune
367	Wickert
388	Miller
435	Vick

When a salesperson makes a sale, a record is created, including the date, time, and dollar amount of the sale. The time is expressed in hours and minutes, based on a 24-hour clock. The sale amount is expressed in whole dollars. Salespeople earn a commission that differs for each sale, based on the rate schedule in the accompanying table.

Sale Amount ($)	Commission Rate (%)
0–50,999	4
51,000–125,999	5
126,000–200,999	6
201,000 and up	7

Design an application that produces each of the following:

a. A list of each salesperson number, name, total sales, and total commissions

b. A list of each month of the year as both a number and a word (for example, "01 January"), and the total sales for the month for all salespeople

c. A list of total sales as well as total commissions earned by all salespeople for each of the following time frames, based on hour of the day: 00–05, 06–12, 13–18, and 19–23

 Find the Bugs

12. Your student disk contains files named DEBUG06-01.txt, DEBUG06-02.txt, and DEBUG06-03.txt. Each file starts with some comments that describe the problem. Comments are lines that begin with two slashes (//). Following the comments, each file contains pseudocode that has one or more bugs you must find and correct.

Game Zone

13. Create the logic for a Magic 8 Ball© game in which the user enters a question such as "What does my future hold?". The computer randomly selects one of eight possible vague answers, such as "It remains to be seen".

14. Create the logic for an application that contains an array of 10 multiple-choice questions related to your favorite hobby. Each question contains three answer choices. Also create a parallel array that holds the correct answer to each question—A, B, or C. Display each question and verify that the user enters only A, B, or C as the answer—if not, keep prompting the user until a valid response is entered. If the user responds to a question correctly, display "Correct!"; otherwise, display "The correct answer is " and the letter of the correct answer. After the user answers all the questions, display the number of correct and incorrect answers.

15. a. Create the logic for a dice game. The application randomly "throws" five dice for the computer and five dice for the player. After each random throw, store the results in an array. The application displays all the values, which can be from 1 to 6 inclusive for each die. Decide the winner based on the following hierarchy of die values. Any higher combination beats a lower one; for example, five of a kind beats four of a kind.

   - Five of a kind

   - Four of a kind

   - Three of a kind

   - A pair

   For this game, the numeric dice values do not count. For example, if both players have three of a kind, it's a tie, no matter what the values of the three dice are.

Figure 6-19 Typical execution of the dice game

Additionally, the game does not recognize a full house (three of a kind plus two of a kind). Figure 6-19 shows how the game might be played in a command-line environment.

b. Improve the dice game so that when both players have the same combination of dice values, the higher value wins. For example, two 6s beats two 5s.

16. Design the logic for the game Hangman, in which the user guesses letters in a hidden word. Store the letters of a word in an array of characters. Display a dash for each missing letter. Allow the user to continuously guess a letter until all the letters in the word are guessed correctly. As the user enters each guess, display the word again, filling in the guess if it was correct. For example, if the hidden word is "computer," first display "--------". After the user guesses "p", the display becomes "---p----". Make sure that when a user makes a correct guess, all the matching letters are filled in. For example, if the word is "banana" and the user guesses "a", all three "a" characters must be filled in.

17. Create two parallel arrays that represent a standard deck of 52 playing cards. One array is numeric and holds the values 1 through 13 (representing Ace, 2 through 10, Jack, Queen, and King). The other array is a string array and holds suits ("Clubs", "Diamonds", "Hearts", and "Spades"). Create the arrays so that all 52 cards are represented. Create a War card game that randomly selects two cards (one for the player and one for the computer) and declares a winner or a tie based on the numeric value of the two cards. The game should play for 26 rounds, dealing a full deck with no repeated cards. For this game, assume that the lowest card is the Ace. Display the values of the player's and computer's cards, compare their values, and determine the winner. When all the cards in the deck are exhausted, display a count of the number of times the player wins, the number of times the computer wins, and the number of ties.

Here are some hints:

- Start by creating an array of all 52 playing cards.

- Select a random number for the deck position of the player's first card and assign the card at that array position to the player.

- Move every higher-positioned card in the deck "down" one to fill in the gap. In other words, if the player's first random number is 49, select the card at position 49 (both the numeric value and the string), move the card that was in position 50 to position 49, and move the card that was in position 51 to position 50. Only 51 cards remain in the deck after the player's first card is dealt, so the available-card array is smaller by one.

- In the same way, randomly select a card for the computer and "remove" the card from the deck.

 Up for Discussion

18. A train schedule is an everyday, real-life example of an array. Think of at least four more.

19. Every element in an array always has the same data type. Why is this necessary?

CHAPTER 7

File Handling and Applications

In this chapter, you will learn about:

- ◎ Computer files
- ◎ The data hierarchy
- ◎ Performing file operations
- ◎ Sequential files and control break logic
- ◎ Merging sequential files
- ◎ Master and transaction file processing
- ◎ Random access files

Understanding Computer Files

In Chapter 1, you learned that computer memory, or random access memory (RAM), is temporary storage. When you write a program that stores a value in a variable, you are using temporary storage; the value you store is lost when the program ends or the computer loses power. This type of storage is volatile.

Permanent storage, on the other hand, is not lost when a computer loses power; it is nonvolatile. When you write a program and save it to a disk, you are using permanent storage.

 When discussing computer storage, *temporary* and *permanent* refer to volatility, not length of time. For example, a *temporary* variable might exist for several hours in a very large program or one that runs in an infinite loop, but a *permanent* piece of data might be saved and then deleted by a user within a few seconds. Because you can erase data from files, some programmers prefer the term *persistent storage* to permanent storage. In other words, you can remove data from a file stored on a device such as a disk drive, so it is not technically permanent. However, the data remains in the file even when the computer loses power, so, unlike in RAM, the data persists.

A **computer file** is a collection of data stored on a nonvolatile device in a computer system. Files exist on **permanent storage devices**, such as hard disks, DVDs, USB drives, and reels of magnetic tape. The two broad categories of files are:

- **Text files**, which contain data that can be read in a text editor because the data has been encoded using a scheme such as ASCII or Unicode. Text files might include facts and figures used by business programs, such as a payroll file that contains employee numbers, names, and salaries. The programs in this chapter will use text files.

- **Binary files**, which contain data that has not been encoded as text. Examples include images and music.

Although their contents vary, files have many common characteristics, as follows:

- Each has a name. The name often includes a dot and a file extension that describes the type of the file. For example, .txt is a plain text file, .dat is a data file, and .jpg is an image file in Joint Pictures Expert Group format.

- Each file has a specific time of creation and a time it was last modified.

- Each file occupies space on a section of a storage device; that is, each file has a size. Sizes are measured in bytes. A **byte** is a small

 Watch the video *Understanding Files.*

Appendix A contains more information on bytes and how file sizes are expressed.

unit of storage; for example, in a simple text file, a byte holds only one character. Because a byte is so small, file sizes usually are expressed in **kilobytes** (thousands of bytes), **megabytes** (millions of bytes), or **gigabytes** (billions of bytes).

Figure 7-1 shows how some files look when you view them in Microsoft Windows.

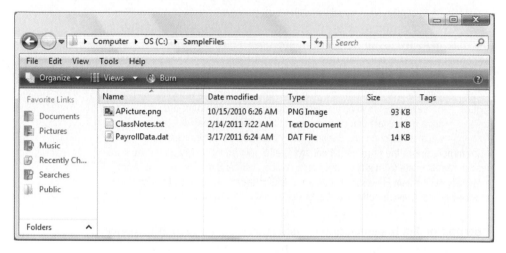

Figure 7-1   Three stored files showing their names, dates of modification, and sizes

Organizing Files

The terms *directory* and *folder* are used synonymously to mean an entity that organizes files. *Directory* is the more general term; the term *folder* came into use in graphical systems. For example, Microsoft began calling directories *folders* with the introduction of Windows 95.

Computer files on a storage device are the electronic equivalent of paper files stored in file cabinets. With a physical file cabinet, the easiest way to store a document is to toss it into a drawer without a folder. However, for better organization, most office clerks place paper documents in folders and most computer users organize their files into folders or directories. **Directories** and **folders** are organization units on storage devices; each can contain multiple files as well as additional directories. The combination of the disk drive plus the complete hierarchy of directories in which a file resides is its **path**. For example, in the Windows operating system, the following line would be the complete path for a file named PayrollData.dat on the C drive in a folder named SampleFiles within a folder named Logic:

`C:\Logic\SampleFiles\PayrollData.dat`

TWO TRUTHS & A LIE

Understanding Computer Files

1. Temporary storage is usually volatile.

2. Computer files exist on permanent storage devices, such as RAM.

3. A file's path is the hierarchy of folders in which it is stored.

The false statement is #2. Computer files exist on permanent storage devices, such as hard disks, floppy disks, USB drives, reels or cassettes of magnetic tape, and compact discs.

Understanding the Data Hierarchy

When businesses store data items on computer systems, they are often stored in a framework called the **data hierarchy** that describes the relationships between data components. The data hierarchy consists of the following:

- **Characters** are letters, numbers, and special symbols, such as "A", "7", and "$". Anything you can type from the keyboard in one keystroke (including a space or a tab) is a character. Characters are made up of smaller elements called bits, but just as most human beings can use a pencil without caring whether atoms are flying around inside it, most computer users can store characters without caring about these bits.

 Computers also recognize characters you cannot enter from a standard keyboard, such as foreign-alphabet characters like φ or Σ.

- **Fields** are single useful data items that are composed of one or more characters. Fields include items such as `lastName`, `middleInitial`, `streetAddress`, or `annualSalary`.

- **Records** are groups of fields that go together for some logical reason. A random name, address, and salary aren't very useful, but if they're *your* name, *your* address, and *your* salary, then that's your record. An inventory record might contain fields for item number, color, size, and price; a student record might contain ID number, grade point average, and major.

- **Files** are groups of related records. The individual records of each student in your class might go together in a file called Students. dat. Similarly, records of each person at your company might be in a file called Personnel.dat. Some files can have just a few records. For example, a student file for a college seminar might have only 10 records. Others, such as the file of credit-card holders for a major department-store chain or policy holders of a large insurance company, can contain thousands or even millions of records.

A **database** holds groups of files, often called **tables**, that together serve the information needs of an organization. Database software establishes and maintains relationships between fields in these tables, so that users can pull related data items together in a format that allows businesspeople to make managerial decisions efficiently. Chapter 14 of the comprehensive version of this text covers database creation.

280

TWO TRUTHS & A LIE

Understanding the Data Hierarchy

1. In the data hierarchy, a field is a single data item, such as lastName, streetAddress, or annualSalary.

2. In the data hierarchy, fields are grouped together to form a record; records are groups of fields that go together for some logical reason.

3. In the data hierarchy, related records are grouped together to form a field.

The false statement is #3. Related records form a file.

Performing File Operations

To use data files in your programs, you need to understand several file operations:

- Declaring a file
- Opening a file
- Reading from a file
- Writing to a file
- Closing a file

Declaring a File

The InputFile and OutputFile types are capitalized in this book because their equivalents are capitalized in most programming languages. This approach helps to distinguish these complex types from simple types such as num and string.

Most languages support several types of files, but the broadest types are files that can be used for input and files that can be used for output. Each type of file has a data type defined in the language you are using. You declare files in the same way you declare variables and constants—by giving each file a data type and an identifier. For example, you might declare two files as follows:

```
InputFile employeeData
OutputFile updatedData
```

The identifiers given to files, such as `employeeData` and `updatedData`, are internal to the program, just as variable names are. To make a program read a file's data from a storage device, you also need to associate the program's internal filename with the operating system's name for the file. Often, this association is accomplished when you open the file.

Opening a File

In most programming languages, before an application can use a data file, it must **open the file**. Opening a file locates it on a storage device and associates a variable name within your program with the file. For example, if the identifier `employeeData` has been declared as type `InputFile`, then you might make a statement similar to the following:

```
open employeeData "EmployeeData.dat"
```

This statement associates the file named "EmployeeData.dat" on the storage device with the program's internal name `employeeData`. Usually, you can also specify a more complete path when the data file is not in the same directory as the program, as in the following:

```
open employeeData "C:\CompanyFiles\CurrentYear\
    EmployeeData.dat"
```

Reading Data From a File

Before you can use stored data within a program, you must load the data into computer memory. You never use the data values that are stored on a storage device directly. Instead, you use a copy that is transferred into memory. When you copy data from a file on a storage device into RAM, you **read from the file**.

Especially when data items are stored on a hard disk, their location might not be clear to you—data just seems to be "in the computer." To a casual computer user, the lines between permanent storage and temporary memory are often blurred because many newer programs automatically save data for you periodically without asking your permission. However, at any moment in time, the version of a file in memory might differ from the version that was last saved to a storage device.

If data items have been stored in a file and a program needs them, you can write separate programming statements to input each field, as in the following example:

```
input name from employeeData
input address from employeeData
input payRate from employeeData
```

Most languages also allow you to write a single statement in the following format:

```
input name, address, payRate from employeeData
```

 Most programming languages provide a way for you to use a group name for record data, as in the following statement:

```
input EmployeeRecord from employeeData
```

When this format is used, you need to define the separate fields that compose an EmployeeRecord when you declare the variables for the program.

The way the program knows how much data to input for each variable differs among programming languages. In many languages, a delimiter such as a comma is stored between data fields. In other languages, the amount of data retrieved depends on the data types of the variables in the input statement.

You usually do not want to input several items in a single statement when you read data from a keyboard, because you want to prompt the user for each item separately as you input it. However, when you retrieve data from a file, prompts are not needed. Instead, each item is retrieved in sequence and stored in memory at the appropriate named location.

Figure 7-2 shows how an input statement works. When the input statement executes, each field is copied and placed in the appropriate variable in computer memory. Nothing on the disk indicates a field name associated with any of the data; the variable names exist within the program only. For example, another program could use the same file as input and call the fields surname, street, and salary.

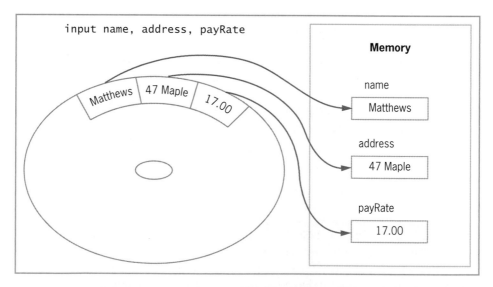

Figure 7-2   Reading three data items from a storage device into memory

When you read data from a file, you must read all the fields that are stored even though you might not want to use all of them. For example, suppose you want to read an employee data file that contains names, addresses, and pay rates for each employee, and you want to output a list of names. Even though you are not concerned with the address or pay rate fields, you must read them into your program for each employee before you can get to the name for the next employee.

Writing Data to a File

When you store data in a computer file on a persistent storage device, you **write to the file**. This means you copy data from RAM to the file. When you write data to a file, you write the contents of the fields using a statement such as the following:

```
output name, address, payRate to updatedData
```

When you write data to a file, you usually do not include explanations that make data easier for humans to interpret; you just write facts and figures. For example, you do not include column headings or write explanations such as "The pay rate is ", nor do you include commas, dollar signs, or percent signs in numeric values. Those embellishments are appropriate for output on a monitor or on paper, but not for storage.

Closing a File

When you finish using a file, the program should **close the file**—that is, the file is no longer available to your application. Failing to close an input file (a file from which you are reading data) usually does not present serious consequences; the data still exists in the file. However, if you fail to close an output file (a file to which you are writing data), the data might become inaccessible. You should always close every file you open, and you should close the file as soon as you no longer need it. When you leave a file open for no reason, you use computer resources, and your computer's performance suffers. Also, particularly within a network, another program might be waiting to use the file.

A Program that Performs File Operations

Figure 7-3 contains a program that opens two files, reads employee data from the input file, alters the employee's pay rate, writes the updated record to an output file, and closes the files. The statements that use the files are shaded.

In most programming languages, if you read data from a keyboard or write it to the display monitor, you do not need to open the device. The keyboard and monitor are the **default input and output devices**, respectively.

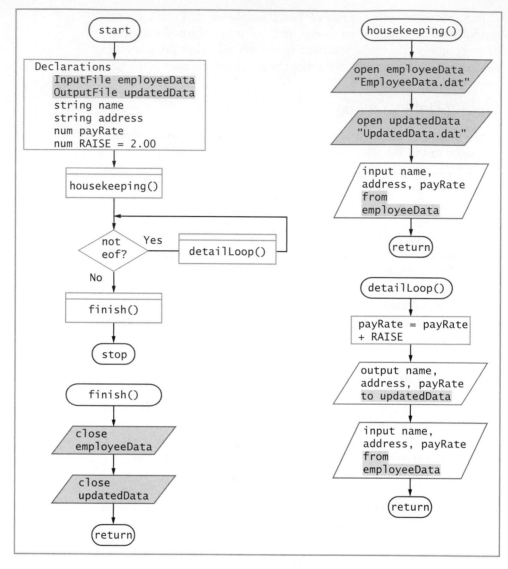

Figure 7-3 Flowchart and pseudocode for program that uses a file

```
start
   Declarations
      InputFile employeeData
      OutputFile updatedData
      string name
      string address
      num payRate
      num RAISE = 2.00
   housekeeping()
   while not eof
      detailLoop()
   endwhile
   finish()
stop

housekeeping()
   open employeeData "EmployeeData.dat"
   open updatedData "UpdatedData.dat"
   input name, address, payRate from employeeData
return

detailLoop()
   payRate = payRate + RAISE
   output name, address, payRate to updatedData
   input name, address, payRate from employeeData
return

finish()
   close employeeData
   close updatedData
return
```

Figure 7-3   Flowchart and pseudocode for program that uses a file (continued)

 The convention in this book is to place file open and close statements in parallelograms in flowcharts, because they are operations closely related to input and output.

In the program in Figure 7-3, each employee's data is read into memory. Then the payRate variable in memory is increased by $2.00. The value of the pay rate on the input storage device is not altered. After the employee's pay rate is increased, the name, address, and newly altered pay rate values are stored in the output file. When processing is complete, the input file retains the original data and the output file contains the revised data. Many organizations would keep the original file as a backup file. A **backup file** is a copy that is kept in case values need to be restored to their original state. The backup copy is called a **parent file** and the newly revised copy is a **child file**.

 Watch the video
File Operations.

 Logically, the verbs "print," "write," and "display" mean the same thing—all produce output. However, in conversation, programmers usually reserve the word "print" for situations in which they mean "produce hard copy output." Programmers are more likely to use "write" when talking about sending records to a data file, and "display" when sending records to a monitor. In some programming languages, there is no difference in the verb you use for output, no matter what type of hardware you use; you simply assign different output devices (such as printers, monitors, and disk drives) as needed to programmer-named objects that represent them.

In many organizations, both data files and printed report files are sent to disk storage devices when they are created. Later, as time becomes available on an organization's busy printers (often after business hours), the report disk files are copied to paper.

Throughout this book you have been encouraged to think of input as basically the same process, whether it comes from a user typing interactively at a keyboard or from a stored file on a disk or other media. That concept remains a valid one as you read the rest of this chapter, which discusses applications that commonly use stored file data. Such applications could be executed by a data-entry operator from a keyboard, but it is more common for the data used in these applications to have been entered, validated, and sorted earlier in another application, and then processed as input from files to achieve the results discussed in this chapter.

TWO TRUTHS & A LIE

Performing File Operations

1. The identifiers given to files are internal to the program; you must associate them with the operating system's name for the file.

2. When you read from a file, you copy values from memory to a storage device.

3. If you fail to close an input file, usually no serious consequences will occur; the data still exists in the file.

The false statement is #2. When you read from a file, you copy values from a storage device into memory. When you write to a file, you copy values from memory to a storage device.

Understanding Sequential Files and Control Break Logic

A **sequential file** is a file in which records are stored one after another in some order. Frequently, records in a sequential file are organized based on the contents of one or more fields. Examples of sequential files include:

- A file of employees stored in order by ID number

- A file of parts for a manufacturing company stored in order by part number

- A file of customers for a business stored in alphabetical order by last name

 Files that are stored in order by some field have been sorted; they might have been sorted manually before they were saved, or a program might have sorted them. You can learn about sorting techniques in Chapter 8 of the comprehensive version of this book.

Understanding Control Break Logic

A **control break** is a temporary detour in the logic of a program. In particular, programmers use a **control break program** when a change in the value of a variable initiates special actions or causes special or unusual processing to occur. You usually write control break programs to organize output for programs that handle data records organized logically in groups based on the value in a field. As you read records, you examine the same field in each record, and when you encounter a record that contains a different value from the ones that preceded it, you perform a special action. For example, you might generate a report that lists all company clients in order by state of residence, with a count of clients after each state's client list. See Figure 7-4 for an example of a **control break report** that breaks after each change in state.

Company Clients by State of Residence

Name	City	State	
Albertson	Birmingham	Alabama	
Davis	Birmingham	Alabama	
Lawrence	Montgomery	Alabama	
		Count for Alabama	3
Smith	Anchorage	Alaska	
Young	Anchorage	Alaska	
Davis	Fairbanks	Alaska	
Mitchell	Juneau	Alaska	
Zimmer	Juneau	Alaska	
		Count for Alaska	5
Edwards	Phoenix	Arizona	
		Count for Arizona	1

Figure 7-4 A control break report with totals after each state

Other examples of control break reports produced by control break programs could include:

- All employees listed in order by department number, with a new page started for each department

- All books for sale in a bookstore listed in order by category (such as reference or self-help), with a count following each category of book

- All items sold in order by date of sale, with a different ink color for each new month

Each of these reports shares two traits:

- The records used in each report are listed in order by a specific variable: state, department, category, or date.

- When that variable changes, the program takes special action: starts a new page, prints a count or total, or switches ink color.

 With some newer languages, such as SQL, the details of control breaks are handled automatically. Still, understanding how control break programs work improves your competence as a programmer.

To generate a control break report, your input records must be organized in sequential order based on the field that will cause the breaks. In other words, to write a program that produces a report of customers by state, like the one in Figure 7-4, the records must be grouped by state before you begin processing. Frequently, this grouping will mean placing the records in alphabetical order by state, although they could just as easily be ordered by population, governor's name, or any other factor, as long as all of one state's records are together.

Suppose you have an input file that contains client names, cities, and states, and you want to produce a report like the one in Figure 7-4. The basic logic of the program works like this:

- Each time you read a client's record from the input file, you determine whether the client resides in the same state as the previous client.

- If so, you simply output the client's data, add 1 to a counter, and read another record, without any special processing. If there are 20 clients in a state, these steps are repeated 20 times in a row—read a client's data, count it, and output it.

- Eventually you will read a record for a client who is not in the same state. At that point, before you output the data for the first client in the new state, you must output the count for the previous state. You must also reset the counter to 0 so it is ready to start counting customers in the next state. Then, you can proceed to handle client records for the new state, and you continue to do so until the next time you encounter a client from a different state. This type of program contains a **single-level control break**, a break in the logic of the program (in this case, pausing or detouring to output a count) that is based on the value of a single variable (in this case, the state).

The technique you must use to "remember" the old state so you can compare it with each new client's state is to create a special variable, called a **control break field**, to hold the previous state. As you read each new record, comparing the new and old state values determines when it is time to output the count for the previous state.

Figure 7-5 shows the mainline logic and getReady() module for a program that produces the report in Figure 7-4. In the mainline logic, the control break variable oldState is declared in the shaded statement. In the getReady() module, the report headings are output, the file is opened, and the first record is read into memory. Then, the state value in the first record is copied to the oldState variable. (See shading.) Note that it would be incorrect to initialize oldState when it is declared. When you declare the variables at the beginning of the main program, you have not yet read the first record; therefore, you don't know what the value of the first state will be. You might assume it is "Alabama" because that is the first state alphabetically, and you might be right, but perhaps the first state is "Alaska" or even "Wyoming". You are assured of storing the correct first state value if you copy it from the first input record.

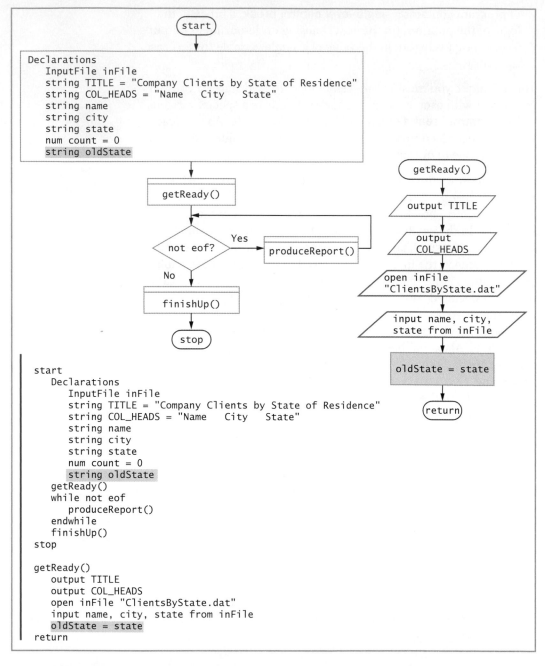

Figure 7-5   Mainline logic and `getReady()` module for the program that produces clients by state report

Within the produceReport() module in Figure 7-6, the first task is to check whether state holds the same value as oldState. For the first record, on the first pass through this method, the values are equal (because you set them to be equal right after getting the first input record in the getReady() module). Therefore, you proceed by outputting the first client's data, adding 1 to count, and inputting the next record.

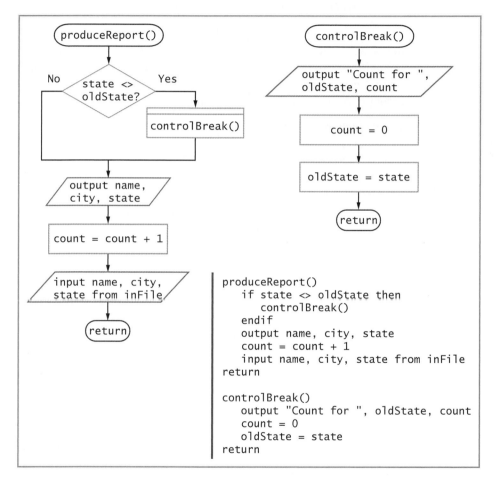

Figure 7-6 The produceReport() and controlBreak() modules for the program that produces clients by state

As long as each new record holds the same state value, you continue outputting, counting, and inputting, never pausing to output the count. Eventually, you will read in data for a client whose state is different from the previous one. That's when the control break occurs. Whenever a new state differs from the old one, three tasks must be performed:

- The count for the previous state must be output.

- The count must be reset to 0 so it can start counting records for the new state.

- The control break field must be updated.

When the produceReport() module receives a client record for which **state** is not the same as **oldState**, you cause a break in the normal flow of the program. The new client record must "wait" while the count for the just-finished state is output and **count** and the control break field **oldState** acquire new values.

Watch the video *Control Break Logic*.

The produceReport() module continues to output client names, cities, and states until the end of file is reached; then the finishUp() module executes. As shown in Figure 7-7, the module that executes after processing the last record in a control break program must complete any required processing for the last group that was handled. In this case, the finishUp() module must display the count for the last state that was processed. After the input file is closed, the logic can return to the main program, where the program ends.

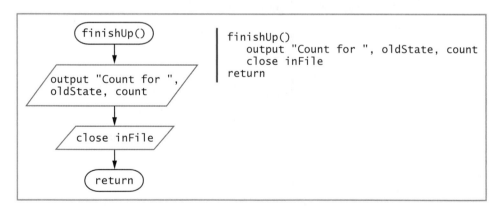

Figure 7-7 The finishUp() module for the program that produces clients by state report

TWO TRUTHS & A LIE

Understanding Sequential Files and Control Break Logic

1. In a control break program, a change in the value of a variable initiates special actions or causes special or unusual processing to occur.

2. When a control break variable changes, the program takes special action.

3. To generate a control break report, your input records must be organized in sequential order based on the first field in the record.

The false statement is #3. Your input records must be organized in sequential order based on the field that will cause the breaks.

Merging Sequential Files

Businesses often need to merge two or more sequential files. **Merging files** involves combining two or more files while maintaining the sequential order. For example:

- Suppose you have a file of current employees in ID number order and a file of newly hired employees, also in ID number order. You need to merge these two files into one combined file before running this week's payroll program.

- Suppose you have a file of parts manufactured in the Northside factory in part-number order and a file of parts manufactured in the Southside factory, also in part-number order. You need to merge these two files into one combined file, creating a master list of available parts.

- Suppose you have a file that lists last year's customers in alphabetical order and another file that lists this year's customers in alphabetical order. You want to create a mailing list of all customers in order by last name.

Before you can easily merge files, two conditions must be met:

- Each file must contain the same record layout.

- Each file used in the merge must be sorted in the same order (ascending or descending) based on the same field.

For example, suppose your business has two locations, one on the East Coast and one on the West Coast, and each location maintains a customer file in alphabetical order by customer name. Each file contains fields for name and customer balance. You can call the fields in the East Coast file eastName and eastBalance, and the fields in the West Coast file westName and westBalance. You want to merge the two files, creating one combined file containing records for all customers. Figure 7-8 shows some sample data for the files; you want to create a merged file like the one shown in Figure 7-9.

East Coast File		West Coast File	
eastName	eastBalance	westName	westBalance
Able	100.00	Chen	200.00
Brown	50.00	Edgar	125.00
Dougherty	25.00	Fell	75.00
Hanson	300.00	Grand	100.00
Ingram	400.00		
Johnson	30.00		

Figure 7-8 Sample data contained in two customer files

mergedName	mergedBalance
Able	100.00
Brown	50.00
Chen	200.00
Dougherty	25.00
Edgar	125.00
Fell	75.00
Grand	100.00
Hanson	300.00
Ingram	400.00
Johnson	30.00

Figure 7-9 Merged customer file

The mainline logic for a program that merges two files is similar to the main logic you've used before in other programs: it contains preliminary, housekeeping tasks; a detail module that repeats until the end of the program; and some clean-up, end-of-job tasks. However, most programs you have studied processed records until an eof condition was met, either because an input data file reached its end or because a user entered a sentinel value in an interactive program. In a program that merges files, there are two input files, so checking for eof in one of them is insufficient. Instead, the program can check a flag variable with a name such as bothAtEnd. For example, you might initialize bothAtEnd to N, but change its value to Y after you have encountered eof in both input files.

Figure 7-10 shows the mainline logic for a program that merges the files shown in Figure 7-8. After the getReady() module executes, the shaded question that sends the logic to the finishUp() module tests the bothAtEnd variable. When it holds Y, the program ends.

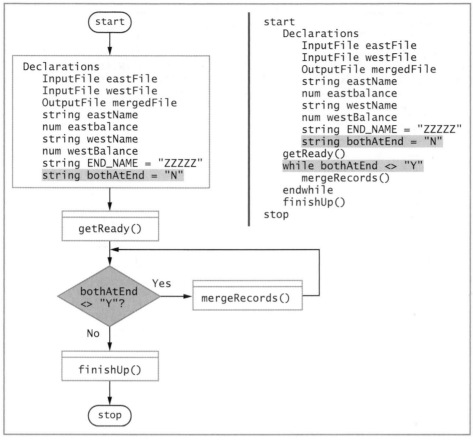

Figure 7-10 Mainline logic of a program that merges files

The getReady() module is shown in Figure 7-11. It opens three files—the input files for the east and west customers, and an output file in which to place the merged records. The program then reads one record from each input file. If either file has reached its end, the END_NAME constant is assigned to the variable that holds that file's customer name. The getReady() module then checks to see whether both files are finished (admittedly, a rare occurrence in the getReady() portion of the program's execution) and sets the bothAtEnd flag variable to Y if they are. Assuming there is at least one record available, the logic would then enter the mergeRecords() module.

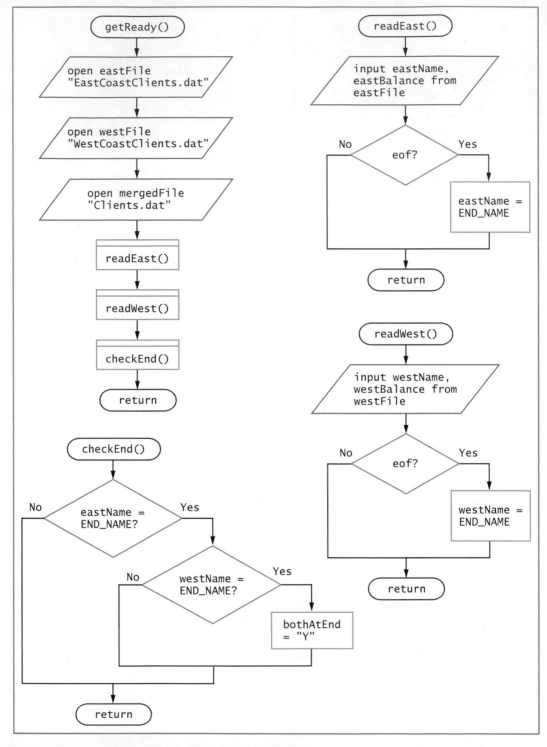

Figure 7-11 The getReady() method for a program that merges files, and the methods it calls

```
getReady()
    open eastFile "EastCoastClients.dat"
    open westFile "WestCoastClients.dat"
    open mergedFile "Clients.dat"
    readEast()
    readWest()
    checkEnd()
return

readEast()
    input eastName, eastBalance from eastFile
    if eof then
        eastName = END_NAME
    endif
return

readWest()
    input westName, westBalance from westFile
    if eof then
        westName = END_NAME
    endif
return

checkEnd()
    if eastName = END_NAME then
        if westName = END_NAME then
            bothAtEnd = "Y"
        endif
    endif
return
```

Figure 7-11 The getReady() method for a program that merges files, and the methods it calls (continued)

When you begin the mergeRecords() module in the program using the files shown in Figure 7-8, two records—one from eastFile and one from westFile—are sitting in the memory of the computer. One of these records needs to be written to the new output file first. Which one? Because the two input files contain records stored in alphabetical order, and you want the new file to store records in alphabetical order, you first output the input record that has the lower alphabetical value in the name field. Therefore, the process begins as shown in Figure 7-12.

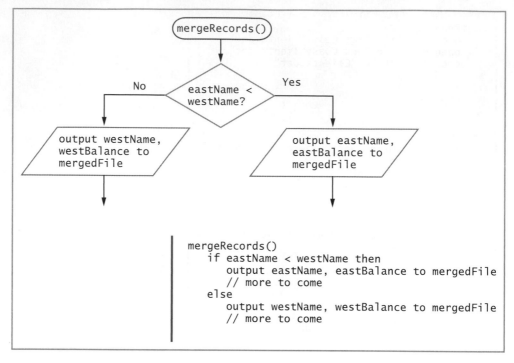

Figure 7-12   Start of merging process

Using the sample data from Figure 7-8, you can see that the "Able" record from the East Coast file should be written to the output file, while Chen's record from the West Coast file waits in memory. The eastName value "Able" is alphabetically lower than the westName value "Chen".

After you write Able's record, should Chen's record be written to the output file next? Not necessarily. It depends on the next eastName following Able's record in eastFile. When data records are read into memory from a file, a program typically does not "look ahead" to determine the values stored in the next record. Instead, a program usually reads the record into memory before making decisions about its contents. In this program, you need to read the next eastFile record into memory and compare it to "Chen". Because in this case the next record in eastFile contains the name "Brown", another eastFile record is written; no westFile records are written yet.

After the first two eastFile records, is it Chen's turn to be written now? You really don't know until you read another record from eastFile and compare its name value to "Chen". Because this record contains the name "Dougherty", it is indeed time to write

Chen's record. After Chen's record is written, should you now write Dougherty's record? Until you read the next record from westFile, you don't know whether that record should be placed before or after Dougherty's record.

Therefore, the merging method proceeds like this: Compare two records, write the record with the lower alphabetical name, and read another record from the *same* input file. See Figure 7-13.

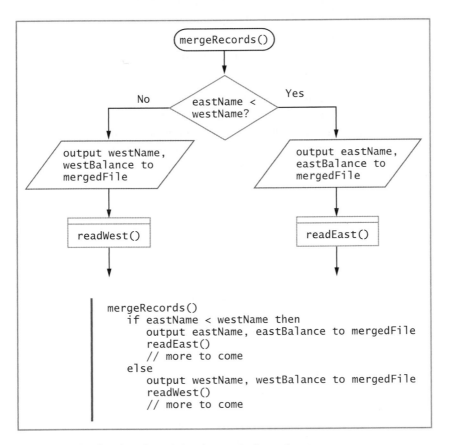

```
mergeRecords()
    if eastName < westName then
        output eastName, eastBalance to mergedFile
        readEast()
        // more to come
    else
        output westName, westBalance to mergedFile
        readWest()
        // more to come
```

Figure 7-13 Continuation of development of merging process

Recall the names from the two original files in Figure 7-8, and walk through the processing steps.

1. Compare "Able" and "Chen". Write Able's record. Read Brown's record from eastFile.

2. Compare "Brown" and "Chen". Write Brown's record. Read Dougherty's record from eastFile.

3. Compare "Dougherty" and "Chen". Write Chen's record. Read Edgar's record from westFile.

4. Compare "Dougherty" and "Edgar". Write Dougherty's record. Read Hanson's record from eastFile.

5. Compare "Hanson" and "Edgar". Write Edgar's record. Read Fell's record from westFile.

6. Compare "Hanson" and "Fell". Write Fell's record. Read Grand's record from westFile.

7. Compare "Hanson" and "Grand". Write Grand's record. Read from westFile, encountering eof. This causes westName to be set to END_NAME.

What happens when you reach the end of the West Coast file? Is the program over? It shouldn't be because records for Hanson, Ingram, and Johnson all need to be included in the new output file, and none of them is written yet. Because the westName field is set to END_NAME, and END_NAME has a very high alphabetic value ("ZZZZZ"), each subsequent eastName will be lower than the value of westName, and the rest of the eastName file will be processed. With a different set of data, the eastFile might have ended first. In that case, eastName would be set to END_NAME, and each subsequent westFile record would be processed.

Figure 7-14 shows the complete mergeRecords() module and the finishUp() module.

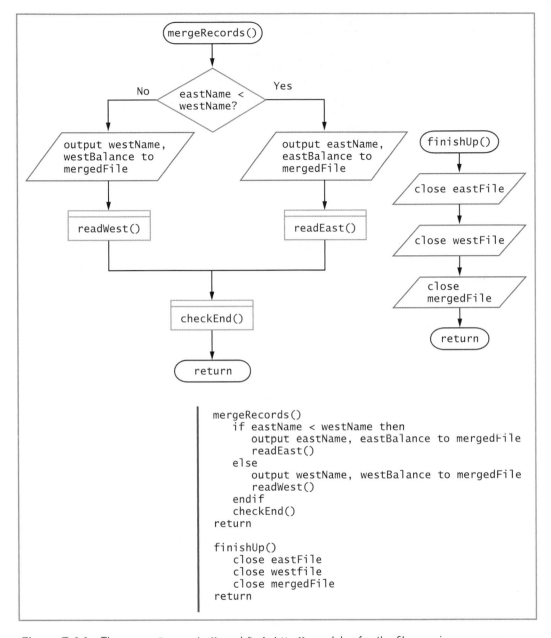

Figure 7-14 The mergeRecords() and finishUp() modules for the file-merging program

As the value for **END_NAME**, you might choose to use 10 or 20 Zs instead of only five. Although it is unlikely that a person will have the last name ZZZZZ, you should make sure that the high value you choose is actually higher than any legitimate value.

After Grand's record is processed, `westFile` is read and `eof` is encountered, so `westName` gets set to END_NAME. Now, when you enter the loop again, `eastName` and `westName` are compared, and `eastName` is still "Hanson". The `eastName` value (Hanson) is lower than the `westName` value (ZZZZZ), so the data for `eastName`'s record writes to the output file, and another `eastFile` record (Ingram) is read.

The complete run of the file-merging program now executes the first six of the seven steps listed previously, and then proceeds, as shown in Figure 7-14 and as follows, starting with a modified Step 7:

7. Compare "Hanson" and "Grand". Write Grand's record. Read from `westFile`, encountering `eof` and setting `westName` to "ZZZZZ".

8. Compare "Hanson" and "ZZZZZ". Write Hanson's record. Read Ingram's record.

9. Compare "Ingram" and "ZZZZZ". Write Ingram's record. Read Johnson's record.

10. Compare "Johnson" and "ZZZZZ". Write Johnson's record. Read from `eastFile`, encountering `eof` and setting `eastName` to "ZZZZZ".

11. Now that both names are "ZZZZZ", set the flag `bothAtEnd` equal to Y.

 Watch the video *Merging Files.*

When the `bothAtEnd` flag variable equals Y, the loop is finished, the files are closed, and the program ends.

 If two names are equal during the merge process—for example, when there is a "Hanson" record in each file—then both Hansons will be included in the final file. When `eastName` and `westName` match, `eastName` is not lower than `westName`, so you write the `westFile` "Hanson" record. After you read the next `westFile` record, `eastName` will be lower than the next `westName`, and the `eastFile` "Hanson" record will be output. A more complicated merge program could check another field, such as first name, when last name values match.

 You can merge any number of files. To merge more than two files, the logic is only slightly more complicated; you must compare the key fields from all the files before deciding which file is the next candidate for output.

TWO TRUTHS & A LIE

Merging Sequential Files

1. A sequential file is a file in which records are stored one after another in some order. Most frequently, the records are stored based on the contents of one or more fields within each record.

2. Merging files involves combining two or more files while maintaining the sequential order.

3. Before you can easily merge files, each file must contain the same number of records.

The false statement is #3. Before you can easily merge files, each file must contain the same record layout and each file used in the merge must be sorted in the same order based on the same field.

Master and Transaction File Processing

In the last section, you learned how to merge related sequential files in which each record in each file contained the same fields. Some related sequential files, however, do not contain the same fields. Instead, some related files have a master-transaction relationship. A **master file** holds complete and relatively permanent data; a **transaction file** holds more temporary data. For example, a master customer file might hold customers' names, addresses, and phone numbers, and a customer transaction file might contain data that describes a customer's most recent purchase.

Commonly, you gather transactions for a period of time, store them in a file, and then use them one by one to update matching records in a master file. You **update the master file** by making appropriate changes to the values in its fields based on the recent transactions. For example, a file containing transaction purchase data for a customer might be used to update each balance due field in a customer record master file.

Here are a few other examples of files that have a master-transaction relationship:

- A library maintains a master file of all patrons and a transaction file with information about each book or other items checked out.

When a child file is updated, it becomes a parent, and its parent becomes a grandparent. Individual organizations create policies concerning the number of generations of backup files they will save before discarding them.

The terms "parent" and "child" refer to file backup generations, but they are used for a different purpose in object-oriented programming. When you base a class on another using inheritance, the original class is the parent and the derived class is the child. You can learn about these concepts in Chapters 10 and 11 of the comprehensive version of this book.

- A college maintains a master file of all students and a transaction file for each course registration.

- A telephone company maintains a master file for every telephone line (number) and a transaction file with information about every call.

When you update a master file, you can take two approaches:

- You can actually change the information in the master file. When you use this approach, the information that existed in the master file prior to the transaction processing is lost.

- You can create a copy of the master file, making the changes in the new version. Then, you can store the previous, parent version of the master file for a period of time, in case there are questions or discrepancies regarding the update process. The updated, child version of the file becomes the new master file used in subsequent processing. This approach is used in a program later in this chapter.

The logic you use to perform a match between master and transaction file records is similar to the logic you use to perform a merge. As with a merge, you must begin with both files sorted in the same order on the same field. Figure 7-15 shows the mainline logic for a program that matches files. The master file contains a customer number, name, and a field that holds the total dollar amount of all purchases the customer has made previously. The transaction file holds data for sales, including a transaction number, the number of the customer who made the transaction, and the amount of the transaction.

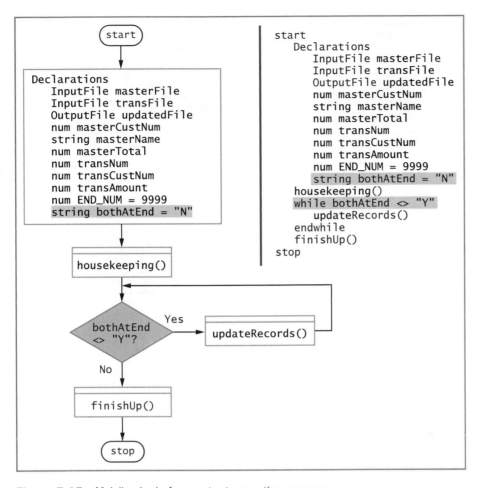

Figure 7-15   Mainline logic for master-transaction program

Figure 7-16 contains the housekeeping() module for the program, and the modules it calls. These modules are very similar to their counterparts in the file-merging program earlier in the chapter. When the program begins, one record is read from each file. When any file ends, the field used for matching is set to a high value, 9999, and when both files are at end, a flag variable is set so the mainline logic can test for the end of processing.

In the file-merging program presented earlier in this chapter, you placed "ZZZZZ" in the customer name field at the end of the file because string fields were being compared. In this example, because you are using numeric fields (customer numbers), you can store 9999 in them at the end of the file. The assumption is that 9999 is higher than any valid customer number.

306

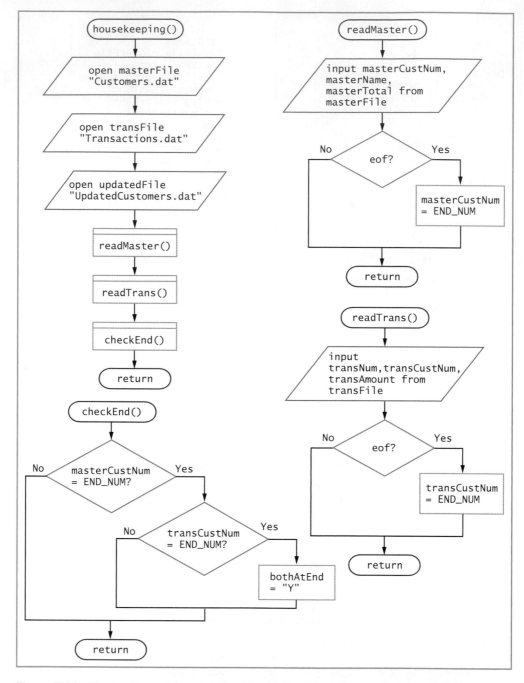

Figure 7-16   The housekeeping() module for master-transaction program, and the modules it calls

Imagine that you will update master file records by hand instead
of using a computer program, and imagine that each master and
transaction record is stored on a separate piece of paper. The easiest way
to accomplish the update is to sort all the master records by customer

number and place them in a stack, and then sort all the transactions by customer number (not transaction number) and place them in another stack. You then would examine the first transaction, and look through the master records until you found a match. Any master records without transactions would be placed in a "completed" stack without changes. When a transaction matched a master record, you would correct the master record using the new transaction amount, and then go on to the next transaction. Of course, if there is no matching master record for a transaction, then you would realize an error had occurred, and you would probably set the transaction aside before continuing. The updateRecords() module works exactly the same way.

In the file-merging program presented earlier in this chapter, your first action in the program's detail loop was to determine which file held the record with the lower value; then, you wrote that record. In a matching program, you are trying to determine not only whether one file's comparison field is larger than another's; it's also important to know if they are *equal*. In this example, you want to update the master file record's masterTotal field only if the transaction record transCustNum field contains an exact match for the customer number in the master file record. Therefore, you compare masterCustNum from the master file and transCustNum from the transaction file. Three possibilities exist:

- The transCustNum value equals masterCustNum. In this case, you add transAmount to masterTotal, and then write the updated master record to the output file. Then, you read in both a new master record and a new transaction record.

- The transCustNum value is higher than masterCustNum. This means a sale was not recorded for that customer. That's all right; not every customer makes a transaction every period, so you simply write the original customer record with exactly the same information it contained when input. Then, you get the next customer record to see if this customer made the transaction currently under examination.

- The transCustNum value is lower than masterCustNum. This means you are trying to apply a transaction for which no master record exists, so there must be an error, because a transaction should always have a master record. You can handle this error in a variety of ways; here, you will write an error message to an output device before reading the next transaction record. A human operator can then read the message and take appropriate action.

 The logic used here assumes there can be only one transaction per customer. In the exercises at the end of this chapter, you will develop the logic for a program in which the customer can have multiple transactions.

Whether transCustNum was higher than, lower than, or equal to masterCustNum, after reading the next transaction or master record (or both), you check whether both `masterCustNum` and `transCustNum` have been set to 9999. When both are 9999, you set the `bothAtEnd` flag to Y.

Figure 7-17 shows the `updateRecords()` module that carries out the logic of the file-matching process. Figure 7-18 shows some sample data you can use to walk through the logic for this program.

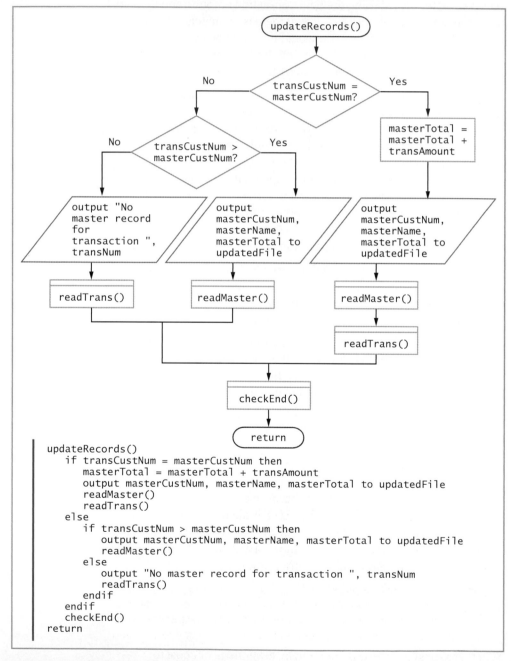

```
updateRecords()
   if transCustNum = masterCustNum then
      masterTotal = masterTotal + transAmount
      output masterCustNum, masterName, masterTotal to updatedFile
      readMaster()
      readTrans()
   else
      if transCustNum > masterCustNum then
         output masterCustNum, masterName, masterTotal to updatedFile
         readMaster()
      else
         output "No master record for transaction ", transNum
         readTrans()
      endif
   endif
   checkEnd()
return
```

Figure 7-17   The `updateRecords()` module for the master-transaction program

Master File		Transaction File	
masterCustNum	masterTotal	transCustNum	transAmount
100	1000.00	100	400.00
102	50.00	105	700.00
103	500.00	108	100.00
105	75.00	110	400.00
106	5000.00		
109	4000.00		
110	500.00		

Figure 7-18   Sample data for the file-matching program

The program proceeds as follows:

1. Read customer 100 from the master file and customer 100 from the transaction file. Customer numbers are equal, so 400.00 from the transaction file is added to 1000.00 in the master file, and a new master file record is written with a 1400.00 total sales figure. Then, read a new record from each input file.

2. The customer number in the master file is 102 and the customer number in the transaction file is 105, so there are no transactions today for customer 102. Write the master record exactly the way it came in, and read a new master record.

3. Now, the master customer number is 103 and the transaction customer number is still 105. This means customer 103 has no transactions, so you write the master record as is and read a new one.

4. Now, the master customer number is 105 and the transaction number is 105. Because customer 105 had a 75.00 balance and now has a 700.00 transaction, the new total sales figure for the master file is 775.00, and a new master record is written. Read one record from each file.

5. Now, the master number is 106 and the transaction number is 108. Write customer record 106 as is, and read another master.

6. Now, the master number is 109 and the transaction number is 108. An error has occurred. The transaction record indicates that you made a sale to customer 108, but there is no master record for customer number 108. Either the transaction is incorrect (there is an error in the transaction's customer number) or the transaction is correct but you have failed to create a master record. Either way, write an error message so that a

clerk is notified and can handle the problem. Then, get a new transaction record.

7. Now, the master number is 109 and the transaction number is 110. Write master record 109 with no changes and read a new one.

8. Now, the master number is 110 and the transaction number is 110. Add the 400.00 transaction to the previous 500.00 balance in the master file, and write a new master record with 900.00 in the masterTotal field. Read one record from each file.

9. Because both files are finished, end the job. The result is a new master file in which some records contain exactly the same data they contained going in, but others (for which a transaction has occurred) have been updated with a new total sales figure. The original master and transaction files that were used as input can be saved for a period of time as backups.

Figure 7-19 shows the finishUp() module for the program. After all the files are closed, the updated master customer file contains all the customer records it originally contained, and each holds a current total based on the recent group of transactions.

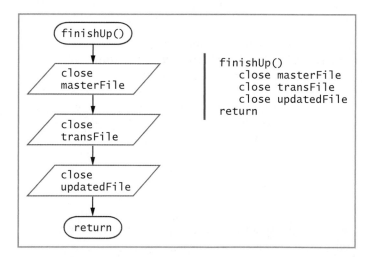

Figure 7-19   The finishUp() module for the master-transaction program

Random Access Files

The examples of files that have been written to and read from in this chapter are sequential access files, which means that you access the records in sequential order from beginning to end. For example, if you wrote an employee record with an ID number 234, and then you created a second record with an ID number 326, you would see when you retrieved the records that they remain in the original data-entry order. Businesses store data in sequential order when they use the records for **batch processing**, or processing that involves performing the same tasks with many records, one after the other. For example, when a company produces paychecks, the records for the pay period are gathered in a batch and the checks are calculated and printed in sequence. It really doesn't matter whose check is produced first because none are distributed to employees until all have been printed.

Besides indicating a system that works with many records, the term *batch processing* can also be used to mean a system in which you issue many operating-system commands as a group.

For many applications, sequential access is inefficient. These applications, known as **real-time** applications, require that a record be accessed immediately while a client is waiting. A program in which the user makes direct requests is an **interactive program**. For example, if a customer telephones a department store with a question about a monthly bill, the customer service representative does not need or want to access every customer account in sequence. With tens of thousands of account records to read, it would take too long to access the customer's record. Instead, customer service representatives require **random access files**, files in which records can be located in any order. Files in which records must be accessed immediately are also called **instant access files**. Because they enable you to locate a particular record directly (without reading all of the preceding records), random access files are also called **direct access files**. You can declare a random access file with a statement similar to the following:

```
RandomFile customerFile
```

You associate this name with a stored file similarly to how you associate an identifier with sequential input and output files. You also can use read, write, and close operations with a random access file similarly to the way you use them with sequential files. However, with random access files you have the additional capability to find a record directly. For example, you might be able to use a statement similar to the following to find customer number 712 on a random access file:

```
seek record 712
```

This feature is particularly useful in random access processing. Consider a business with 20,000 customer accounts. When the customer who has the 14,607th record in the file acquires a new telephone number, it is convenient to directly access the 14,607th record and write the new telephone number to the file in the location in which the old number was previously stored.

TWO TRUTHS & A LIE

Random Access Files

1. A batch program usually uses instant access files.

2. In a real-time application, a record is accessed immediately while a client is waiting.

3. An interactive program usually uses random access files.

The false statement is #1. A batch program usually uses sequential files; interactive programs use random, instant access files.

Chapter Summary

- A computer file is a collection of data stored on a nonvolatile device in a computer system. Although the contents of files differ, each file occupies space on a section of a storage device, and each has a name and a specific time of creation or last modification. Computer files are organized in directories or folders. A file's complete list of directories is its path.

- Data items in a file usually are stored in a hierarchy. Characters are letters, numbers, and special symbols, such as "A", "7", and "$". Fields are single useful data items that are composed of one or more characters. Records are groups of fields that go together for some logical reason. Files are groups of related records.

- When you use a data file in a program, you must declare it and open it; opening a file associates an internal program identifier with the name of a physical file on a storage device. When you read from a file, the data is copied into memory. When you write to a file, the data is copied from memory to a storage device. When you are done with a file, you close it.

- A sequential file is a file in which records are stored one after another in some order. A control break program is one that reads a sequential file and performs special processing based on a change in one or more fields in each record in the file.

- Merging files involves combining two or more files while maintaining the sequential order.

- Some related sequential files are master files that hold relatively permanent data, and transaction files that hold more temporary data. Commonly, you gather transactions for a period of time, store them in a file, and then use them one by one to update matching records in a master file.

- Real-time, interactive applications require random access files in which records can be located in any order. Files in which records must be accessed immediately are also called instant access files and direct access files.

Key Terms

A **computer file** is a collection of data stored on a nonvolatile device in a computer system.

Permanent storage devices hold nonvolatile data; examples include hard disks, DVDs, USB drives, and reels of magnetic tape.

Text files contain data that can be read in a text editor.

Binary files contain data that has not been encoded as text.

A **byte** is a small unit of storage; for example, in a simple text file, a byte holds only one character.

A **kilobyte** is approximately 1000 bytes.

A **megabyte** is a million bytes.

A **gigabyte** is a billion bytes.

Directories are organization units on storage devices; each can contain multiple files as well as additional directories. In a graphic system, directories are often called *folders*.

Folders are organization units on storage devices; each can contain multiple files as well as additional folders. Folders are graphic directories.

A file's **path** is the combination of its disk drive and the complete hierarchy of directories in which the file resides.

The **data hierarchy** is a framework that describes the relationships between data components. The data hierarchy contains characters, fields, records, and files.

Characters are letters, numbers, and special symbols, such as "A", "7", and "$".

Fields are single useful data items that are composed of one or more characters.

Records are groups of fields that go together for some logical reason.

Files are groups of related records.

A **database** holds groups of files and provides methods for easy retrieval and organization.

Tables are files in a database.

Opening a file locates it on a storage device and associates a variable name within your program with the file.

Reading from a file copies data from a file on a storage device into RAM.

Writing to a file copies data from RAM to persistent storage.

Closing a file makes it no longer available to an application.

Default input and output devices are those that do not require opening. Usually they are the keyboard and monitor, respectively.

A **backup file** is a copy that is kept in case values need to be restored to their original state.

A **parent file** is a copy of a file before revision.

A **child file** is a copy of a file after revision.

A **sequential file** is a file in which records are stored one after another in some order.

A **control break** is a temporary detour in the logic of a program.

A **control break program** is one in which a change in the value of a variable initiates special actions or causes special or unusual processing to occur.

A **control break report** is a form of output that includes special processing after each group of records.

A **single-level control break** is a break in the logic of the program to perform special processing based on the value of a single variable.

A **control break field** holds a value that causes special processing in a control break program.

Merging files involves combining two or more files while maintaining the sequential order.

A **master file** holds complete and relatively permanent data.

A **transaction file** holds temporary data that you use to update a master file.

To **update a master file** involves making changes to the values in its fields based on transactions.

Batch processing involves performing the same tasks with many records, one after the other.

Real-time applications require that a record be accessed immediately while a client is waiting.

In an **interactive program**, the user makes direct requests, as opposed to one in which input comes from a file.

In **random access files**, records can be located in any order.

Instant access files are random access files in which records must be accessed immediately.

Direct access files are random access files.

Review Questions

1. Random access memory is _____.

    a. permanent

    b. volatile

    c. persistent

    d. continual

2. Which is true of text files?

    a. Text files contain data that can be read in a text editor.

    b. Text files commonly contain images and music.

    c. Both of the Above.

    d. None of the Above.

3. Every file on a storage device has a _____.

    a. name

    b. size

    c. both of the above

    d. none of the above

4. Which of the following is true regarding the data hierarchy?

    a. Files contain records.

    b. Characters contain fields.

    c. Fields contain files.

    d. Fields contain records.

5. The process of _____ a file locates it on a storage device and associates a variable name within your program with the file.

    a. opening

    b. closing

    c. declaring

    d. defining

6. When you write to a file, you _____.

    a. move data from a storage device to memory

    b. copy data from a storage device to memory

    c. move data from memory to a storage device

    d. copy data from memory to a storage device

7. Unlike when you print a report, when a program's output is a data file, you do not _____.

    a. include headings or other formatting

    b. open the files

    c. include all the fields represented as input

    d. all of the above

8. When you close a file, it _____.

    a. is no longer available to the program

    b. cannot be reopened

    c. becomes associated with an internal identifier

    d. ceases to exist

9. A file in which records are stored one after another in some order is a(n) _____ file.

    a. temporal

    b. sequential

    c. random

    d. alphabetical

10. When you combine two or more sorted files while maintaining their sequential order based on a field, you are _____ the files.

    a. tracking

    b. collating

    c. merging

    d. absorbing

11. A control break occurs when a program _____.

    a. takes one of two alternate courses of action for every record

    b. ends prematurely, before all records have been processed

    c. pauses to perform special processing based on the value of a field

    d. passes logical control to a module contained within another program

12. Which of the following is an example of a control break report?

    a. a list of all customers of a business in zip code order, with a count of the number of customers who reside in each zip code

    b. a list of all students in a school, arranged in alphabetical order, with a total count at the end of the report

    c. a list of all employees in a company, with a message "Retain" or "Dismiss" following each employee record

    d. a list of some of the patients of a medical clinic—those who have not seen a doctor for at least two years

13. A control break field _____.

    a. always is output prior to any group of records on a control break report

    b. always is output after any group of records on a control break report

    c. never is output on a report

    d. causes special processing to occur

14. Whenever a control break occurs during record processing in any control break program, you must _____.

    a. declare a control break field

    b. set the control break field to 0

    c. update the value in the control break field

    d. output the control break field

15. Assume you are writing a program to merge two files named FallStudents and SpringStudents. Each file contains a list of students enrolled in a programming logic course during the semester indicated, and each file is sorted in student ID number order. After the program compares two records and subsequently writes a Fall student to output, the next step is to _____.

    a. read a SpringStudents record

    b. read a FallStudents record

    c. write a SpringStudents record

    d. write another FallStudents record

16. When you merge records from two or more sequential files, the usual case is that the records in the files _____.

    a. contain the same data

    b. have the same format

    c. are identical in number

    d. are sorted on different fields

17. A file that holds more permanent data than a transaction file is a _____ file.

    a. master

    b. primary

    c. key

    d. mega-

18. A transaction file is often used to _____ another file.

    a. augment

    b. remove

    c. verify

    d. update

19. The saved version of a file that does not contain the most recently applied transactions is known as a _____ file.

    a. master

    b. child

    c. parent

    d. relative

20. Random access files are used most frequently in all of the following except _____.

    a. interactive programs

    b. batch processing

    c. real-time applications

    d. programs requiring direct access

Exercises

Your student disk contains one or more comma-delimited sample data files for each exercise in this section and the Game Zone section. You might want to use these files in any of several ways:

- You can look at the file contents to better understand the types of data each program uses.

- You can use the files' contents as sample data when you desk-check the logic of your flowcharts or pseudocode.

- You can use the files as input files if you implement the solutions in a programming language and write programs that accept file input.

- You can use the data as guides for entering appropriate values if you implement the solutions in a programming language and write interactive programs.

- When multiple files are included for an exercise, it reminds you that the problem requires different procedures when the number of data records varies.

1. The Vernon Hills Mail-Order Company often sends multiple packages per order. For each customer order, output enough mailing labels to use on each of the boxes that will be mailed. The mailing labels contain the customer's complete name and address, along with a box number in the form "Box 9 of 9". For example, an order that requires three boxes produces three labels: "Box 1 of 3", "Box 2 of 3", and "Box 3 of 3". Design an

application that reads records that contain a customer's title (for example, "Mrs."), first name, last name, street address, city, state, zip code, and number of boxes. The application must read the records until eof is encountered. Produce enough mailing labels for each order.

2. The Springwater Township School District has two high schools—Jefferson and Audubon. Each school maintains a student file with fields containing student ID, last name, first name, and address. Each file is in student ID number order. Design the logic for a program that merges the two files into one file containing a list of all students in the district, maintaining student ID number order.

3. The Redgranite Library keeps a file of all books borrowed every month. Each file is in Library of Congress number order and contains additional fields for author and title.

    a. Design the logic for a program that merges the files for January and February to create a list of all books borrowed in the two-month period.

    b. Modify the library program so that if a book number has more than one record, you output the book information only once.

    c. Modify the library program so that if a book number has more than one record, you not only output the book information only once, you output a count of the total number of times the book was borrowed.

4. Hearthside Realtors keeps a transaction file for each salesperson in the office. Each transaction record contains the salesperson's first name, date of the sale, and sale price. The records for the year are sorted in ascending sale price order. Two salespeople, Diane and Mark, have formed a partnership. Design the logic that produces a merged list of their transactions (including name of salesperson, date, and price) in descending order by price.

5. Dartmoor Medical Associates maintains two patient files—one for the Lakewood office and one for the Hanover office. Each record contains the name, address, city, state, and zip code of a patient, with the files maintained in zip code order. Design the logic that merges the two files to produce one combined name-and-address file, which the office staff can use for addressing mailings of the practice's monthly Healthy Lifestyles newsletter.

6. a. The Willmington Walking Club maintains a master file that contains a record for each of its members. Fields in the master file include the walker's ID number, first name, last name, and total miles walked to the nearest one-tenth of a mile. Every week, a transaction file is produced. It contains a walker's ID number and the number of miles the walker has logged that week. Each file is sorted in walker ID number order. Design the logic for a program that matches the master and transaction file records and updates the total miles walked for each club member by adding the current week's miles to the cumulative total. Not all walkers submit walking reports each week. The output is the updated master file and an error report that lists any transaction records for which no master record exists.

   b. Modify the walking club program to output a certificate of achievement each time a walker exceeds the 500-mile mark. The certificate, which contains the walker's name and an appropriate congratulatory message, is output during the execution of the update program when a walker's mile total surpasses 500.

7. a. The Timely Talent Temporary Help Agency maintains an employee master file that contains an employee ID number, last name, first name, address, and hourly rate for each temporary worker. The file has been sorted in employee ID number order. Each week, a transaction file is created with a job number, address, customer name, employee ID, and hours worked for every job filled by Timely Talent workers. The transaction file is also sorted in employee ID order. Design the logic for a program that matches the master and transaction file records, and outputs one line for each transaction, indicating job number, employee ID number, hours worked, hourly rate, and gross pay. Assume that each temporary worker works, at most, one job per week; output one line for each worker who has worked that week.

   b. Modify the help agency program so that any temporary worker can work any number of separate jobs in a week. Print one line for each job that week.

   c. Modify the help agency program so that it accumulates the worker's total pay for all jobs in a week and outputs one line per worker.

Find the Bugs

8. Your student disk contains files named DEBUG07-01.txt, DEBUG07-02.txt, and DEBUG07-03.txt. Each file starts with some comments that describe the problem. Comments are lines that begin with two slashes (//). Following the comments, each file contains pseudocode that has one or more bugs you must find and correct.

Game Zone

9. The International Rock Paper Scissors Society holds regional and national championships. Each region holds a semifinal competition in which contestants play 500 games of Rock Paper Scissors. The top 20 competitors in each region are invited to the national finals. Assume you are provided with files for the East, Midwest, and Western regions. Each file contains the following fields for the top 20 competitors: last name, first name, and number of games won. The records in each file are sorted in alphabetical order. Merge the three files to create a file of the top 60 competitors who will compete in the national championship.

10. In the Game Zone section of Chapter 5, you designed a guessing game in which the application generates a random number and the player tries to guess it. After each guess, you displayed a message indicating whether the player's guess was correct, too high, or too low. When the player eventually guessed the correct number, you displayed a score that represented a count of the number of guesses that were required. Modify the game so that when it starts, the player enters his or her name. After a player plays the game exactly five times, save the best (lowest) score from the five games to a file. If the player's name already exists in the file, update the record with the new lowest score. If the player's name does not already exist in the file, create a new record for the player. After the file is updated, display all the best scores stored in the file.

Up for Discussion

11. Suppose you are hired by a police department to write a program that matches arrest records with court records detailing the ultimate outcome or verdict for each case. You have been given access to current files so that you can test the program. Your friend works in the personnel department of a large company and must perform background checks on potential employees. (The job applicants sign a form authorizing the check.) Police records are open to the public and your friend could look up police records at the courthouse, but it would take many hours per week. As a convenience, should you provide your friend with outcomes of any arrest records of job applicants?

12. Suppose you are hired by a clinic to match a file of patient office visits with patient master records to print various reports. While working with the confidential data, you notice the name of a friend's fiancé. Should you tell your friend that the fiancé is seeking medical treatment? Does the type of treatment affect your answer?

Understanding Numbering Systems and Computer Codes

The numbering system with which you are most familiar is the decimal system—the system based on 10 digits, 0 through 9. When you use the decimal system, no other symbols are available; if you want to express a value larger than 9, you must resort to using multiple digits from the same pool of 10, placing them in columns.

When you use the decimal system, you analyze a multicolumn number by mentally assigning place values to each column. The value of the rightmost column is 1, the value of the next column to the left is 10, the next column is 100, and so on, multiplying the column value by 10 as you move to the left. There is no limit to the number of columns you can use; you simply keep adding columns to the left as you need to express higher values. For example, Figure A-1 shows how the value 305 is represented in the decimal system. You simply sum the value of the digit in each column after it has been multiplied by the value of its column.

```
      Column value
  100    10     1
 ┌─────┬─────┬─────┐
 │  3  │  0  │  5  │
 └─────┴─────┴─────┘

 ┌─────────────────────┐
 │ 3 * 100 = 300       │
 │ 0 * 10  =   0       │
 │ 5 * 1   =   5       │
 │           ---       │
 │           305       │
 └─────────────────────┘
```

Figure A-1 Representing 305 in the decimal system

The binary numbering system works in the same way as the decimal numbering system, except that it uses only two digits, 0 and 1. When you use the binary system, if you want to express a value greater than 1, you must resort to using multiple columns, because no single symbol is available that represents any value other than 0 or 1. However, instead of each new column to the left being 10 times greater than

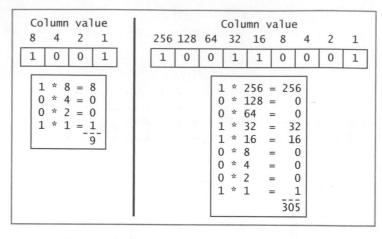

Figure A-2   Representing decimal values 9 and 305 in the binary system

the previous column, when you use the binary system, each new column is only two times the value of the previous column. For example, Figure A-2 shows how the numbers 9 and 305 are represented in the binary system. Notice that in both binary numbers, as well as in the decimal system, it is perfectly acceptable—and often necessary—to create numbers with 0 in one or more columns. As with the decimal system, the binary system has no limit to the number of columns—you can use as many as it takes to express a value.

A computer stores every piece of data it ever uses as a set of 0s and 1s. Each 0 or 1 is known as a bit, which is short for binary digit. Every computer uses 0s and 1s because all values in a computer are stored as electronic signals that are either on or off. This two-state system is most easily represented using just two digits.

Computers use a set of binary digits to represent stored characters. If computers used only one binary digit to represent characters, then only two different characters could be represented, because the single bit could be only 0 or 1. If computers used only two digits, then only four characters could be represented—the four codes 00, 01, 10, and 11, which in decimal values are 0, 1, 2, and 3, respectively. Many computers use sets of eight binary digits to represent each character they store, because using eight binary digits provides 256 different combinations. One combination can represent an "A", another a "B", still others "a" and "b", and so on. Two hundred fifty-six combinations are enough so that each capital letter, small letter, digit, and punctuation mark used in English has its own code; even a space has a code. For example, in some computers 01000001 represents the character "A". The binary number 01000001 has a decimal value of 65, but this numeric value is not important to ordinary computer users; it is simply a code that

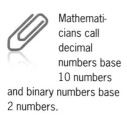

Mathematicians call decimal numbers base 10 numbers and binary numbers base 2 numbers.

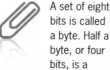

A set of eight bits is called a byte. Half a byte, or four bits, is a nibble. You will learn more about bytes later in this appendix.

stands for "A". The code that uses 01000001 to mean "A" is the American Standard Code for Information Interchange, or ASCII.

The ASCII code is not the only computer code; it is typical, and is the one used in most personal computers. The Extended Binary Coded Decimal Interchange Code, or EBCDIC, is an eight-bit code that is used in IBM mainframe computers. In these computers, the principle is the same—every character is stored as a series of binary digits. However, the actual values used are different. For example, in EBCDIC, an "A" is 11000001, or 193. Another code used by languages such as Java and C# is Unicode; with this code, 16 bits are used to represent each character. The character "A" in Unicode has the same decimal value as the ASCII "A", 65, but it is stored as 0000000001000001. Using 16 bits provides many more possible combinations than using only eight bits—65,536 to be exact. With Unicode, not only are there enough available codes for all English letters and digits, but also for characters from many international alphabets.

Ordinary computer users seldom think about the numeric codes behind the letters, numbers, and punctuation marks they enter from their keyboards or see displayed on a monitor. However, they see the consequence of the values behind letters when they see data sorted in alphabetical order. When you sort a list of names, "Andrea" comes before "Brian," and "Caroline" comes after "Brian" because the numeric code for "A" is lower than the code for "B", and the numeric code for "C" is higher than the code for "B", no matter whether you are using ASCII, EBCDIC, or Unicode.

Table A-1 shows the decimal and binary values behind the most commonly used characters in the ASCII character set—the letters, numbers, and punctuation marks you can enter from your keyboard using a single key press.

Most of the values not included in Table A-1 have a purpose. For example, the decimal value 7 represents a bell—a dinging sound your computer can make, often used to notify you of an error or some other unusual condition.

Each binary number in Table A-1 is shown containing two sets of four digits; this convention makes the long eight-digit numbers easier to read.

Decimal number	Binary number	ASCII character	
32	0010 0000		Space
33	0010 0001	!	Exclamation point
34	0010 0010	"	Quotation mark, or double quote
35	0010 0011	#	Number sign, also called an octothorpe or a pound sign
36	0010 0100	$	Dollar sign
37	0010 0101	%	Percent
38	0010 0110	&	Ampersand
39	0010 0111	'	Apostrophe, single quote
40	0010 1000	(	Left parenthesis
41	0010 1001	)	Right parenthesis
42	0010 1010	*	Asterisk
43	0010 1011	+	Plus sign
44	0010 1100	,	Comma
45	0010 1101	-	Hyphen or minus sign
46	0010 1110	.	Period or decimal point
47	0010 1111	/	Slash or front slash
48	0011 0000	0	
49	0011 0001	1	
50	0011 0010	2	
51	0011 0011	3	
52	0011 0100	4	
53	0011 0101	5	
54	0011 0110	6	
55	0011 0111	7	
56	0011 1000	8	
57	0011 1001	9	
58	0011 1010	:	Colon
59	0011 1011	;	Semicolon
60	0011 1100	<	Less-than sign
61	0011 1101	=	Equal sign
62	0011 1110	>	Greater-than sign
63	0011 1111	?	Question mark
64	0100 0000	@	At sign
65	0100 0001	A	

Table A-1   Decimal and binary values for common ASCII characters

Decimal number	Binary number	ASCII character	
66	0100 0010	B	
67	0100 0011	C	
68	0100 0100	D	
69	0100 0101	E	
70	0100 0110	F	
71	0100 0111	G	
72	0100 1000	H	
73	0100 1001	I	
74	0100 1010	J	
75	0100 1011	K	
76	0100 1100	L	
77	0100 1101	M	
78	0100 1110	N	
79	0100 1111	O	
80	0101 0000	P	
81	0101 0001	Q	
82	0101 0010	R	
83	0101 0011	S	
84	0101 0100	T	
85	0101 0101	U	
86	0101 0110	V	
87	0101 0111	W	
88	0101 1000	X	
89	0101 1001	Y	
90	0101 1010	Z	
91	0101 1011	[	Opening or left bracket
92	0101 1100	\	Backslash
93	0101 1101	]	Closing or right bracket
94	0101 1110	^	Caret
95	0101 1111	_	Underline or underscore
96	0110 0000	`	Grave accent
97	0110 0001	a	
98	0110 0010	b	
99	0110 0011	c	
100	0110 0100	d	

Table A-1   Decimal and binary values for common ASCII characters (continued)

Decimal number	Binary number	ASCII character	
101	0110 0101	e	
102	0110 0110	f	
103	0110 0111	g	
104	0110 1000	h	
105	0110 1001	i	
106	0110 1010	j	
107	0110 1011	k	
108	0110 1100	l	
109	0110 1101	m	
110	0110 1110	n	
111	0110 1111	o	
112	0111 0000	p	
113	0111 0001	q	
114	0111 0010	r	
115	0111 0011	s	
116	0111 0100	t	
117	0111 0101	u	
118	0111 0110	v	
119	0111 0111	w	
120	0111 1000	x	
121	0111 1001	y	
122	0111 1010	z	
123	0111 1011	{	Opening or left brace
124	0111 1100	|	Vertical line or pipe
125	0111 1101	}	Closing or right brace
126	0111 1110	~	Tilde

Table A-1 Decimal and binary values for common ASCII characters (continued)

The Hexadecimal System

The hexadecimal numbering system is called the base 16 system because it uses 16 digits. As shown in Table A-2, the digits are 0 through 9 and A through F. Computer professionals often use the hexadecimal system to express addresses and instructions as they are stored in computer memory because hexadecimal provides convenient shorthand expressions for groups of binary values. In Table A-2, each hexadecimal value represents one of the 16 possible combinations of four-digit binary values.

Decimal value	Hexadecimal value	Binary value (shown using four digits)
0	0	0000
1	1	0001
2	2	0010
3	3	0011
4	4	0100
5	5	0101
6	6	0110
7	7	0111
8	8	1000
9	9	1001
10	A	1010
11	B	1011
12	C	1100
13	D	1101
14	E	1110
15	F	1111

Table A-2   Values in the decimal and hexadecimal systems

Therefore, instead of referencing memory contents as a 16-digit binary value, for example, programmers can use a 4-digit hexadecimal value.

In the hexadecimal system, each column is 16 times the value of the column to its right. Therefore, column values from right to left are 1, 16, 256, 4096, and so on. Figure A-3 shows how 171 and 305 are expressed in hexadecimal.

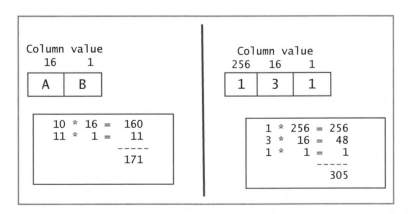

Figure A-3   Representing decimal values 171 and 305 in the hexadecimal system

Measuring Storage

In computer systems, both internal memory and external storage are measured in bits and bytes. Eight bits make a byte, and a byte frequently holds a single character (in ASCII or EBCDIC) or half a character (in Unicode). Because a byte is such a small unit of storage, the size of memory and files is often expressed in thousands or billions of bytes. Table A-3 describes some commonly used terms for storage measurement.

In the metric system, "kilo" means 1000. However, in Table A-3, notice that a kilobyte is 1024 bytes. The discrepancy occurs because everything stored in a computer is based on the binary system, so multiples of two are used in most measurements. If you multiply 2 by itself 10 times, the result is 1024, which is a little over 1000. Similarly, a gigabyte is 1,073,741,624 bytes, which is more than a billion.

Confusion arises because many hard-drive manufacturers use the decimal system instead of the binary system to describe storage. For example, if you buy a hard drive that holds 10 gigabytes, it actually holds exactly 10 billion bytes. However, in the binary system, 10 GB is 10,737,418,240 bytes, so when you check your hard drive's capacity, your computer will report that you don't quite have 10 GB, but only 9.31 GB.

Term	Abbreviation	Number of bytes using binary system	Number of bytes using decimal system	Example
Kilobyte	KB or kB	1024	one thousand	This appendix occupies about 85 kB on a hard disk.
Megabyte	MB	1,048,576 (1024 × 1024 kilobytes)	one million	One megabyte can hold an average book in text format. A 3½ inch diskette you might have used a few years ago held 1.44 megabytes.
Gigabyte	GB	1,073,741,824 (1,024 megabytes)	one billion	The hard drive on a fairly new laptop computer might be 160 gigabytes. An hour of HDTV video is about 4 gigabytes.
Terabyte	TB	1024 gigabytes	one trillion	The entire Library of Congress can be stored in 10 terabytes.
Petabyte	PB	1024 terabytes	one quadrillion	Popular Web sites such as YouTube and Google have 20 to 30 petabytes of activity per month.
Exabyte	EB	1024 petabytes	one quintillion	A popular expression claims that all words ever spoken by humans could be stored in text form in 5 exabytes.
Zettabyte	ZB	1024 exabytes	one sextillion	A popular expression claims that all words ever spoken by humans could be stored in audio form in 42 zettabytes.
Yottabyte	YB	1024 zettabytes	one septillion (a 1 followed by 24 zeros)	All data accessible on the Internet and in corporate networks is estimated to be 1 yottabyte.

Table A-3 Commonly used terms for computer storage

Flowchart
Symbols

This appendix contains the flowchart symbols used in this book.

Terminal	⬭
Flowline	→
Input/Output	▱
Process	▭
Decision	◇
Internal module call	▭
External module call	▯

Structures

This appendix contains diagrams of the structures allowed in structured programming. Although all logical problems can be solved using the three fundamental structures, the additional structures provide convenience in some situations. Each structure has one entry point and one exit point. At these points, structures can be stacked and nested.

Three Fundamental Structures

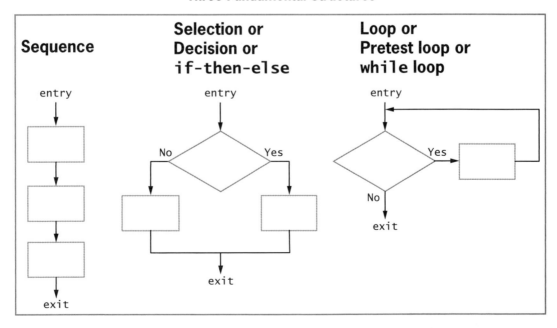

Additional Selection Structures

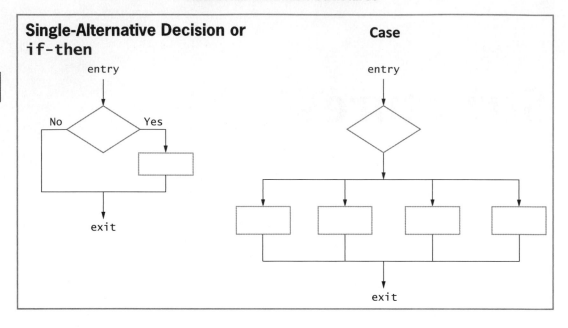

Single-Alternative Decision or `if-then`

Case

For more information on the case structure and posttest loops, see Appendix F.

Additional Loop Structure

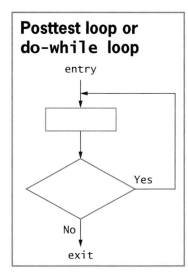

Posttest loop or `do-while` loop

Solving Difficult Structuring Problems

In Chapter 3, you learned that you can solve any logical problem using only the three standard structures—sequence, selection, and loop. Modifying an unstructured program to make it adhere to structured rules often is a simple matter. Sometimes, however, structuring a more complicated program can be challenging. Still, no matter how complicated, large, or poorly structured a problem is, the same tasks can *always* be accomplished in a structured manner.

Consider the flowchart segment in Figure D-1. Is it structured?

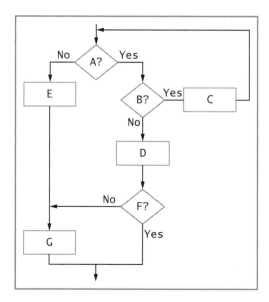

Figure D-1 Unstructured flowchart segment

No, it is not structured. To straighten out the flowchart segment, making it structured, you can use the "spaghetti" method. Using this method, you untangle each path of the flowchart as if you were attempting to untangle strands of spaghetti in a bowl. The objective is to create a new flowchart segment that performs exactly the same tasks as the first, but using only the three structures—sequence, selection, and loop.

To begin to untangle the unstructured flowchart segment, you start at the beginning with the decision labeled A, shown in Figure D-2. This step must represent the beginning of either a selection or a loop, because a sequence would not contain a decision.

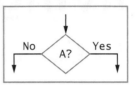

Figure D-2 Structuring, Step 1

If you follow the logic on the No, or left, side of the question in the original flowchart, you can pull up on the left branch of the decision. You encounter process E, followed by G, followed by the end, as shown in Figure D-3. Compare the "No" actions after Decision A in the first flowchart (Figure D-1) with the actions after Decision A in Figure D-3; they are identical.

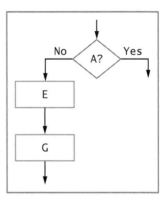

Figure D-3 Structuring, Step 2

Now continue on the right, or Yes, side of Decision A in Figure D-1. When you follow the flowline, you encounter a decision symbol, labeled B. Pull on B's left side, and a process, D, comes up next. See Figure D-4.

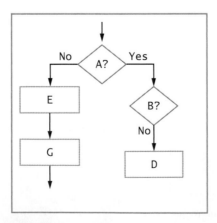

Figure D-4 Structuring, Step 3

After Step D in the original diagram, a decision labeled F comes up. Pull on its left, or No, side and you get a process, G, and then the end. When you pull on F's right, or Yes, side in the original flowchart, you simply reach the end, as shown in Figure D-5. Notice in Figure D-5 that the G process now appears in two locations. When you improve unstructured flowcharts so that they become structured, you often must repeat steps. This eliminates crossed lines and difficult-to-follow spaghetti logic.

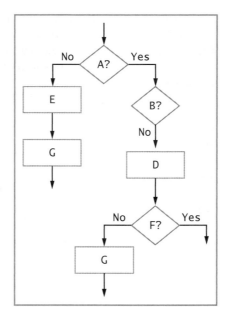

Figure D-5   Structuring, Step 4

The biggest problem in structuring the original flowchart segment from Figure D-1 follows the right, or Yes, side of the B decision. When the answer to B is Yes, you encounter process C, as shown in both Figures D-1 and D-6. The structure that begins with Decision C looks like a loop because it doubles back, up to Decision A. However, the rules of a structured loop say that it must have the appearance shown in Figure D-7: a question, followed by a structure, returning

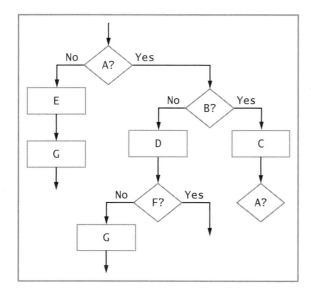

Figure D-6   Structuring, Step 5

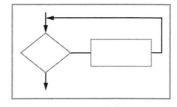

Figure D-7   A structured loop

right back to the question. In Figure D-1, if the path coming out of C returned right to B, there would be no problem; it would be a simple, structured loop. However, as it is, Question A must be repeated. The spaghetti technique says if things are tangled up, start repeating them. So repeat an A decision after C, as Figure D-6 shows.

In the original flowchart segment in Figure D-1, when A is Yes, Question B always follows. So, in Figure D-8, after A is Yes and B is Yes, Step C executes, and A is asked again; when A is Yes, B repeats. In the original, when B is Yes, C executes, so in Figure D-8, on the right side of B, C repeats. After C, A occurs. On the right side of A, B occurs. On the right side of B, C occurs. After C, A should occur again, and so on. Soon you should realize that, to follow the steps in the same order as in the original flowchart segment, you will repeat these same steps forever.

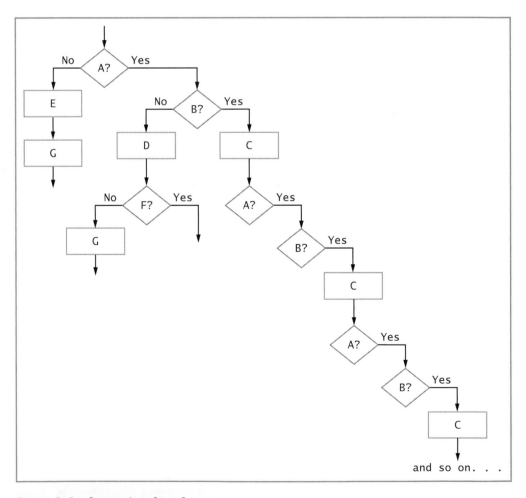

Figure D-8   Structuring, Step 6

If you continue with Figure D-8, you will never be able to end; every C is always followed by another A, B, and C. Sometimes, to make a program segment structured, you have to add an extra flag variable to get out of an infinite mess. A flag is a variable that you set to indicate a true or false state. Typically, a variable is called a flag when its only purpose is to tell you whether some event has occurred. You can create a flag variable named `shouldRepeat` and set its value to "Yes" or "No", depending on whether it is appropriate to repeat Decision A. When A is No, the `shouldRepeat` flag should be set

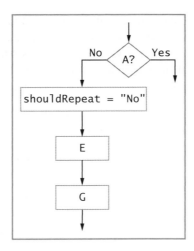

Figure D-9   Adding a flag to the flowchart

to "No" because, in this situation, you never want to repeat Question A again. See Figure D-9.

Similarly, after A is Yes, but when B is No, you never want to repeat Question A again, either. Figure D-10 shows that you set `shouldRepeat` to "No" when the answer to B is No. Then you continue with D and the F decision that executes G when F is No.

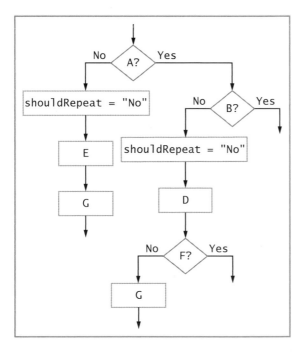

Figure D-10   Adding a flag to a second path in the flowchart

However, in the original flowchart segment in Figure D-1, when the B decision result is Yes, you *do* want to repeat A. So when B is Yes, perform the process for C and set the `shouldRepeat` flag equal to "Yes", as shown in Figure D-11.

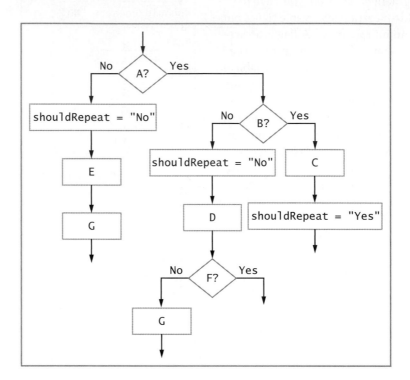

Figure D-11 Adding a flag to a third path in the flowchart

Now all paths of the flowchart can join together at the bottom with one final question: Is `shouldRepeat` equal to "Yes"? If it isn't, exit; but if it is, extend the flowline to go back to repeat Question A. See Figure D-12. Take a moment to verify that the steps that would execute following Figure D-12 are the same steps that would execute following Figure D-1.

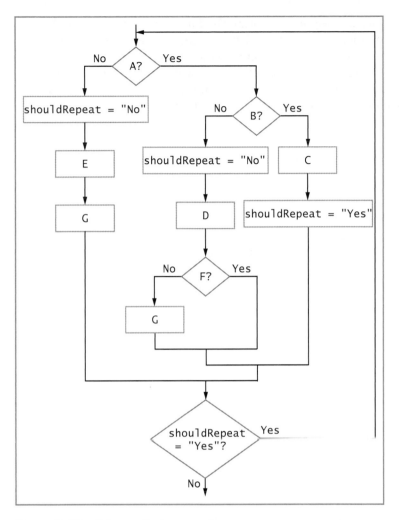

Figure D-12 Tying up the loose ends

- When **A** is No, **E** and **G** always execute.
- When **A** is Yes and **B** is No, **D** and decision **F** always execute.
- When **A** is Yes and **B** is Yes, **C** always executes and **A** repeats.

Figure D-12 contains three nested selection structures. Notice how the **F** decision begins a complete selection structure whose Yes and No paths join together when the structure ends. This **F** selection structure is within one path of the **B** decision structure; the **B** decision begins a complete selection structure, the Yes and No paths of which join together at the bottom. Likewise, the **B** selection structure resides entirely within one path of the **A** selection structure.

The flowchart segment in Figure D-12 performs identically to the original spaghetti version in Figure D-1. However, is this new flowchart segment structured? There are so many steps in the diagram, it is hard to tell. You may be able to see the structure more clearly if you create a module named **aThroughG()**. If you create the module shown in Figure D-13, then the original flowchart segment can be drawn as in Figure D-14.

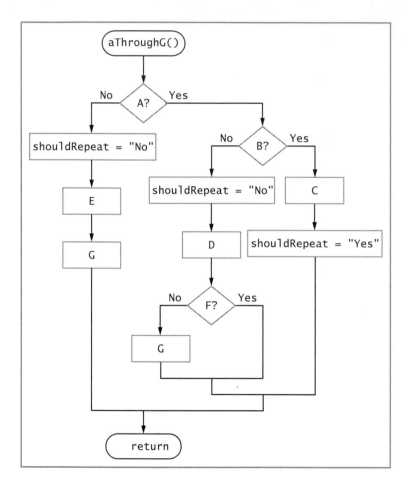

Figure D-13 The **aThroughG()** module

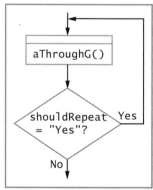

Figure D-14 Logic in Figure D-12, substituting a module for Steps A through G

Now you can see that the completed flowchart segment in Figure D-14 is a do-until loop. If you prefer to use a while loop, you can redraw Figure D-14 to perform a sequence followed by a while loop, as shown in Figure D-15.

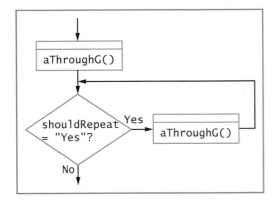

Figure D-15 Logic in Figure D-14, substituting a sequence and while loop for the do-until loop

It has taken some effort, but any logical problem can be made to conform to structured rules. It may take extra steps, including repeating specific steps and using some flag variables, but every logical problem can be solved using the three structures: sequence, selection, and loop.

Creating Print Charts

A printed report is a very common type of output. You can design a printed report on a printer spacing chart, which is also called a print chart or a print layout. Many modern-day programmers use various software tools to design their output, but you can also create a print chart by hand. This appendix provides some of the details for creating a traditional handwritten print chart. Even if you never design output on your own, you might see print charts in the documentation of existing programs.

Figure E-1 shows a printer spacing chart, which basically looks like graph paper. The chart has many boxes, and in each box the designer

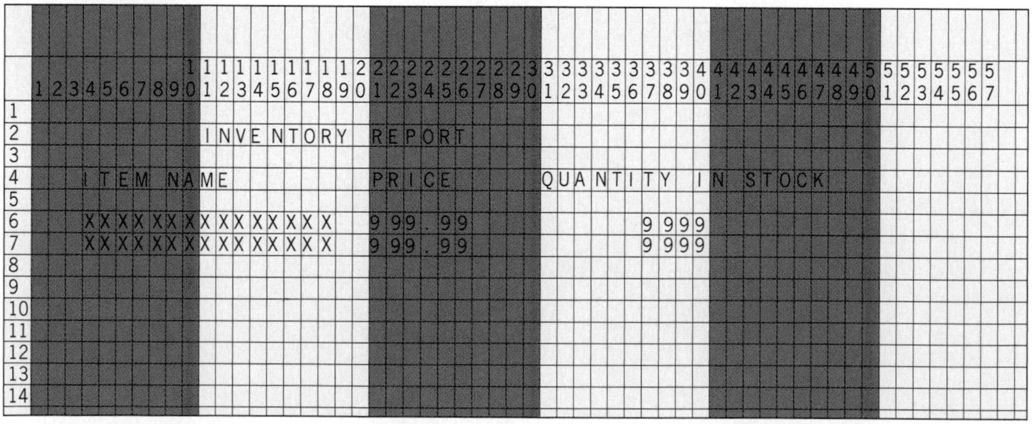

Figure E-1 A printer spacing chart

places one character that will be printed. The rows and columns in the chart usually are numbered for reference.

For example, suppose you want to create a printed report with the following features:

- A printed title, INVENTORY REPORT, that begins 11 spaces from the left edge of the page and one line down

- Column headings for ITEM NAME, PRICE, and QUANTITY IN STOCK, two lines below the title and placed over the actual data items that are displayed

- Variable data appearing below each of the column headings

The exact spacing and the use of uppercase or lowercase characters in the print chart make a difference. Notice that the constant data in the output—the items that remain the same in every execution of the report—do not need to follow the same rules as variable names in the program. Within a report, constants like INVENTORY REPORT and ITEM NAME can contain spaces. These headings exist to help readers understand the information presented in the report, not for a computer to interpret; there is no need to run the names together, as you do when choosing identifiers for variables.

A print layout typically shows how the variable data will appear on the report. Of course, the data will probably be different every time the program is executed. Thus, instead of writing in actual item names and prices, the users and programmers usually use Xs to represent generic variable characters, and 9s to represent generic variable numeric data. (Some programmers use Xs for both character and numeric data.) Each line containing Xs and 9s is a detail line, or a line that displays the data details. Detail lines typically appear many times per page, as opposed to heading lines, which contain the title and any column headings, and usually appear only once per page.

Even though an actual inventory report might eventually go on for hundreds or thousands of detail lines, writing two or three rows of Xs and 9s is sufficient to show how the data will appear. For example, if a report contains employee names and salaries, those data items will occupy the same print positions on output for line after line, whether the output eventually contains 10 employees or 10,000. A few rows of identically positioned Xs and 9s are sufficient to establish the pattern.

Two Variations on the Basic Structures— case and do-while

You can solve any logic problem you might encounter using only the three structures: sequence, selection, and loop. However, many programming languages allow two more structures: the case structure and the do-while loop. These structures are never *needed* to solve any problem—you can always use a series of selections instead of the case structure, and you can always use a sequence plus a while loop in place of the do-while loop. However, sometimes these additional structures are convenient. Programmers consider them all to be acceptable, legal structures.

The case Structure

You can use the case structure when there are several distinct possible values for a single variable you are testing and each value requires a different course of action. Suppose you work at a school at which tuition varies per credit hour, depending on whether a student is a freshman, sophomore, junior, or senior. The structured flowchart and pseudocode in Figure F-1 show a series of decisions that assigns different tuition values depending on the value of year.

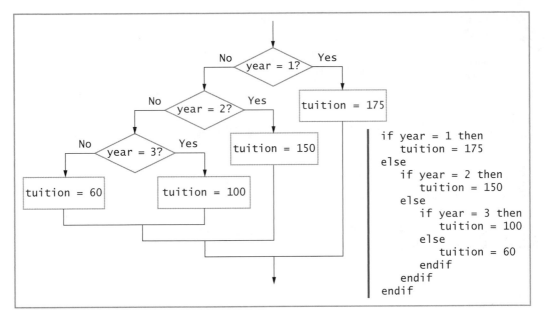

Figure F-1 Flowchart and pseudocode of tuition decisions

The logic shown in Figure F-1 is absolutely correct and completely structured. The year = 3? selection structure is contained within the year = 2? structure, which is contained within the year = 1? structure. (In this example, if year is not 1, 2, or 3, it is assumed that the student receives the senior tuition rate.)

Even though the program segments in Figure F-1 are correct and structured, many programming languages permit using a **case** structure, as shown in Figure F-2. When using the **case** structure, you test a variable against a series of values, taking appropriate action based on the variable's value. Many people feel such programs are easier to read, and the **case** structure is allowed because the same results *could*

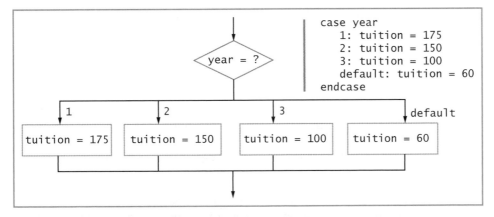

Figure F-2 Flowchart and pseudocode of **case** structure that determines tuition

The term *default* used in Figure F-2 means "if none of the other cases is true." Various programming languages you learn may use different syntaxes for the default case.

 You use the case structure only when a series of decisions is based on different values stored in a single variable. If multiple variables are tested, then you must use a series of decisions.

be achieved with a series of structured selections (thus making the program structured). That is, if the first program is structured and the second one reflects the first one point by point, then the second one must be structured also.

Even though a programming language permits you to use the case structure, you should understand that the case structure is just a convenience that might make a flowchart, pseudocode, or actual program code easier to understand at first glance. When you write a series of decisions using the case structure, the computer still makes a series of individual decisions, just as though you had used many if-then-else combinations. In other words, you might prefer looking at the diagram in Figure F-2 to understand the tuition fees charged by a school, but a computer actually makes the decisions as shown in Figure F-1—one at a time. When you write your own programs, it is always acceptable to express a complicated decision-making process as a series of individual selections.

The do-while Loop

Recall that a structured loop (often called a while loop) looks like Figure F-3. A special-case loop called a do-while loop looks like Figure F-4.

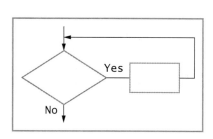

Figure F-3 The while loop, which is a pretest loop

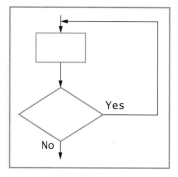

Figure F-4 Structure of a do-while loop, which is a posttest loop

 Notice that the word "do" begins the name of the do-while loop. This should remind you that the action you "do" precedes testing the condition.

An important difference exists between these two structures. In a while loop, you ask a question and, depending on the answer, you might or might not enter the loop to execute the loop's procedure. Conversely, in do-while loops, you ensure that the procedure executes at least once; then, depending on the answer to the controlling question, the loop may or may not execute additional times.

In a while loop, the question that controls a loop comes at the beginning, or "top," of the loop body. A while loop is a pretest loop because a condition is tested before entering the loop even once. In a do-while loop, the question that controls the loop comes at the end, or "bottom," of the loop body. Do-while loops are posttest loops because a condition is tested after the loop body has executed.

You encounter examples of do-while looping every day. For example:

```
do
    pay a bill
while more bills remain to be paid
```

As another example:

```
do
    wash a dish
while more dishes remain to be washed
```

In these examples, the activity (paying bills or washing dishes) must occur at least one time. With a do-while loop, you ask the question that determines whether you continue only after the activity has been executed at least once.

You never are required to use a posttest loop. You can duplicate the same series of actions generated by any posttest loop by creating a sequence followed by a standard, pretest while loop. Consider the flow-charts and pseudocode in Figure F-5.

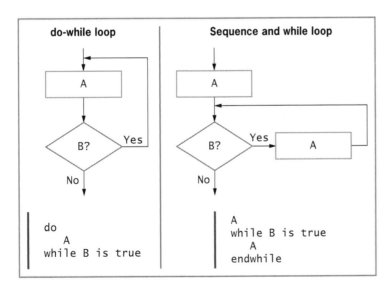

Figure F-5 Flowchart and pseudocode for do-while loop and while loop that do the same thing

On the left side of Figure F-5, A executes, and then B is asked. If B is yes, then A executes and B is asked again. On the right side of the figure, A executes, and then B is asked. If B is yes, then A executes and B is asked again. In other words, both sets of flowchart and pseudocode segments do exactly the same thing.

Because programmers understand that any posttest loop (do-while) can be expressed with a sequence followed by a while loop, most languages allow at least one of the versions of the posttest loop for convenience. Again, you are never required to use a posttest loop; you can always accomplish the same tasks with a sequence followed by a pretest while loop.

Recognizing the Characteristics Shared by All Structured Loops

As you examine Figures F-3 and F-4, notice that with the while loop, the loop-controlling question is placed at the beginning of the steps that repeat. With the do-while loop, the loop-controlling question is placed at the end of the sequence of the steps that repeat.

All structured loops, both pretest and posttest, share these two characteristics:

- The loop-controlling question must provide either entry to or exit from the repeating structure.

- The loop-controlling question provides the *only* entry to or exit from the repeating structure.

In other words, there is exactly one loop-controlling value, and it provides either the only entrance to or the only exit from the loop.

Some languages support a do-until loop, which is a posttest loop that iterates until the loop-controlling question is false. The do-until loop follows structured loop rules.

Recognizing Unstructured Loops

Figure F-6 shows an unstructured loop. It is not a while loop, which begins with a decision and, after an action, returns to the decision. It is also not a do-while loop, which begins with an action and ends with a decision that might repeat the action. Instead, it begins like a posttest loop (a do-while loop), with a process followed by a decision, but one branch of the decision does not repeat the initial process. Instead, it performs an additional new action before repeating the initial process.

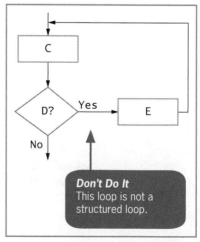

Figure F-6   Unstructured loop

If you need to use the logic shown in Figure F-6—performing a task, asking a question, and perhaps performing an additional task before looping back to the first process—then the way to make the logic structured is to repeat the initial process within the loop, at the end of the loop. Figure F-7 shows the same logic as Figure F-6, but now it is structured logic, with a sequence of two actions occurring within the loop.

Especially when you are first mastering structured logic, you might prefer to use only the three basic structures—sequence, selection, and `while` loop. Every logical problem can be solved using only these three structures, and you can understand all of the examples in this book using only these structures.

353

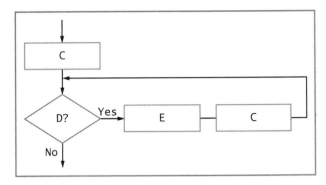

Figure F-7 Sequence and structured loop that accomplish the same tasks as Figure F-6

Glossary

A

abstraction The process of paying attention to important properties while ignoring nonessential details.

accumulator A variable that you use to gather or accumulate values.

algorithm The sequence of steps necessary to solve any problem.

alphanumeric values The set of values that includes alphabetic characters, numbers, and punctuation.

AND decision A decision in which two conditions must both be true for an action to take place.

annotation symbol A flowcharting symbol that contains information that expands on what appears in another flowchart symbol; it is most often represented by a three-sided box that is connected to the step it references by a dashed line.

application software Programs that carry out a task for the user.

array A series or list of variables in computer memory, all of which have the same name but are differentiated with subscripts.

assignment operator The equal sign; it always requires the name of a memory location on its left side.

assignment statement A statement that stores the result of any calculation performed on its right side to the named location on its left side.

B

backup file A copy that is kept in case values need to be restored to their original state.

batch processing Processing that performs the same tasks with many records in sequence.

binary decision A yes-or-no decision; so called because there are two possible outcomes.

binary files Files that contain data that has not been encoded as text.

binary language Computer language represented using a series of 0s and 1s.

binary operator An operator that requires two operands—one on each side.

binary search A search that starts in the middle of a sorted list, and then determines whether it should continue higher or lower to find a target value.

block A group of statements that executes as a single unit.

Boolean expression An expression that represents only one of two states, usually expressed as true or false.

byte A unit of computer storage. It can contain any of 256 combinations of 0s and 1s that often represent a character.

C

camel casing The format for naming variables in which the initial letter is lowercase, multiple-word variable names are run together, and each new word within the variable name begins with an uppercase letter.

cascading if statement A series of nested if statements.

central processing unit (CPU) The piece of hardware that processes data.

character A letter, number, or special symbol such as "A", "7", or "$".

child file A copy of a file after revision.

closing a file An action that makes a file no longer available to an application.

coding the program The act of writing the statements of a program in a programming language.

command line The location on your computer screen at which you enter text to communicate with the computer's operating system.

compiler Software that translates a high-level language into machine language and tells you if you have used a programming language incorrectly. A compiler is similar to an interpreter; however, a compiler translates all the statements in a program prior to executing them.

compound condition A condition constructed when you need to ask multiple questions before determining an outcome.

computer file A collection of data stored on a nonvolatile device in a computer system.

computer memory The temporary, internal storage within a computer.

computer system A combination of all the components required to process and store data using a computer.

conditional AND operator A symbol that you use to combine decisions so that two (or more) conditions must be true for an action to occur. Also called an AND operator.

conditional OR operator A symbol that you use to combine decisions when any one condition can be true for an action to occur. Also called an OR operator.

control break A temporary detour in the logic of a program.

control break field A variable that holds the value that signals a break in a program.

control break program A program in which a change in the value of a variable initiates special actions or causes special or unusual processing to occur.

control break report A report that lists items in groups. Frequently, each group is followed by a subtotal.

conversion The entire set of actions an organization must take to switch over to using a new program or set of programs.

counter Any numeric variable you use to count the number of times an event has occurred.

D

data dictionary A list of every variable name used in a program, along with its type, size, and description.

data hierarchy Represents the relationship of databases, files, records, fields, and characters.

data type The characteristic of a variable that describes the kind of values the variable can hold and the types of operations that can be performed with it.

database A logical container that holds a group of files, often called tables, that together serve the information needs of an organization.

dead path A logical path that can never be traveled.

debugging The process of finding and correcting program errors.

decision structure A program structure in which you ask a question, and, depending on the answer, you take one of two courses of action. Then, no matter which path you follow, you continue with the next task.

decision symbol A symbol that represents a decision in a flowchart, and is shaped like a diamond.

declaration A statement that names a variable and its data type.

declaring variables The process of naming program variables and assigning a type to them.

decrementing The act of changing a variable by decreasing it by a constant value, frequently 1.

default input and output devices Hardware devices that do not require opening. Usually they are the keyboard and monitor, respectively.

defensive programming A technique with which you try to prepare for all possible errors before they occur.

definite loop A loop for which the number of repetitions is a predetermined value.

desk-checking The process of walking through a program solution on paper.

detail loop tasks The steps that are repeated for each set of input data.

direct access files Random access files.

directories Organization units on storage devices; each can contain multiple files as well as additional directories. In a graphic system, directories are often called *folders*.

documentation All of the supporting material that goes with a program.

dual-alternative `if` or **dual-alternative selection** A selection structure that defines one action to be taken when the tested condition is true, and another action to be taken when it is false.

dummy value A preselected value that stops the execution of a program.

E

echoing input The act of repeating input back to a user either in a subsequent prompt or in output.

element A separate array variable.

`else` clause A part of a decision that holds the action or actions that execute only when the Boolean expression in the decision is false.

encapsulation The act of containing a task's instructions and data in the same method.

end-of-job task A step you take at the end of the program to finish the application.

end-structure statements Statements that designate the ends of pseudocode structures.

eof An end-of-data file marker, short for "end of file."

executing Having a computer use a written and compiled program. See also *running*.

external documentation All the external material that programmers develop to support a program. Contrast with *program comments*, which are internal program documentation.

F

field A single data item, such as `lastName`, `streetAddress`, or `annualSalary`.

file A group of records that go together for some logical reason.

flag A variable that you set to indicate whether some event has occurred.

floating-point value A fractional, numeric variable that contains a decimal point.

flowchart A pictorial representation of the logical steps it takes to solve a problem.

flowline An arrow that connects the steps in a flowchart.

folders Organization units on storage devices; each can contain multiple files as well as additional folders. Folders are graphic directories.

`for` statement A statement that can be used to code definite loops. It contains a loop control variable that it automatically initializes, evaluates, and increments. Also called a `for` loop.

G

garbage Describes the unknown value stored in an unassigned variable.

gigabyte A billion bytes.

GIGO Acronym for "garbage in, garbage out"; it means that if your input is incorrect, your output is worthless.

global Describes variables that are known to an entire program.

goto-less programming A name to describe structured programming, because structured programmers do not use a "go to" statement.

graphical user interface (GUI) A program interface that uses screens to display program output and allows users to interact with a program in a graphical environment.

H

hardware The equipment of a computer system.

hierarchy chart A diagram that illustrates modules' relationships to each other.

high-level programming language A programming language that is like English, as opposed to a low-level programming language.

housekeeping tasks Tasks that include steps you must perform at the beginning of a program to get ready for the rest of the program.

Hungarian notation A variable-naming convention in which a variable's data type or other information is stored as part of its name.

I

identifier A variable name.

if-then A structure similar to an if-then-else, but no alternative or "else" action is necessary.

if-then-else Another name for a selection structure.

in scope The characteristic in which variables and constants apply only within the method in which they are declared.

incrementing Changing a variable by adding a constant value to it, frequently 1.

indefinite loop A loop for which you cannot predetermine the number of executions.

indirect relationship Describes the relationship between parallel arrays in which an element in the first array does not directly access its corresponding value in the second array.

infinite loop A repeating flow of logic without an ending.

initializing a variable The act of assigning the first value to a variable, often at the same time the variable is created.

inner loop When loops are nested, the loop that is contained within the other loop.

input Describes the entry of data items into computer memory using hardware devices such as keyboards and mice.

input symbol A symbol that indicates an input operation, and is represented as a parallelogram in flowcharts.

input/output symbol A parallelogram in flowcharts.

I/O symbol An input/output symbol.

instant access files Random access files in which records must be accessed immediately.

integer A whole number.

integrated development environment (IDE) A software package that provides an editor, compiler, and other programming tools.

interactive program A program in which a user makes direct requests, as opposed to one in which input comes from a file.

internal documentation Documentation within a program. See also *program comments*.

IPO chart A program development tool that delineates input, processing, and output tasks.

iteration Another name for a loop structure.

K

keywords The limited word set that is reserved in a language.

kilobyte Approximately 1000 bytes.

L

left-to-right associativity Describes operators that evaluate the expression to the left first.

linear search A search through a list from one end to the other.

logic Instructions given to the computer in a specific sequence, without leaving any instructions out or adding extraneous instructions.

logical error An error that occurs when incorrect instructions are performed, or when instructions are performed in the wrong order.

logical NOT operator A symbol that reverses the meaning of a Boolean expression.

loop A structure that repeats actions while a condition continues.

357

loop body The set of actions that occurs within a loop.

loop control variable A variable that determines whether a loop will continue.

loop structure A structure that repeats actions based on the answer to a question.

low-level language A programming language not far removed from machine language, as opposed to a high-level programming language.

lvalue The memory address identifier to the left of an assignment operator.

M

machine language A computer's on/off circuitry language; the low-level language made up of 1s and 0s that the computer understands.

magic number An unnamed numeric constant.

main program A program that runs from start to stop and calls other modules. Also called a main program method.

mainline logic The overall logic of the main program from beginning to end.

maintenance All the improvements and corrections made to a program after it is in production.

making a decision The act of testing a value.

making declarations The process of naming program variables and assigning a type to them.

master file A file that holds complete and relatively permanent data.

megabyte A million bytes.

merging files The act of combining two or more files while maintaining the sequential order.

Microsoft Visual Studio IDE A software package that contains useful tools for creating programs in Visual Basic, C++, and C#.

mnemonic A memory device; variable identifiers act as mnemonics for hard-to-remember memory addresses.

modularization The process of breaking down a program into modules.

module A small program unit that you can use with other modules to make a program. Programmers also refer to modules as subroutines, procedures, functions, and methods.

module's body Part of a module that contains all the statements in the module.

module's header Part of a module that includes the module identifier and possibly other necessary identifying information.

module's return statement Part of a module that marks the end of the module and identifies the point at which control returns to the program or module that called the module.

N

named constant A named memory location, similar to a variable, except its value never changes during the execution of a program. Conventionally, constants are named using all capital letters.

nested decision A decision "inside of" another decision. Also called a nested if.

nested loop A loop structure within another loop structure; nesting loops are loops within loops.

nesting structures Placing a structure within another structure.

nonvolatile Describes storage whose contents are retained when power is lost.

null case The branch of a decision in which no action is taken.

numeric constant A specific numeric value.

numeric variable A variable that holds numeric values.

O

object code Code that has been translated to machine language.

object-oriented programming A programming technique that focuses on objects, or "things," and describes their features, or attributes, and their behaviors.

opening a file The process of locating a file on a storage device, physically preparing it for reading, and associating it with an identifier inside a program.

OR decision A decision that contains two (or more) decisions; if at least one condition is met, the resulting action takes place.

order of operations Describes the rules of precedence.

out of bounds Describes an array subscript that is not within the range of acceptable subscripts.

outer loop The loop that contains a nested loop.

output Describes the operation of retrieving information from memory and sending it to a device, such as a monitor or printer, so people can view, interpret, and work with the results.

output symbol A symbol that indicates an output operation, and is represented as a parallelogram in flowcharts.

overhead All the resources required by an operation.

P

parallel arrays Two or more arrays in which each element in one array is associated with the element in the same relative position in the other array or arrays.

parent file A copy of a file before revision.

Pascal casing The format for naming variables in which the initial letter is uppercase, multiple-word variable names are run together, and each new word within the variable name begins with an uppercase letter.

path The combination of the disk drive and the complete hierarchy of directories in which the file resides.

permanent storage devices Hardware devices that hold nonvolatile data; examples include hard disks, DVDs, USB drives, and reels of magnetic tape.

populating an array The act of assigning values to array elements.

portable Describes a module that can more easily be reused in multiple programs.

priming input or **priming read** The statement that reads the first input data record prior to starting a structured loop.

procedural programming A programming technique that focuses on the procedures that programmers create.

processing The acts of organizing data items, checking them for accuracy, and performing mathematical operations on them.

processing symbol Represented as a rectangle in flowcharts.

program A set of instructions for a computer.

program code The set of instructions a programmer writes in a programming language.

program comments Nonexecuting statements that programmers place within their code to explain program statements in English. See also *internal documentation*.

program development cycle The steps that occur during a program's lifetime.

program level The level at which global variables are declared.

programming The act of developing and writing programs.

programming language A language such as Visual Basic, C#, C++, Java, or COBOL, used to write programs.

prompt A message that is displayed on a monitor, asking the user for a response.

pseudocode An English-like representation of the logical steps it takes to solve a problem.

R

random access files Files that contain records that can be located in any order.

random access memory (RAM) Temporary, internal computer storage.

range check Comparing a variable to a series of values that marks the limiting ends of ranges.

reading from a file The act of copying data from a file on a storage device into RAM.

real numbers Floating-point numbers.

real-time Describes applications that require a record to be accessed immediately while a client is waiting.

record A group of fields that go together for some logical reason.

relational comparison operator A symbol that expresses Boolean comparisons. Examples include =, >, <, >=, <=, and <>. These operators are also called relational operators or comparison operators.

reliability The feature of modular programs that assures you a module has been tested and proven to function correctly.

repetition Another name for a loop structure.

reusability The feature of modular programs that allows individual modules to be used in a variety of applications.

right-associativity and **right-to-left associativity** Describes operators that evaluate the expression to the right first.

rules of precedence Rules that dictate the order in which operations in the same statement are carried out.

running Having a computer use a written and compiled program. See also *executing*.

S

scripting language A language such as Python, Lua, Perl, or PHP, used to write programs that are typed directly from a keyboard and stored as text rather than as binary executable files. Also called scripting programming languages or script languages.

selection structure A program structure in which you ask a question, and, depending on the answer, you take one of two courses of action. Then, no matter which path you follow, you continue with the next task.

self-documenting Term used for a program that contains meaningful data and module names that describe the program's purpose.

semantic error An error that occurs when a correct word is used in an incorrect context.

sentinel value A value that represents an entry or exit point.

sequence structure A program structure in which you perform an action or task, and then you perform the next action, in order. A sequence can contain any number of tasks, but there is no chance to branch off and skip any of the tasks.

sequential file A file in which records are stored one after another in some order.

short-circuit evaluation A logical feature in which expressions in each part of a larger expression are evaluated only as far as necessary to determine the final outcome.

single-alternative if or **single-alternative selection** A selection structure in which action is required for only one branch of the decision. You call this form of the selection structure an if-then, because no "else" action is necessary.

single-level control break A break in the logic of a program based on the value of a single variable.

size of the array The number of elements the array can hold.

software Programs that tell a computer what to do.

source code The readable statements of a program, written in a programming language.

spaghetti code Snarled, unstructured program logic.

stack A memory location in which the computer keeps track of the correct memory address to which it should return after executing a module.

stacking structures Attaching program structures end to end.

step value A number you use to increase a loop control variable on each pass through a loop.

storage device Hardware apparatus that holds information for later retrieval.

string constant (or literal string constant) A specific group of characters enclosed within quotation marks.

string variable A variable that can hold text that includes letters, digits, and special characters such as punctuation marks.

structure A basic unit of programming logic; each structure is a sequence, selection, or loop.

structured programs Programs that follow the rules of structured logic.

stub A method without statements that is used as a placeholder.

subscript A number that indicates the position of a particular item within an array.

summary report A report that lists only totals, without individual detail records.

syntax The rules of a language.

syntax error An error in language or grammar.

system software The programs that you use to manage your computer.

T

tables Files in a database.

temporary variable A working variable that you use to hold intermediate results during a program's execution.

terminal symbol A symbol used at each end of a flowchart. Its shape is a lozenge. Also called a start/stop symbol.

text editor A program that you use to create simple text files; it is similar to a word processor, but without as many features.

text files Files that contain data that can be read in a text editor.

then clause Part of a decision that holds the action that results when the Boolean expression in the decision is true.

TOE chart A program development tool that lists tasks, objects, and events.

transaction file A file that holds temporary data that you use to update a master file.

trivial expression An expression that always evaluates to the same value.

truth table A diagram used in mathematics and logic to help describe the truth of an entire expression based on the truth of its parts.

U

unnamed constant A literal numeric or string value.

unstructured programs Programs that do not follow the rules of structured logic.

update a master file To change the values in a file's fields based on transactions.

users (or end users) People who employ and benefit from computer programs.

V

validating data Making sure data falls within an acceptable range.

variable A named memory location of a specific data type, whose contents can vary or differ over time.

visible A characteristic of data items in which they "can be seen" only within the method in which they are declared.

volatile A characteristic of internal memory, which loses its contents every time the computer loses power.

W

while loop or **while...do loop** A loop in which a process continues while some condition continues to be true.

writing to a file The act of copying data from RAM to persistent storage.

Index

Special Characters

> (left angle bracket), 138
> (right angle bracket), 138
() (parentheses), 56
<> (not equal to operator), 138
% (percent sign), 49
& (ampersand), 147
* (asterisk), 49, 51
+ (plus sign), 49, 51
- (minus sign), 49, 51
= (equal sign), 48–50, 51, 138
>= (greater-than or equal-to operator), 138
<= (less-than or equal-to operator), 138
^ (caret), 49
| (pipe), 153
/ (slash), 51, 49

A

abbreviations, precautions about using, 71
abstraction, modularization providing, 53–54
accumulating totals using loops, 208–211
accumulators, 208–211
addition operator (+), 49, 51
algorithms, 10
alphanumeric values, 46
American Standard Code for Information Interchange (ASCII) code, 327, 328–330
ampersand (&), 147

AND decisions, 141–150
    avoiding common errors, 148–150
    nesting for efficiency, 144–146
    AND operator. *See* conditional AND operator (&&)
annotation symbols, 69–70
application software, 2
arithmetic operations, 49–51
arithmetic operators, 49–51
arrays, 228–263
    constants, 240–241
    declaring, 231
    efficiency, 239
    elegance, 239
    elements. *See* elements of arrays
    initializing, 230–231
    for loops to process, 261
    manner of occupying computer memory, 229–231
    parallel, 246–253
    populating, 230
    remaining within bounds, 258–260
    replacing nested decisions, 232–239
    searching. *See* searching arrays
    size. *See* size of the array
    subscripts (indexes). *See* subscripts, arrays

ASCII (American Standard Code for Information Interchange) code, 327, 328–330
asking unnecessary questions, 164–165
assignment operator (=), 48–50, 51
assignment statements, 48
associativity
    left-to-right, 51
    right, 48
    right-to-left, 48, 51
asterisk (*), multiplication operator, 49, 51

B

backup files, 285
base 10 numbers, 325, 326
base 2 numbers, 325–326
batch processing, 311
binary decisions, 21
binary files, 277
binary languages, 4
binary numbering system, 325–326, 327, 328–330
binary operators, 48
binary searches, 253
bits, 326
blocks, statements, 99
body
    loops, 97
    modules, 55
Boole, George, 134
Boolean data type, 72

Boolean expressions, 134–137
bytes, 277–278, 326

C

calling modules, 56
camel casing, 44
caret (^), arithmetic operator, 49
cascading if statements, 143
case sensitivity, comparisons, 190
case structure, 144, 348–350
central processing unit (CPU), 3
chained calls, modules, 56
characters, 279
child files, 285, 304
clarity
    statements, 72–73
    structure to provide, 110
closing files, 283
coding the program, 3, 10–11
command line, 25
comments, 69–70
comparison(s)
    case sensitivity, 190
    negative, 139–140
comparison operators,
        relational, 137–141
compilers, 4
compound conditions, 141
computer files, 276–314,
        277–278, 279
    backup, 285
    binary, 277
    child, 285, 304
    closing, 283
    declaring, 280–281
    grandparent, 304
    master, 303
    master-transaction
        processing, 303–310
    merging, 293–302
    opening, 281
    organizing, 278
    parent, 285, 304
    program to perform file
        operations and,
        283–286
    random access (direct access
        or instant access),
        311–312
    reading data, 281–283

sequential. See sequential
    files
text, 277
transaction, 303
writing data to, 283
computer memory, 3–4
    manner of occupation by
        arrays, 229–231
computer systems, 2–5
conditional AND operator (&&),
        146–148
    combining with OR operator,
        precedence, 166–168
conditional OR operator (||),
        152, 153–154
    combining with AND
        operator, precedence,
        166–168
confusing line breaks, 73
constants
    choosing identifiers, 71–72
    declaring. See declaring
        constants
    global, 61
    local, 59
    named, declaring, 47
    numeric (literal numeric),
        45–46
    in scope, 59
    as size of array, 240–241
    string (literal string), 46
    unnamed, 46
    uppercase letters in
        identifiers, 241
control break(s), 287–292
    single-level, 289
control break fields, 289
control break programs, 287
control break reports, 287–288
conversion, 14
counted (counter-controlled)
        loops, 187–188
counters, 188
CPU (central processing unit), 3

D

data
    information versus, 3
    validating reasonableness
        and consistency using
        loops, 216

validating using loops,
        211–213
data dictionaries, 72
data hierarchy, 279–280
data items, 2
    visibility, 59
data types, 43, 46–47
    Boolean, 72
    validating using loops,
        215–216
dead paths, 162–164
debugging, 13
decimal system, 325, 326
decision(s), 133–171
    binary, 21
    Boolean expressions, 134–137
    AND logic. See AND
        decisions
    making, 21
    nested, 142. See nested
        decisions
    OR logic. See OR decisions
    precedence when combining
        AND and OR
        operators, 166–168
    range checks, 159–165
    relational comparison
        operators, 137–141
decision structure, 96–97, 102,
        335–336
decision symbol, 21, 334
declarations, 43
declaring
    arrays, 231
    constants. See declaring
        constants
    files, 280–281
    variables. See declaring
        variables
declaring constants
    within modules, 59–61
    named constants, 47
    program level, 61
declaring variables, 43–44
    within modules, 59–61
    program level, 61
decrementing, 188
default input and output
        devices, 283
defensive programming, 211
definite loops, 187–188

desk-checking, 10
detail loop tasks, 62
dialog boxes, 280
direct access files, 311–312
directories, 278
displaying, defined, 285–286
division operator (/), 49, 51
documentation, 9
    internal and external, 69
double-sided decisions, 134
`do-until` loops, 352
`do-while` loops, 207, 336, 350–352
dual-alternative `if`s (decisions or selections), 96–97, 134
dummy values, 22

E

EB (exabytes), 333
EBCDIC (Extended Binary Coded Decimal Interchange Code) code, 327
echoing input, 74–76
efficiency
    arrays, 239
    searches of arrays, 251–253
    structure to provide, 110
elegance, 203
    arrays, 239
elements of arrays, 229
    constants as values, 241
`else` clauses, 136
encapsulated statements, 57
end users, 8–9
end-of-job tasks, 62
end-structure statements, 99
environments
    programming, 23–25
    user, 25–26
eof, 22
equal sign (=)
    assignment operator, 48–50, 51
    equivalency operator, 138
equivalency operator (= or ==), 138
errors
    debugging, 13
    logical, 5
    semantic, 5
    syntax, 11

exabytes (EB), 333
executing programs, 4
Extended Binary Coded Decimal Interchange Code (EBCDIC) code, 327
external documentation, 69
external module call symbol, 334

F

fields, 279
    control break, 289
files. *See* computer files
floating-point numeric variables, 46
flowcharts, 15
    drawing, 17–18
    indicating relationships, 139
    pseudocode compared, 18
    structure, 99
    symbols, 69–70, 334
flowline(s), 17
flowline symbol, 334
folders, 278
`for` loops (`for` statements), 206–207
    processing arrays, 261
forcing data items, 214
function(s), 52
functional cohesion, 59
functional decomposition, 52

G

garbage, 44
gigabytes (GB), 278
global variables and constants, 61
goto-less programming, selection structures compared, 110
grandparent files, 304
graphical user interfaces (GUIs), 26
greater-than operator (>), 138
greater-than or equal-to operator (>=), 138
GUIs (graphical user interfaces), 26

H

hardware, 2
hexadecimal notation, 7
hexadecimal system, 330–331

hierarchy charts, 66–68
high-level programming languages, 11
housekeeping tasks, 61–62
Hungarian notation, 72

I

identifiers, 43
    choosing, 71–72
IDEs (integrated development environments), 24–25
`if-then` decisions (selections), 134, 336
`if-then-else` structure, 96–97, 335
in scope variables and constants, 59
incrementing, 188
indefinite loops, 188–190
indexes, arrays. *See* subscripts, arrays
indirect relationships, 251
infinite loops, 19–20
information, data versus, 3
initializing arrays, 230–231
initializing variables, 43
    neglecting to initialize loop control variables, 197–198
inner loops, 192
input, 2–3
    from user, echoing, 74–76
input devices, default, 283
input operations, 6
input statements, priming, 103–109, 189
input symbol, 17
input/output (I/O) symbol, 17, 334
instant access files, 311–312
instructions, repeating, 18–20
integers, 46
integrated development environments (IDEs), 24–25
    automatic statement-completion feature, 71
interactive programs, 311
internal documentation, 69
internal module call symbol, 334
interpreters, 4
invalid entries, testing for, 260

I/O (input/output) symbol, 17, 334
IPO charts, 10
iteration, 97

K

keywords, 44
kilobytes (KB or kB), 278, 333

L

left angle bracket (>), less-than operator, 138
left-to-right associativity, 51
less-than operator (>), 138
less-than or equal-to operator (<=), 138
line breaks, confusing, 73
linear searches, 242–243
literal numeric constants, 45–46
literal string constants, 46
local variables and constants, 59
logic
    computer programs, 5–7
    mainline. *See* mainline logic
    planning, 10
    unstructured, structuring and modularizing, 115–121
logical errors, 5
logical NOT operator, 158
long statements, temporary variables to clarify, 73
loop(s), 19–20, 184–218
    accumulating totals, 208–211
    advantages, 185–186
    avoiding common mistakes, 196–205
    counted (counter-controlled), 187–188
    definite, 187–188
    do-until, 352
    including statements inside that belong outside the loop, 201–205
    indefinite, 188–190
    infinite, 19–20
    inner, 192
    loop control variables. *See* loop control variables
    for loops, 206–207
    mainline logic, 190–191
    nested, 192–196

outer, 192
posttest (do-while), 207, 336, 350–352
pretest, 207
reprompting, limiting, 213–214
structured, characteristics shared by, 352
unstructured, recognizing, 352–353
validating data, 211–213
validating data types, 215–216
validating reasonableness and consistency of data, 216
loop body, 97
loop control variables, 186–191
    decrementing, 188
    definite loops with counters, 187–188
    incrementing, 188
    indefinite loops with sentinel values, 188–190
    mainline logic, 190–191
    neglecting to alter, 198–199
    neglecting to initialize, 197–198
    using wrong comparison with, 200–201
loop structures, 97–98, 102, 335
    selection structures compared, 105
Lovelace, Ada Byron, 27
low-level machine languages, 11
lvalues, 49

M

machine language, 4
    translating program into, 11–12
magic numbers, 47
main program, 55
mainline logic, 55
    loops, 190–191
    most common configuration, 61–65
maintenance, 14
    structure to facilitate, 111
making decisions, 21

master files, 303
    master-transaction processing and, 303–310
    updating, 303
MB (megabytes), 278, 333
measuring storage, 332–333
megabytes (MB), 278, 333
memory. *See* computer memory
merging sequential files, 293–302
methods, 52
Microsoft Visual Studio IDE, 24
minus sign (-), subtraction operator, 49, 51
mnemonics, 44
modularization, 52–61
    advantages, 52–55, 57–58
    drawbacks, 59
    functional cohesion, 59
    process, 55–61
    structure to facilitate, 111
    unstructured logic, 115–121
modules, 52
    body, 55
    calling, 56
    chained calls, 56
    choosing identifiers, 71–72
    declaring variables and constants within, 59–61
    hierarchy charts, 66–68
    naming, 55–56
    parentheses following, 56
    portability, 60
    return statements, 55
multiple programmers, modularization permitting, 54
multiplication operator (*), 49, 51

N

named constants, 47
naming
    constants, 71–72
    modules, 55–56, 71–72
    subscripts in arrays, 251
    variables, 44–45, 71–72
negative comparisons, 139–140
nested if, 142

nested loops, 192–196
nesting decisions, 142
    nesting AND decisions for
        efficiency, 144–146
    replacing with arrays,
        232–239
nesting structures, 99–101
nibbles, 326
nonvolatile storage, 4
not equal to operator (<>), 138
null case, 97
numbering systems, 325–333
numeric constants, 45–46
numeric variables, 46
    floating-point, 46

O
object code, 4
object-oriented programming,
    27
opening files, 281
OR decisions, 150–159
    avoiding common errors,
        155–159
    OR operator. *See* conditional
        OR operator (||)
    writing for efficiency,
        152–153
OR operator (||). *See* conditional
    OR operator (||)
order of operations, 50, 51
out of bounds, array subscripts,
    260
outer loops, 192
output, 3
output devices, default, 283
output operations, 7
output symbol, 17
overhead, 47

P
parallel arrays, 246–253
parent files, 285, 304
parentheses (()), following
    modules, 56
Pascal casing, 45
paths, 278
PB (petabytes), 333
percent sign (%), arithmetic
    operator, 49
permanent storage, 277

permanent storage devices, 277
petabytes (PB), 333
pipe (|), 153
planning program logic, 10
plus sign (+), addition operator,
    49, 51
populating arrays, 230
portability of modules, 60
posttest loops, 207, 336,
    350–352
precedence, combining AND
    and OR operators,
    166–168
pretest loops, 207, 335
priming input (priming read)
    statements, 189
    structuring programs,
        103–109
print charts, 346–347
printing, defined, 285–286
problems, understanding, in
    program development
    cycle, 8–10
procedural programming, 27
procedures, 52
process symbol, 334
processing, 3
processing operations, 6–7
processing symbol, 17
professionalism, structure to
    provide, 110
program(s), 2
    coding, 3, 10–11
    control break, 287
    ending with a sentinel value,
        20–23
    interactive, 311
    logic, 5–7
    main, 55
    maintaining, 14
    modularizing. *See*
        modularization
    planning logic, 10
    putting into production, 14
    running (executing), 4
    structured, 93. *See also*
        structure(s)
    testing, 12–14
    translating into machine
        language, 11–12
    unstructured, 93–94

program code, 3
program comments, 69–70
program design, good, features
    of, 68–69
program development cycle,
    8–15
program level, declaring
    variables and constants,
    61
programming, 2
    good habits, 76
    object-oriented, 27
    procedural, 27
programming environments,
    23–25
programming languages, 3
programming models, evolution,
    27–28
prompts, 74–76
pseudocode, 15–16
    flowcharts compared, 18
    indicating relationships, 139
    structure, 99
    writing, 15–16

Q
questions, unnecessary, asking,
    164–165

R
random access files, 311–312
random access memory
    (RAM), 4
range checks, 159–165
    avoiding common errors,
        162–165
range matches, searching arrays,
    254–257
reading from files, 281–283
real numbers, 46
real-time applications, 311
records, 279
relational comparison operators,
    137–141
relationships, indirect, 251
reliability, 55
repeating instructions, 18–20
repetition, 97
reports
    control break, 287–288
    summary, 208

reprompting loops, limiting, 213–214
return statements, modules, 55
reusability, modularization permitting, 54–55
right angle bracket (>), greater-than operator, 138
right-associativity, 48
right-to-left associativity, 48, 51
rules of precedence, 50, 51
running programs, 4

S

script languages, 4
scripting languages, 4
scripting programming languages, 4
searching arrays, 242–257
    binary searches, 253
    flags, 246
    improving efficiency, 251–253
    linear searches, 242–243
    range matches, 254–257
selection structure, 96–97, 102, 335–336
    loop structures compared, 105
self-documenting programs, 71
semantic errors, 5
sentinel values
    ending programs, 20–23
    indefinite loops with, 188–190
sequence structure, 95–96, 102, 325
sequential files, 286–302
    control break logic, 287–292
    merging, 293–302
short-circuit evaluation, 147
single-alternative ifs (decisions or selections), 97, 134, 336
single-level control breaks, 289
single-sided decisions, 134
size of the array, 229
    constant as, 240–241
    remaining within array bounds, 258–260
slash (/), division operator, 49, 51
software, 2. *See also* program(s)
    translating program into machine language using, 11–12

solving difficult structuring problems, 337–345
source code, 4
spaghetti code, 93–94
stack(s), 59
stacking structures, 98
statements
    blocks, 99
    clarity, 72–73
    encapsulated, 57
    long, temporary variables to clarify, 73
step values, 207
storage
    measuring, 332–333
    temporary and permanent, 277
storage devices, 3
string constants, 46
string variables, 46
    equal, 139
structure(s), 92–123, 335–336
    case, 348–350
    definition, 95
    flowcharts, 99
    if-then-else, 96–97, 335
    loop, 97–98, 102, 335
    nesting, 99–101
    pretest loop, 335
    priming input, 103–109
    process, 115–121
    pseudocode, 99
    reasons for using, 110–111
    recognizing, 111–115
    selection (decision), 96–97, 102, 335–336
    sequence, 95–96, 102, 325
    solving difficult structuring problems, 337–345
    spaghetti code, 93–94
    stacking, 98
    while loop, 97–98, 335
stubs, 195
subroutines, 52
subscripts, arrays, 229–230
    constants, 241
    naming, 251
    out of bounds, 260
subtraction operator (-), 49, 51
summary reports, 208

syntax, 3, 10, 11
syntax errors, 11
system software, 2

T

tables, 280
TB (terabytes), 333
temporary storage, 277
temporary variables to clarify long statements, 73
terabytes (TB), 333
terminal symbol, 18, 334
testing
    for invalid entries, 260
    programs, 12–14
text editors, 24
text files, 277
then clauses, 136
TOE charts, 10
totals, accumulating using loops, 208–211
transaction files, master-transaction processing and, 303–310
trivial expressions, 139
truth tables, 147

U

Unicode, 327
uninitialized variables, 210–211
unknown values, variables, 44
unnamed constants, 46
unnecessary questions, asking, 164–165
unreachable paths, 162–164
unstructured programs, 93–94
updating master files, 303
user(s), 8–9
user environments, 25–26

V

validating data
    loops, 211–213
    using loops, 211–213
values
    assigning to variables, 48–51
    dummy, 22
    sentinel. *See* sentinel values
    step, 207
    testing, 21
    unknown, variables, 44

variables, 6, 42–45
    assigning values,
        48–51
    choosing identifiers,
        71–72
    data types, 46–47
    declaring. *See* declaring
        variables
    global, 61
    initializing, 43
    local, 59
    loop control. *See* loop control
        variables
    naming, 44–45

    numeric, 46
    range checks, 159–165
    in scope, 59
    string, 46
    temporary (work), to clarify
        long statements, 73
    uninitialized, 210–211
    unknown values, 44
visibility of data items, 59
volatile storage, 4

W
`while` (`while...do`) loops,
    97–98, 335

work variables, to clarify long
    statements, 73
writing
    defined, 285–286
    to files, 283
    pseudocode, 15–16

Y
yottabytes (YB), 333

Z
zettabytes (ZB), 333